Lighthouses of Maine

Lighthouses of Maine

Bill Caldwell

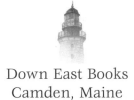

Down East Books
Camden, Maine

Copyright © 1986 by Bill Caldwell
Reprinted by arrangement with Susan Caldwell.
*Some of the original text of this book has been altered to reflect factual updates since it was first written.

Cover painting: *Owls Head Light Under Lowering Sky*
© 2002 by Christopher Cart

Printed and bound at Versa Press, East Peoria, IL.
5   4   3   2   1

Down East Books
Camden, ME
BOOK ORDERS: 800-685-7962
www.downeastbooks.com

ISBN: 0-89272-585-0

Grateful acknowledgement is made to Philip Ziegler for permission to reproduce his pencil sketches of some of Maine's most popular and memorable lighthouses.

Library of Congress Control Number: 2002107843

Originally published in 1986
by Guy Gannett Publishing Co., Portland, ME

For lights and lightkeepers
who guide voyagers
toward their destinies

Lighthouses Along the Coast of Maine

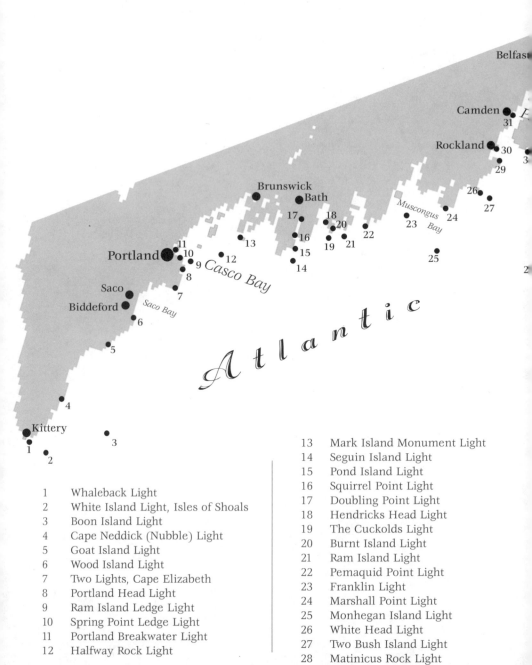

1 Whaleback Light
2 White Island Light, Isles of Shoals
3 Boon Island Light
4 Cape Neddick (Nubble) Light
5 Goat Island Light
6 Wood Island Light
7 Two Lights, Cape Elizabeth
8 Portland Head Light
9 Ram Island Ledge Light
10 Spring Point Ledge Light
11 Portland Breakwater Light
12 Halfway Rock Light
13 Mark Island Monument Light
14 Seguin Island Light
15 Pond Island Light
16 Squirrel Point Light
17 Doubling Point Light
18 Hendricks Head Light
19 The Cuckolds Light
20 Burnt Island Light
21 Ram Island Light
22 Pemaquid Point Light
23 Franklin Light
24 Marshall Point Light
25 Monhegan Island Light
26 White Head Light
27 Two Bush Island Light
28 Matinicus Rock Light

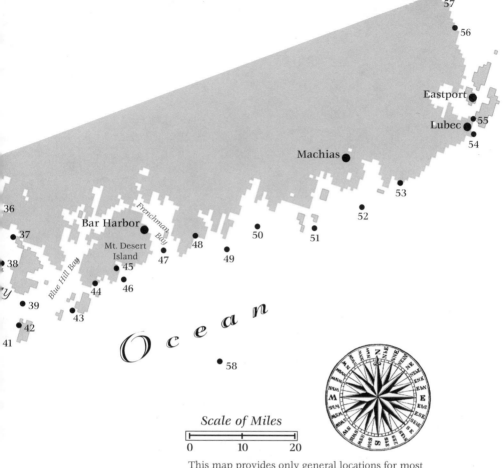

Machias

Eastport

Lubec

Bar Harbor

Frenchman Bay

Mt. Desert Island

Blue Hill Bay

Ocean

57
56
55
54
53
52
51
50
49
48
47
46
45
44
43
42
41
40
39
38
37
36
58

Scale of Miles

0   10   20

This map provides only general locations for most of Maine's lighthouses. Consult a more detailed map for specific directions.

29	Owls Head Light	45	Bear Island Light
30	Rockland Breakwater Light	46	Baker Island Light
31	Curtis Island Light	47	Egg Rock Light
32	Browns Head Light	48	Prospect Harbor Point Light
33	Goose Rocks Light	49	Petit Manan Light
34	Grindel Point Light	50	Nash Island Light
35	Fort Point Light	51	Moose Peak Light
36	Dice Head Light	52	Libby Island Light
37	Pumpkin Island Light	53	Little River Light
38	Eagle Island Light	54	West Quoddy Head Light
39	Mark Island Light	55	Lubec Channel Light
40	Heron Neck Light	56	St. Croix Light
41	Saddleback Ledge Light	57	Whitlock Mill Light
42	Isle au Haut Light	58	Mt. Desert Rock Light
43	Burnt Coat Harbor Light		
44	Bass Harbor Head Light		

Contents

One of the best feelings in the world is the feeling of getting home.

Sometimes a smell tells you: the smell of pines or wild roses as you turn into the drive, or of carbolic soap in a rooming-house hall.

In other times and places, noise may tell you: traffic noise on New York streets, the growl of diesel buses, or the sound of surf breaking across a ledge.

Other times, sight tells you: a familiar landmark signals you are close to home and your pulse steps up its beat.

But the king of all homecoming signals is the sight of a lighthouse or the noise of its fog signal.

A lighthouse, seen from a distance on a calm and clear day, is like a congratulatory pat on the back: like someone saying, "Bill, your navigation was on the nose! You held your compass course true through all the chop and tide!"

At night, the sight of a lighthouse beacon is like a loving kiss in the dark. You had been hoping for it, but when it came it was a lovely surprise.

In thick fog or in blinding snow or rain, the sound of the foghorn from a lighthouse is God's welcome home. You feel almost blessed; you feel grateful, and above all, you feel relieved. The tension drains out of the neck muscles and forearms and you have time to turn and smile in the dark at your mate and to ask for the reward of hot coffee.

No welcome-home handshake, no welcome-home hug, can surpass a sailor's contact with the lighthouse he's been searching for.

Ancient Lighthouses

"Let there be light."

The famous phrase might have been the prayer of a mariner looking for landfall on a black night thousands of years ago.

He'd be astonished by the number of lighthouses that guide seafarers today. There are thousands of lighthouses in the world, not counting those on navigable rivers and inland seas.

Today, it is easy to assume lighthouses were built for the benefit of ships and sailors, generous gifts from their fellow men safe on shore.

Not so. Lighthouses were built mostly by the people on shore so that they and their communities could prosper, bringing more trade their way. Commerce meant ships and ships meant commerce—and ships sought out the safest routes. Where there were lighthouses to guide them, ships sailed. So the goal of growing nations with seacoasts was to build enough lighthouses so that a vessel along their coast should never be out of sight of a light.

Today, the goal is the same, but the techniques have changed. With the advent of radio direction finders, radar, loran, and global-positioning satellites, nations are building these kinds of aids to navigation instead of lighthouses. Port cities have built modern ship-handling terminals to move cargoes, pipelines to move oil inland, and highways for trailer trucks to transport goods to customers. They have built greater airports and air-traffic-control systems to guide passenger and cargo planes to them.

But the goal is the same as when they first built lighthouses—to attract commerce and to grow. Lighthouses were built by landsmen to line their pockets, more than for the safety of men at sea. Congress and local governments were largely unmoved by lost lives and lost ships, and the cries from seafarers for lights. Only after public outcry from angry voters, or when pressure was put on by ship owners who contributed to political war chests, did Congress appropriate funds for new lighthouses during the 19th century.

Politics are the same today. Airline pilots and passengers demand more safety in air controls, but Congress disregards them until a midair crash or other air disaster so rouses voter opinion that it appropriates the needed money.

If money has been the root of most lighthouses, love played a big part in one of the very first, built by the Greeks. In Greek mythology, Leander fell in love with the beautiful priestess Hero. She lived on the opposite shore from him, on the other side of the Hellespont, the ancient name for the Straits of Dardanelles. Each night she would burn a light on her shore and Leander would dive into the Hellespont and swim across to visit her, guided by her light. One night a storm put out the light, and Leander was drowned. In her grief at losing her lover, Hero then drowned herself. This legend may be the first proof of the tragedy that happens when a light goes out.

Homer in his *Iliad* refers to lighthouses in these lines, translated by Pope:

> So to night-wandering sailors pale with fears
> Wide o'er the watery waste a light appears,
> Which on the far-seen mountain blazing high
> Streams from a lonely watch-tower to the sky.

Greek Lights

The Colossus of Rhodes, built about 300 B.C., standing with its huge legs astride the harbor entrance to Rhodes, may have been the first lighthouse of the Western world. The figure of Apollo, cast in bronze, stood more than one hundred and fifty feet above the water, and at night a fire burned in Apollo's torch to guide ships to the harbor entrance. But the famed Colossus of Rhodes was short-lived, demolished in an earthquake in 224 B.C., after serving the harbor a mere fifty-six years.

The greatest lighthouse ever built in the world was the one built at the island of Pharos offshore from Alexandria. Construction began in 261 B.C. and went on for nineteen years. The base was 100 feet square. It stood more than 550 feet high, and the open fire at the top could be seen for twenty-nine miles. This light endured for fifteen centuries. The Pharos of Alexandria was ranked as one of the Seven Wonders of the World. The enormous structure has been credited to Alexander the Great and to Cleopatra, but it is fairly certain that it was built by King Ptolemy II and that the architect was a man named Sostratus.

The bottom tier was of gleaming white marble, square in shape. The second tier was octagonal and the uppermost tier was circular. At the 400-foot level was a meat and vegetable market. The long climb may

Made of bronze, the Colossus of Rhodes took twelve years (292–280 B.C.) to build and stood 400 feet high. It was a lighthouse and a statue to honor the sun god. In 224 B.C. it was toppled by an earthquake and lay where it fell for 878 years, until invading Arabs broke up the statue for scrap.

have been worth it because it was a huge terrace from which shoppers could view the world around them, and also see the great lamp burning above.

A wood fire was kept burning day and night, thus providing ships with a column of smoke to steer by in daylight, and a pillar of fire to steer by in darkness. There are no records showing how the light's constant appetite for wood was satisfied, nor how wood in vast quantities was hauled to the top. If indeed the fire was kept burning for fifteen hundred years, as we are told, it must have consumed entire forests.

More than fifteen centuries after it was built, the Arabian geographer Edrisi visited the Pharos of Alexandria and wrote this description:

"This lighthouse has not its equal in the world for excellence of construction and for strength—the various blocks of quality stone are so strongly cemented together with melted lead, that the whole is imperishable, although waves of the sea continually break against its northern face.

This technique of joining blocks of stone together with melted lead was used two thousand years later in the construction of the famous Eddystone Light of Plymouth, England.

One of the Seven Wonders of the Ancient World, the Pharos lighthouse at Alexandria, Egypt, stood more than 500 feet high. It endured for 1,500 years before being toppled by a massive earthquake sometime in the 13th century.

It is no surprise that the architect of this magnificent lighthouse at Pharos Island wanted to put his name on it, and somehow, someday, get credit for the masterpiece. Architect Sostratus knew he could never get away with simply engraving his name on one stone block. That impertinence would anger his lord and master, King Ptolemy. The king's name alone was permitted to appear. So the crafty Sostratus engraved the king's name visible to all. But upon another great base stone he cut the following words: "Sostratus of Gnidus, son of Dixphanus, to the Gods protecting those upon the sea." Then he covered these words with cement to hide them. And on the surface he wrote the name of his master, King Ptolemy, knowing full well that the cement would wear away soon after the king and Sostratus were dead, but that for centuries thereafter, the inscription underneath would last and give credit where credit was due.

So famous was the Pharos of Alexandria that "Pharos" became the generic word for lighthouses around the world. The Latin word for lighthouse is *pharus*; in Italian, Spanish, and Portuguese, it is *faro*; in French, it is *phare*; and the word pharos stayed in the English language until the 1600s. The science of lighthouse engineering is called pharology.

The Pharos of Alexandria, after enduring fifteen hundred years, was finally toppled by a massive earthquake in the 13th century.

Roman Lights

The Romans were magnificent builders and brilliant engineers. Proof lies throughout Europe and the British Isles: Romans built the Great North Road leading out from London; the Great Roman Wall, across the waist of Scotland, built to keep the pesky Picts and Scots from raiding the Roman outpost of England; the great amphitheaters like the Coliseum; bridges like the one at Avignon in France; baths like those at Bath, England; and all the glories of ancient Rome. But what about lighthouses?

They built nothing to match the Pharos or the Colossus at Rhodes, but Romans, a practical people, built thirty lighthouses from the Black Sea to the Atlantic, and up the coast of Europe to the English Channel. Their far-flung Roman Empire had to be supplied by ship, and lighthouses were needed to make those voyages safer.

The Emperor Caligula built two facing lighthouses on either side of the English Channel about 40 A.D. The lights were built at Boulogne on the French side and at Dover on the English side. The logical Romans chose these sites to avoid building high light towers, for each was built atop cliffs almost four hundred feet above the sea. The towers themselves were only eight feet high. A Roman medal cast about 185 A.D. clearly shows the light at Boulogne, which the Emperor Charlemagne restored 770 years after Caligula had erected it. There Charlemagne's combination lighthouse and fortress stood for another eight hundred years, until the cliff on which it was built fell into the sea in 1645. Historian Pliny the Elder, in his book *Natural History*, wrote that a "light burned brightly" at Ravenna in 77 A.D., a seaport so spacious that two hundred and fifty ships coming in from the Adriatic Sea could ride at anchor in its harbor. Two years after he wrote this, Pliny was killed when Mt. Vesuvius violently erupted.

The biggest light built by the Romans, also mentioned by historian Pliny, was the light at Ostia at the mouth of the River Tiber, which brought ships to Rome. This light was built about 50 A.D., under Claudius, the fourth emperor of the Roman Empire. It stood less than one-quarter as high as the Greek-built light at Pharos, but the Emperor Claudius crowned it with a statue of himself.

After the fall of the Roman Empire under attack from the barbarians, all of Europe fell back into the Dark Ages. Gone entirely for centuries were the Roman skills of building, the stability of Roman law, and Roman government. The brutal barbarian bullies seized Europe by the throat and devastated civilization on land and sea. Pirates captured and burned ships at sea. Commerce dwindled to a trickle. Shipbuilding stopped. For hundreds of years, no new lighthouses were built. The lights of Europe went out. The Dark Ages took over the Western world.

──The First American Light Was For Boston──

The lighthouses in this book begin in Boston and end at the Canadian border. But the focus is on Maine, because those are the lights I have used the most and know the best.

The starting place is the Boston Light, because this was America's first lighthouse. Between Boston and Eastport, Maine are thousands of miles of indented coast—rocky, dangerous, often ledge-pocked, always beautiful—thousands of islands, some only big enough for a seal to sunbathe or a cormorant to dry its wings. Here, I believe, are the finest cruising waters in the world for small boats with adventurous but cautious hands at the helm.

The first lighthouse in America was lit without fanfare on September 14, 1716. Even in 1716, Boston and New England went about their business close-mouthed.

This entry in the *Boston News Letter* reported the event:

> By virtue of an Act of Assembly made in the First Year of His Majesty's Reign, For Building and Maintaining a Light House upon the Great Brewster (called Beacon-Island) at the entrance of the Harbor of Boston, in order to prevent the loss of the Lives and Estates of His Majesty's Subjects; The said Light House has been built; and on Fryday last the 14th Currant of Light was kindled, which will be very useful for all Vessels going out and coming in to the Harbor of Boston, or any other harbors in Massachusetts Bay, for which all Masters shall pay to the Receiver of Impost, one Penny per Ton Inwards, and another Penny Outwards, except Coasters, who are to pay Two Shillings each, at their Clearance Out, and all Fishing Vessels, Wood Sloops, etc. Five Shillings each by the year.

Cost mattered most in this report. Ship owners in 1716 gave first priority to cost, as they do today.

But how did America's first light look? And who was first keeper of the first light in America?

It towered tall, narrow, and conical. This was an expensive light to build with public money: the price in English pounds was £2,285, 17 shillings, 8 pence halfpenny. (Even more than 285 years ago, the English ragtailed their bills with halfpennies, seldom rounding them off to a penny!) It was built at the order of and the expense of the general court of the Province of Massachusetts Bay. The Boston Light began with a petition. The merchants of Boston petitioned the General Court of the Massachusetts Bay Colony in 1713 that a light be built for ships entering Boston Harbor. The court approved, chose Brewster Island as the site, and, on July 23, 1715, passed an act for building at the expense of the province (about $12,000). The light was first lit on September 14, 1716.

The first keeper in America was George Worthylake, who was paid fifty pounds a year, later increased to seventy pounds ($350) "because he had lost 59 sheep by drowning in a severe storm, his attendance at the light preventing him from saving them." Worthylake's bad luck persisted. In November 1718, after only two years and two months as keeper, Worthylake, his wife, his daughter, and his African-American servant were all drowned when his boat was capsized as he rowed to a nearby island.

This tragic death of the first keeper and his family caught public sympathy. Benjamin Franklin, then a boy of thirteen, wrote a commemorative ballad. In his *Autobiography*, Franklin says he printed his ballad himself and hawked it on the streets of Boston, where it "sold wonderfully well." No copy of the ballad exists, and Franklin called it "wretched stuff." In 1719, the new keeper petitioned the General Court "that a great Gun be placed on the Island to answer Ships in a Fog." The Court approved, and the first fog signal in America was installed. Though it seems strange, the records indicate that the gun served as the only fog signal in Boston Harbor for one hundred and thirty-two years. This cannon is now a historic monument at the U.S. Coast Guard Academy in New London, Connecticut.

The next mention of a fog signal being built is in a report from 1851. This describes a fog bell weighing 1,375 pounds, "lately erected at the outer Light." It states that the new bell would run for six hours with a single winding, striking every forty-seven seconds. This ancient fog signal can still be seen on display at the Boston Light Station, with the date of its manufacture stamped on—1700. America's first light fared badly in the Revolution. British and American soldiers captured and recaptured it several times. When in June 1776 the British sailed out of Boston, they left a trail of gunpowder that blew up the light tower an hour later.

For the next seven years, Boston had no lighthouse. But after the Revolution, the legislature ordered a new one built on the same site in 1783. The lantern stood at a height of 75 feet—later raised to 89 feet in 1859—and the base of the tower was eight feet thick. The lighthouse was ceded by Massachusetts to the United States, along with five other lights in Massachusetts, on June 10, 1790.

Minot's Ledge Light

Minot's Ledge Light, off the southeastern chop of Boston Bay, is one of the world's most famous lighthouses and one of the great engineering feats in marine construction. But the light that stands there today is not the one that stood there in 1847, built by Captain W. H. Swift. That was destroyed in a terrible storm in 1851, only three years after it had been built with awful hardships. Here, briefly, is the story.

Minot's Rocks, also called Cohasset Ledges, have been the terror of seamen and the cause of countless wrecks. In nine years, forty vessels were wrecked on Minot's Rocks and from six of these wrecks, there were no survivors. These devilish ledges are exposed only at three-quarters ebb tide. So sailing vessels bound with the wind heavy at the northeast were liable to be driven east of Boston Light, and too often were driven upon the submerged Minot's Rocks.

Captain Swift began the hard job of building a lighthouse there in 1847. He had to erect his beacon on a small granite rock in open sea, only about three feet above the water; at dead low tide, the exposed surface was no more than twenty-five square feet; the rest of the time the ledge was submerged.

It took Swift two years of hazardous work. First, he and his crew could get onto the rock only at low tide in calm seas. Second, they had to mount his machinery for biting into the granite high out of the reach of waves. He drilled nine holes, each five feet deep, into the granite to hold nine-inch wrought iron pipes. This provided an octagon twenty-five feet in diameter at the bottom, narrowing to fourteen feet on top. It reached sixty feet high, and the lantern was placed on top, making the light seventy feet high. Then Swift strengthened the entire structure with a complex system of diagonal bracings.

In November 1848 the light was lit and, for the first time, a beacon shone to warn vessels away from the dangers of Minot's Ledge.

But it was a hard, miserable, and dangerous life for the keepers. The two keepers lived in a small iron room beneath the lantern, alone with the endless din of breaking waves.

Within three years, tragedy struck. The keepers were drowned and their bodies were never found. The lighthouse was demolished. The killer storm broke over Massachusetts on April 14, 1851, increased to a violent gale on the 15th, and by the 16th had grown to a hurricane of such violence that it enveloped the lighthouse in torrents of ocean. Yet people on shore that night saw the light shining from Minot's Rocks, indicating the keepers were still alive.

Then at 10 p.m. the light disappeared. The bell stopped and was not heard again. At daylight, the seas dropped, so men on land could see Minot's Rocks, but they could see no sign of a lighthouse or its keepers.

Yet in those three years, Minot's Light had proved itself, saving lives and ships. So Congress appropriated funds to build a new and stronger light on the same spot. This was to be the first light built by the newly established United States Lighthouse Board and it took time to make sure the lighthouse would be a winner. The responsibility for designing the new light went to General G. J. Totten, chief of the U.S. Army Engineers and a member of the Lighthouse Board. The job of actually building it went to his subordinate, Captain B. S. Alexander.

Alexander must have been a remarkable engineer, who knew not only engineering but also how to handle men and control costs. The Army Corps of Engineers would welcome a man of Alexander's stripe today. Alexander made his first trip to Minot's Ledge on May 1, 1855, and on May 31 he made his frank report to the Lighthouse Board. He told them that, even in summer, it would be impossible to land and work on the ledge for weeks at a time; that most of the ledge was under water all the time, and the rest was exposed only three or four hours at low tide. He said it would be expensive and wasteful, therefore, to station a stone-cutting crew aboard vessels near the ledge, when they would be idle most of the time, and very hard to discipline. He thus proposed to billet his crew on shore and employ them year-round. Weather and tide permitting, he would send a crew out to the ledge to drill the rock. During high tides or bad weather, the entire crew would work on shore, cutting the granite blocks and preparing the masonry for the 114-foot tower.

The Lighthouse Board quickly accepted Alexander's idea. They gave him the go-ahead before June was out, and Major Alexander immediately went to work. On July 1, a Sunday, he landed with a small work party on the ledge, and started cutting foundations.

It was a long, slow job, as he had predicted. During the first two years, the crews could work at the ledge only 134 hours one year, and 157 hours the next. It was 1857 before the first masonry blocks could be laid. Getting the first course of masonry laid was difficult, since the surface was underwater most of the time. Alexander built small coffer dams of sandbags around each granite block, and sponged out the water be-

Stormy seas off Minot's Ledge Light—from a 19th-century painting.

hind them. When this area was dry, he covered it with a layer of cement and then laid a sheet of muslin over the cement to protect it from the incoming tide. Alexander found, by experimenting, that cement penetrated through the muslin and made a good bond to the first tier of granite blocks.

During 1858 the work went faster, and the masonry reached the sixth course. The next year saw the thirty-second course finished, after 337 hours of labor. In 1860, five years after the job was started, the new Minot's Light was finished. The price tag for the light, with the tower, including the labor and materials and the berthing of the men on shore, totaled $300,000.

Alexander had built a massively strong tower of granite blocks—1,079 of them—each secured to its neighbors by heavy iron dogs, while the first twelve courses were further reinforced by iron rods. The tower contains 3,514 tons of granite.

It has withstood the assault of some of the highest waves ever recorded. Some of the most awesome were the gigantic waves that momentarily submerged the 114-foot-high tower.

But there is a romantic side to Minot's Light. Its nickname is "The I Love You Light," because its beam flashes out a sequence of one-four-three flashes of light spaced over forty-five seconds. This sequence spells out in code "I love you." There is even a catchy love song about "the light which spells 'I love you.'"

The new Minot's Ledge Light was lit in November of 1860 and has shone its much-needed warning ever since, tended by generations of keepers, until the light was automated in 1947.

This is one of the most remarkable examples of lighthouse building under terrible conditions, and became a watershed of technique. It merits a place in this book devoted mostly to the lighthouses of Maine.

The Lighthouse Board

The following chapter about the start of the Lighthouse Board is based on the book, The Modern Lighthouse, *by Arthur Burges Johnson, Chief Clerk of the United States Lighthouse Board, published by the U.S. Government Printing Office in 1890. An interesting footnote for Mainers is that the first page is a Letter of Transmittal from the Secretary of State to the President of the Senate. The secretary of state was Maine's James G. Blaine (the Blaine House is now the official residence of the governor of Maine).*

There were twelve lighthouses in existence when the federal government took over the responsibility for operating and maintaining them on August 7, 1789. I'm glad to report all twelve are still in existence 213 years later. Those lights ranged along the Atlantic coast from Portsmouth Harbor Light in New Hampshire to the Charleston Harbor Light in South Carolina. The lighthouses were under the direction of the Secretary of the Treasury, who at the time was Alexander Hamilton. But the President himself took personal interest in lights and lightkeepers; witness this letter from George Washington to Hamilton, dated October 12, 1790:

Sir:

I have received your letter of the 5th inst. the public service arrangement which you have made relative to the lighthouses at Newport and Portland, they are perfectly agreeable to me, and receive my approbation. I am, sir, your most obedient servant,

George Washington

About this time in the young life of our nation, a political quirk occurred, which some might enjoy seeing repeated today. In May 1792, the office of the Commissioner of Revenue was established. Ten years later it was abolished. Then, unhappily, it was established again in 1813. In 1820, it was again abolished. And all the duties of the Commissioner of Revenue were transferred to the Fifth Auditor of the Treasury, a Mr. Stephen Pleasonton, about whom there will be more to say.

The reason for this aside is that whenever there was a Commissioner of Revenue, he got the responsibility for the lighthouses. And when there wasn't, the responsibility went back to the Secretary of the Treasury.

During the thirty years since the government had taken charge of the twelve original lighthouses, their numbers had increased to fifty-five. During the thirty-two years that Stephen Pleasonton was in charge, the number rocketed up from 55 lighthouses to 325, plus lightships, buoys, monuments, and other aids to navigation. Pleasonton, being an auditor by training, arranged to contract out to the low bidder the maintenance of lighthouse buildings, repairs of the lights themselves, and the supply of oil, wicks, chimney stoves, and cleaning stores. This was an easy job when fifty-five lights were involved, but by the time there were 325, it was big business. Pleasonton signed a contract for five years with the low bidder, who agreed to keep the lights supplied with everything necessary to keep them burning at a fixed price of $35.87 a year per light.

So many new lighthouses were built each year, the General Superintendent of Lights was unable to keep track of how well or poorly the lights were doing their job. Congress began to get bombarded with complaints and, as has always been true with Congress, it set up committees to study the complaints, and then more committees were established to propose changes in the organization of the lighthouses. Study groups were sent to find out how European nations ran their lighthouses, and to evaluate the equipment they used, particularly the new lenses.

By 1852 the studies were done. The report contained 760 pages and scores of illustrations. As a result, Congress established a Lighthouse Board, to which the President would appoint two high-ranking officers from the Navy, two engineers from the Army, and two civilians of high scientific attainments. This board would be attached to the Treasury.

The board was instructed to divide the Atlantic, Gulf, and Pacific coasts into twelve lighthouse districts and to appoint an officer of the Navy or Army to serve as lighthouse inspector in each district. It proved a sound arrangement, for the essence of it has lasted for more than 150 years.

Construction of Early Lights and the Pioneers of Lenses

If there was beauty to our early lighthouses, it came more from their good work than their good looks. They were designed and built by low-budget engineers rather than high-priced architects. So long as their light shone and they functioned, few cared about their appearance.

Until 1840, lighthouses along the New England coast were made two ways: from rubble stone shaped like a cone, or from wooden-frame towers built on the roof of a keeper's house. Stones for the towers were hacked from nearby ledges or from loose stones collected on the beach—whatever sturdy material was close to hand. The walls were usually three feet thick at the base, where the seas hit hard, and tapered to two feet at the top, with the tower reaching twenty to thirty feet high.

Then came a dome of brick and a flat roof of stone slabs overhanging the walls of the tower by six inches or a foot. The lanterns were mounted here, by iron angle posts sunk into the masonry walls three or four feet deep.

The lantern itself was part of the keeper's house. The angle posts supporting the light rested on the attic beams. So the roof of a lightkeeper's house was often strange looking. When the tower swayed in high winds and heavy rain, the keeper and his family below got drenched because of leaks caused by the strain on the roof.

Then in 1847, the Congress gave the Army engineers the job of building six different lighthouses.

They began using iron pilings drilled into rock. Later, they built whole lighthouses from cast-iron plates, as high as 165 feet. Then came tubular foundations and underwater stone foundations put in place by divers. When building began in the open sea, they pioneered work in underwater caissons.

In other parts of this book, the stories will be briefly told of the building of some of the Maine coast lights, and they will be specific about the difficulties and hardships. But here let it be said that many men died in terrible conditions, and scores of others suffered for months on end to build lighthouses at sea.

Many times lights had to be built on remote, wave-beaten ledges that were submerged under seas twelve feet deep at high tide. It was perilous to get ashore on those ledges even at low water, and certain death for men marooned on them as the tides poured in. When these laborers were not working on the ledge in peril, they were often seasick, cold, and frightened as they huddled out a storm on a small boat nearby, their only living quarters for months. Yet these lighthouses are marvelous feats of engineering. Their beauty is incidental to their strength. Their prime duty is to withstand destruction, to be pummeled and beaten by hurricanes and immense destructive seas—and to survive intact, year after year, decade after decade.

This is why lighthouses were built circular and tapered. Their circular form offers the least resistance to wind and sea, regardless of the direction from which they assault the light. They are tapered so the vertical walls recede at the precise angle that will most effectively throw the seas back to themselves, thereby reducing their battering force.

Four of the most remarkable wave-battered lighthouses, built on ledges far at sea, are in Maine: Saddleback Ledge, off Isle au Haut in Penobscot Bay; Halfway Rock, between Seguin and Portland Head Light; Ram Island Ledge, at the entrance to Casco Bay; and Whaleback Ledge at the entrance to Portsmouth Harbor.

The height of a light is determined by two factors. One is the estimated force and height of the waves that will smash against it. The light tower must be out of reach, whenever possible, of breaking seas. The second factor is the distance at which the light should be visible to ships at sea. For example, a lantern fifty feet in the air can be seen 8.5 miles away; at a hundred feet, visibility increases to 11.7 miles; at a height of two hundred feet, visibility is 16 miles. Of course, the magnifying power of lenses and the strength of the light source affect such figures, too.

The destructive battering force of immense seas is hard to summarize in lay terms because so many complex forces are at work. But seas along the Maine coast are often strong enough to toss huge rocks—weighing more than seventy tons—as though they were tennis balls. The force of a hurricane wind is simpler to state. In a hurricane, the pressure exerted on each square inch of a lighthouse reaches forty-six thousand pounds. By comparison, the pressure is only one pound per square inch in a fifteen mile-per-hour breeze. It is astonishing that many Maine lights have withstood the killing forces of hurricane winds and stormy seas for well over one hundred fifty years.

"Keep the light burning!" That is the first commandment among lightkeepers. To comprehend how hard that can be, try to keep a candle lit for a night on the porch of your house or the deck of your boat, then multiply that single night by 365 nights a year and that single year by scores or hundreds of years.

Open fires were the first light signals. It sounds simple—but think of how many men it took to cut and haul the needed wood to the base of the light, and how many more hours it took to haul even one night's wood by rope to the top, and stack it there in readiness. And in the mornings, how to get rid of the ashes before the accumulation overflowed the small space.

In 1673, the beacon at Point Allerton, Massachusetts, was lit by "fiery bales of pitch and occum" burned in open braziers. The first light in Boston Harbor was lit in 1715 by tallow candles. Then came the spider lamp. Then in 1812, the government paid Winslow Lewis $20,000 for the patent on his "magnifying and reflecting lantern." Arnold Johnson, in his encyclopedic report to Congress on lighthouses in 1890, gave it low marks.

However, the Lewis lantern, with a few improvements, clung on for forty years. In 1852, the new Lighthouse Board began using the Fresnel lens, a French invention already used throughout most of the world. This lens gave about four times as much light to a navigator than the old reflector light, and furthermore, it used less costly oil. The Lighthouse Board scored points with Congress over this economy in their annual report for 1858. The average cost per light with reflector lamps had been $1,302 per year, when oil cost $1.13 per gallon. After Fresnel lenses, the cost was down to $1,286 a year, even though the price of oil had increased to $1.62 per gallon.

Lamps, Oils, and Lenses

Lighthouses were moneymakers—not for the sailors or the keepers—but for the contractors who built them, the inventors who patented lenses and lamps, and the oil dealers who won a government contract to supply the illuminating oil.

Winslow Lewis, for one, did well by lighthouses, and they did well by Winslow Lewis. Lewis is an important man in the story of our lighthouses. He was born in Wellfleet, Massachusetts, in 1770, the year of the Boston Massacre by British redcoats. As a young man, he went seafaring and stayed long enough to learn firsthand the need for lighthouses and the urgent need for better equipment in them. On his voyages, he began designing ways to make the light shine brighter and farther to ships at sea. So in 1810, at the age of forty, he swallowed the anchor and came ashore. This was the year he got a patent for the Lewis reflector and magnifying lens to use with lighthouse lanterns. In 1811, he installed his first reflector lantern in the Boston Light.

This was an ideal showcase for Lewis's invention. He had plenty of personal influence around Boston Harbor because he had become commander of a group of mariners there called the Boston Sea-Fencibles, who had organized to defend the inshore islands, Boston Harbor, and the city's waterfront in the War of 1812.

The Boston Light was a conspicuous seamark for trying out a new invention. Ship captains, many of whom were friends and colleagues of Lewis, were able to report to their owners on the efficiency of Lewis's invention. They reported that its light could be seen more clearly and at a greater distance than the previous lantern. More importantly, lighthouse officials ashore liked it because it saved money. Lewis's lantern used only half as much oil.

Secretary of the Treasury Albert Gallatin heard about this economy, and enthused over it because the money for maintaining lights came out of his budget. So, Gallatin contracted with Lewis to install his new invention in all the lighthouses operated by the government.

Lewis was paid $20,000 for his invention. This handsome lump sum was sweetened by an agreement that stated he would receive half of all the money saved on oil. Seven years later, Lewis signed another government contract that allowed him to keep 33 percent of all the money saved on oil over the next seven years. By this time, the number of lighthouses had increased to seventy.

Under another contract, Lewis got the exclusive franchise to supply the high-quality sperm oil required by all seventy lights, and under yet another contract, was retained to inspect every light once a year. By 1820, Lewis was a very busy and prospering man, selling his lanterns, installing them, providing the sperm oil, and inspecting every light in the nation. But there was a thorn in his side—his own nephew, I.P. Lewis, an inspector for the Lighthouse Board. He continually found fault with his uncle's work and said so publicly in his reports to the Secretary of the Treasury and to the Congress.

After Winslow Lewis had enjoyed a virtual monopoly for twenty-two years, the government opened his oil-supply contract to public bidding. And Lewis was underbid by other New Englanders. In 1832, the winners were a group of well-to-do oil dealers from New Bedford, Connecticut, a big whaling port. The group that underbid Lewis was made up of Charles W. Morgan, Samuel Rodman, William R. Rodman, and Edward Merrill. These men contracted to supply best-quality strained spermaceti oil at the rate of $31.98 a year per lamp to every lighthouse in the country. There were 1,932 lamps in 1832 and five years later, when the New Bedford group was awarded the contract again, there were 2,147 lamps, and the contract price per lamp was raised to $35.87. The contract was worth $77,000.

As inspector of lighthouses, Lewis's duties brought him to Maine regularly. In 1817, Lewis installed one of his inventions at Seguin Light, off the mouth of the Kennebec River. In 1822, Lewis, writing as a lighthouse authority, claimed his flashing beacon at Boon Island Light could be seen eighteen to twenty-one miles at sea—an exaggeration. Lewis, God bless him, had a long and fine impact on the growth and upgrading of American lights. But then, they came from a low bottom. Back in 1623, the beacon at Point Allerton, Massachusetts, was a "fire of pitch and occum," which burned in an open brazier. Tallow candles provided the illumination for the light in Boston Harbor in 1715, replaced by a spider lantern hung there as if in a window at home. So when Lewis sold his invention in 1812, almost anything might have been an improvement.

But Arnold Johnson, in his report to Congress in 1890, did not give the Lewis invention high marks:

The patentee of 1812 made no pretension to a knowledge of optics as now understood, and his reflector came about as near a true paraboloid as did a barber's basin. His lamp, burning about 30 to 40 gallons of oil per year, had a three-quarter-inch burner—in front of the lamp was a so-called lens of bottle-green glass—which was supposed to have some magnifying power. This apparatus was enclosed in a massive wrought-iron lantern, glazed with 10 panes, 12 inches in size. The effect of the whole was characterized by one inspector as making a bad light worse.

Critic Johnson was looking back three-quarters of a century when he wrote those unkind words, and he was also writing as a longtime chief clerk to the Lighthouse Board, the board that decided in 1852 to put the Lewis lanterns on the shelf and replace them with Fresnel lenses.

But I feel more kindly towards Winslow Lewis and his invention. He was, after all, a mariner, a man who had suffered from poor lights in the lighthouses he'd steered by. Ashore, he invented an improvement, crude and ugly as his reflector and lantern may have been. Possibly he filled his pockets with the twenty thousand dollars he got selling his patent, and then installing his lanterns and supplying oil for them. But Lewis, responsible for building at least part of a hundred lighthouses before he died, helped to more than double the number of lights along the coast. During his lifetime, no man worked harder, traveled farther, or knew more about lighthouses from both onshore and offshore viewpoints than Winslow Lewis.

Without question, the Fresnel lens was far more effective and far more beautiful. The United States adopted it only long after it had been proven successful in the lighthouses of Europe, where Fresnel's lens had been first used in 1823, nineteen years earlier.

Maine has one of the finest collections of lighthouse lenses at the Lighthouse Museum in Rockland. Visiting there is a must for anyone interested in lighthouses. It is listed in telephone and other directories as the Shore Village Museum. The enchanting and educational display has been largely accumulated as a labor of love by a retired Coast Guard Warrant Officer, Kenneth Black, a man who merits more thanks than he gets. He knows and likes lighthouses, lights, lenses, foghorns, and all their moving parts. Using all the skills of begging, borrowing, and "moonlight requisitioning" learned in his long Coast Guard career, Black has filled his little museum with memorabilia to delight the heart of any lighthouse fancier. What's more, he likes visitors to touch it all, and to make it work. Still more unusual, Black likes the kids to handle everything from immaculate lenses to polished brass. "Hell, we can wipe off their fingerprints! But nobody can erase their memories of what they touch here," says Black.

I'm delighted by the fact that Robert Louis Stevenson, the great storyteller who wrote Treasure Island, came from a long line of lighthouse men. One of them, Alan Stevenson, the great Scottish lighthouse engineer, had a touch of the poet in him. Wrote Alan Stevenson:

> Nothing can be more beautiful than an entire apparatus for a fixed light of the first order. It consists of a belt of refractors, forming a hollow cylinder six feet in diameter and thirty inches high; below it are six triangular rings of glass, ranged in a cylindrical form, and above a crown of thirteen rings of glass, forming by their union a hollow cage, composed of polished glass, ten feet high and six feet in diameter. I know of no work of art more beautiful or creditable to the boldness, ardor, intelligence, and zeal of the artist.

After pulling the family of Robert Louis Stevenson into this book by the ears, I will briefly share my enthusiasm about the Stevensons as lighthouse builders. Robert Stevenson, one of the greatest lighthouse builders of all time, made a tour of all the English lighthouses in 1801, and wrote a book sensibly titled *English Lighthouse Tours*, still a classic reference book today. He came to his career largely through the influence of his father-in-law, a man with the plain name of Thomas Smith, but with the romantic title of "Lighthouse Builder and Engineer to the Commissioners of Northern Lights," the body responsible for all Scottish lighthouses.

At the age of nineteen, Robert Stevenson was assistant to his father-in-law, and was sent by him to superintend the building of a lighthouse off the wild coast of Scotland. After a long apprenticeship, he succeeded his father-in-law as lighthouse builder and engineer to the Commissioners of Northern Lights. For more than a hundred years, this position was held by a Stevenson. Robert's son, Alan Stevenson, quoted above about the beauty of a first-order lens, built the classic tower at Skerrymore, Scotland. He was followed by David Stevenson, who built the North Unst Light. Then came David and Thomas Stevenson, who built Dhu-Heartach Light. They were followed in turn by David and Charles Stevenson, each of whom contributed still more sea lights with such magic names as Rattray Briggs and Sule Skerry. Another member of this distinguished family was Robert Louis Stevenson, who after completing his engineering apprenticeship, abandoned lighthouses for literature.

After this diversion, let us return to the Fresnel lens, the beauty of which turned engineer Alan Stevenson to writing near-poetry. Augustin Jean Fresnel, a French physicist, designed in 1820 what one expert described as "a curtain of prisms in front of a light, and centered around a bull's-eye lens. Each ring of prisms projected slightly beyond the next, with the result that all the light coming from the source was refracted into a horizontal beam." Fresnel later improved his lens by adding reflecting prisms above and below the refracting prisms—this combination of reflection and refraction is called the Catodioptic System.

Fresnel's lens was first used in 1823 at Cordouban Light and quickly thereafter by scores of other lights in Europe. It was not until 1852 that it came to the United States. The Fresnel lens remained in worldwide

This third-order Fresnel lens was removed from Whitehead Light. Built by L. Sauter in Paris, France and installed in 1852, the lens stands eight feet tall and weighs three-quarters of a ton. It is on display at the Shore Village Museum in Rockland, Maine. Gannett file photo

use until the early 1900s. But despite worldwide use of these lenses, they were always ground in France by French lensmakers, at the houses of Henri Lepaut, Barbier and Fenestre, or Sautier, Lemonier et Cie.

Even 150 years ago, the price was high—more than $8,000 for a first-order, beautiful, lenticular lens.

French inventors are to be thanked for the best lamps in the early lighthouses. In 1780, long before Fresnel, Aime Argand invented the burner that is basically the same burner we have more than 220 years later in our household oil lamps. It had a circular wick instead of the old flat wick and it was fed air by a central draft. This was surrounded by a glass chimney and it gave off a brilliant flame, which, when combined with a parabolic reflector to magnify its effect, revolutionized sea lights. With an Argand burner, a beam of very high intensity shone to sea from a relatively small light source.

Like so many inventions, the Argand lamp may have been triggered by an accident. The source of the invention may not have been the scientific brain of Aime Argand, but the clumsiness of his younger brother. He tells the story that Aime had spent years trying various experiments with oil lamps, but in vain.

> One evening, a broken-off neck of a flask was lying on the chimney piece. I happened to reach across the table and placed it over the circular flame of the lamp; immediately the flame rose with brilliancy. My brother jumped from his seat in ecstasy, rushed upon me with a transport of joy, and embraced me with rapture.

That is a translation of the younger brother's version of how the famed Argand lamp came to be invented. The Argand lamp shone from lighthouses for more than thirty years.

KITTERY TO CASCO BAY

White Island Light, Isles of Shoals
Whaleback Light
Nubble Light, Cape Neddick
Boon Island Light
Wood Island Light

White Island Light, Isles of Shoals

The Isles of Shoals are those nine small islands nine miles out to sea from Kittery, which rise strangely white from the ocean. Some belong to Maine, others to New Hampshire. The division was made in 1629, between Captain John Mason, proprietor of the Province of New Hampshire, and Sir Ferdinando Gorges, proprietor of the Province of Maine. Maine took title to Duck, Appledore, Malaga, Cedar, and Smuttynose, and New Hampshire got the remaining islands—Londoner (or Lunging), Star, Seavey's, and White.

The lighthouse, first built in 1820—the year the state of Maine separated from Massachusetts—stands on White Island, an outcrop of barren rocks, uninhabited now since the lighthouse was automated in 1986.

Once these were flourishing islands. They were rather heavily populated, and played a significant role in Maine history; they have been the scene of wonderful stories of Indian raids and shipwrecks. They were once called not the Isles of Shoals, but the Smith Islands.

Captain John Smith—that insatiable seafarer who at age twenty-six had helped settle the Jamestown Colony in Virginia in 1607—spent many years voyaging the coast of Maine, mapping and naming many islands on his charts. He never involved his own name in these christenings until he sailed into this group of barren islands. Their strange whiteness and special beauty won his heart and stirred his ego. He named them for himself—the Smith Islands.

Early fishermen changed the name to the magical one of Isles of Shoals. Some say it's because the group lay close together in the ocean like a shoal of fish. Others say it's because the ocean becomes suddenly shallow—shoals—here.

In 1623, Sir Ferdinando Gorges began a fishing settlement here. By 1628 there were enough sailors in little Gosport Harbor to support two taverns. To cater to the spirit as well as the flesh, a meetinghouse or church was established in 1640, with the Reverend Joseph Hull as the first minister. Three Kelly brothers, three Cutt brothers from Wales, the Oliver brothers, and the Seeleys were playing active roles in life on the fishing settlements of the Shoals in the 1640s. They did not enjoy women in their midst.

In a strange court order of 1647, Richard Cutt, a settler on Hog Island (whose rude name was later beautified to Appledore) complained,

John Reynolds has brought his wife hither with the intention that she live and abide here, contrary to an act of court which says that no woman shall live upon the Isles of Shoals ... he has also brought upon Hog Island a great stock of goats and swine which spoil the spring water ... our petitioners therefore pray that the Act of Court be put in execution for the removal of women from inhabiting here.

The court ordered that the goats and swine go, but allowed the woman to stay.

A young sailor from Cornwall, England, whose family was to become the richest in Maine, settled here on Appledore in 1676. He was William Pepperell, and his moneymaking specialty was to cure fish the Appledore way: light on the salt (it was scarce and expensive), and heavy on the sun, then buried in salt hay until the flesh turned a handsome sherry brown. This specialty of Pepperell's tickled the palates of Spanish grandees who paid fancy prices for his Appledore fish.

This William had a son called William Pepperell who was born at nearby Kittery Point in 1696, and led three thousand men in battle to capture the French fortress of Louisburg, on Cape Breton, in 1745. For this, the boy from the Isles of Shoals was made a baronet by King George II and became Sir William Pepperell. He amassed a fortune and built the Pepperell mansion. Much later, Lady Pepperell built her lovely house on Kittery Point, still an architectural gem and landmark.

The winds of politics changed. During the American Revolution, all the Pepperell wealth and estates were confiscated because the Pepperells stayed loyal to King George III of England. Today the sheets that millions of people sleep between are named for this Pepperell family.

Now, not even lightkeepers live on the Isles of Shoals in winter. But the population was large three hundred years ago. In 1702, a French ship visiting the Shoals reported that there were two hundred and eighty men, plus women and children, on these islands—which would mean at least five hundred people in all.

During and after the War of Independence, these islands hit the skids. Because their people were thought to be loyal to England and therefore the enemy, the islanders were forced to leave. Once they had dispersed and set down roots elsewhere, they were not inclined to return. The Isles of Shoals became a roughneck, disreputable hideaway for the depraved, the outcast, and the drunken thieves who preyed on wrecks.

The lighthouse, erected in 1820, became the focal point of the comeback, after Thomas Laighton became keeper in 1839. Laighton had an odd background for a keeper when he applied for the job, and he used his political pull to get it. Thomas B. Laighton, candidate for governor of New Hampshire, lost his political race badly, by means he thought underhanded and unfair. In what seemed like a bitter revenge for his rejection, Laighton sold his business in Portsmouth and applied for the job of lightkeeper out on the Isles of Shoals. He may have had a businessman's eye on the real estate there. Five years earlier, in 1834, Laighton had purchased four of the nine islands—Appledore, Smuttynose, Malaga, and Cedar—and he now became keeper on the fifth island, White. Treasure was rumored to be buried out there, hidden by the legendary Captain Kidd.

The man from whom Laighton bought the islands was a Captain Samuel Haley, who, when trying to interest Laighton in buying the islands from him, told him he had found bars of silver buried beneath a stone. Haley had sold the silver for three thousand dollars, and used part of his profit to build a seawall, a breakwater, and a wharf. Haley built a

Storm-ravaged seas batter Isles of Shoals Light a day after the big storm of September 1978. Gannett file photo.

rope walk, a windmill, and a salt works. He kept open house for fishermen and buyers, and to help guide ships; before the days of a lighthouse, he hung a lantern every night in an upstairs window.

Thus in 1839, Thomas Laighton, his wife, and two children, Oscar and Celia, moved offshore to keep the light. A retainer-friend named Ben Whaling went with them. The two men shared the watches of four hours each, keeping the light. In 1841, two years after the Laightons had moved into the keeper's house, a baby son was born, christened Cedric. Nearby on Smuttynose lived a Captain Becker, his wife, and six children—tenants of Laighton. Becker, a German, was a war veteran who had fought against Napoleon at Waterloo.

Laighton was a go-getter. He turned over lightkeeper duties to others, while he kept his finger in business and political pies on the mainland. In 1841, he was elected to the New Hampshire Legislature, perhaps the only lightkeeper in the United States to serve in a state legislature. He was also elected to the Board of Selectmen in Portsmouth. Out on the islands, he worked hard to revive the fishing and took the wild step of building a little hotel on Appledore, which he called the Mid Ocean. He moved his family out of the keeper's cottage and into the hotel.

Daughter Celia, later to become a famous poet, essayist, and hotel manager, was now twelve. She had come out here as a baby. Growing up, she had learned to help her father and Ben Whaling trim and keep the lights. She witnessed and later wrote a poem about the wreck of the brig *Pocohantas*, which occurred at Christmastime 1839, while the brig was sailing from Cadiz, Spain, for Newburyport. The brig sailed so close to the light on White Island in the storm of December 22 that Celia and her mother could hear the ship's signal gun as it swept past to destruction on the sandbar at nearby Plum Island. All aboard perished.

Celia herself lit the lamps that fateful night. I quote a few of the verses from the poem she wrote later:

> I lit the lamps in the lighthouse tower
> For the sun dropped down and the day was dead.
> They shone like a glorious clustered flower,
> Ten golden and five red.
>
> The sails that flecked the ocean floor
> From east to west leaned low and fled:
> They knew what came in the distant roar.
>
> Flung by a fitful gust, there beat
> Against the window a dash of rain;

Steady as the tramp of marching feet
Strode on the hurricane.

It smote the waves for a moment still.
Level and deadly white for fear;
The bar rock shuddered,—an awful thrill
Shook even my tower of cheer.

When morning dawned, above the din
Of gale and breaker boomed a gun!
Another! We who sat within
Answered with cries each one.

The thick storm seemed to break apart
To show us, staggering to her grave,
The fated brig. We had no heart
To look, for naught could save.

By 1847, keeper Laighton retired from the lighthouse service to work full-time on his fast-growing hotel. Celia, sixteen, married Levi Thaxter in 1851 and became the lovely and talented hostess of the hotel. The register was soon filled with the lions of the literary and art worlds of New England: Nathaniel Hawthorne, Henry Longfellow, James Russell Lowell, Sarah Orne Jewett, Harriet Beecher Stowe, William Dean Howells, Frances Burnett (of *Little Lord Fauntleroy* fame); and artists such as Childe Hassam, A.T. Bircher, and William Morris Hunt came to paint on Appledore.

The hotel, now called Appledore House, was enlarged and made more grand many times, so more than three hundred people were staying in it at a time. Attracted by its success, competitor hotels sprang up and the Isles of Shoals became a major resort, first of the great resorts on this coast.

Lighthouse keeper Thomas Laighton died in 1866. His son expanded the hotel empire until it all came to an abrupt end in 1914 when the famed Appledore House burned. Celia, her father, mother, and brothers are all buried in the family cemetery on Appledore, in graves that can still be seen today.

Today, in the summer months, other hotels are now filled with meetings of religious congregations, and the Shoals Marine Laboratory of Cornell and the University of New Hampshire are located there.

Whaleback Light

The first Whaleback Light should have toppled and sunk. And it nearly did.

The first light, built in 1829 at the mouth of the Piscataqua River near the Maine–New Hampshire boundary, was shoddily built, but survived—miraculously—for some forty years, though many keepers felt they and their lighthouse would be drowned together.

The stone tower and pier cost $20,000, which in 1829 should have been money enough to build a strong, substantial light. But the contractor skimped in places his cheating might not be easily detected.

Where the lowest stones were laid for the light tower, the ledge should have been leveled off evenly to take the first course of masonry. Instead, the contractor laid the first foundation stones of the tower on an uneven surface of the ledge, and skimped by filling the holes with small stones.

When the first storm seas washed across, out went the loose stones and the underpinnings of the light were washed away. Another bit of cheating was that the contractor failed to bolt the bottom of the tower into the ledge. It is a wonder that the first storms did not wash away the entire lighthouse.

Colonel Sylvanus Thayer, the father of West Point, was sent from Boston to check on the trouble at Whaleback Light. His engineering report was clear and blunt. He advised tearing the shoddy structure down and starting again from scratch. That, he said, would require an appropriation of $75,000.

Written in the 1840s, Thayer's report gathered dust for twenty years. All that while, by the skin of their teeth and lots of good luck, Whaleback keepers escaped death by drowning. Some metal sheathing had been added to the structure, because the keeper swore he could not otherwise survive the seas, which came pouring in. The sheathing may have kept the keeper from drowning, but it did not stop the tower from shaking and shivering each time the seas piled up around it.

Washington bureaucrats, far from the seas and the scene, gained confidence as the years went by and the tower did not fall into the sea, as Colonel Thayer had predicted. This way of ignoring the problem saved $75,000 in new construction. So confident were the bureaucrats that they spent money in 1855 to install a new lens and lantern in the old tower. Then in 1859 they added a new fog signal.

Meanwhile the lighthouse was falling apart structurally. After iron clamps were placed to strengthen the base, they snapped off one by one.

At last, in 1869, about a quarter-century after Colonel Thayer had said the lighthouse should be torn down and replaced, Congress appropriated the money he had asked for to build a new light. This time, the new tower was built in what was known as "the Eddystone style"—the method used to soundly build the famed Eddystone Light on a barren ledge at sea in the English Channel.

The new light was finished in 1872, made out of great granite blocks, dovetailed to each other, with the bottom tiers laid on leveled ledge and heavily bolted into the ledge. The new light was built beside the old tower, which was finally cut down to house a new Daboll trumpet as the fog signal.

But even the new light could not resist the fierce strength of every Atlantic storm. A horrific storm in 1886 battered in one of the windows in the thick granite tower and the sea poured in, almost drowning the keeper, Leander White of Newcastle. Terrified, White fled to the uppermost landing of the light for safety. There he hung a blanket out into the storm, as a distress signal for any passing ship. None saw it because the gale shredded the blanket to ribbons. Luckily, Captain Walter S. Ames on Kittery Point spotted the tatters blowing in the wind. After the gale winds dropped, Ames set out to see what was wrong at Whaleback Light. Ames found Keeper White half-drowned, frightened, and helpless to do anything but whimper at his plight. Ames got him ashore safely and found medical help for him. To remedy the danger, the broken window was taken out and replaced by a solid granite block. What was lost in light was gained in safety.

Two years later, the terrible gale of November 1888 swept over Whaleback into Portsmouth and Kittery. This time the foundations of the old tower, which now housed the fog signal, were swept off by giant waves. The keeper reported that two thousand tons of rocks had been ripped from the old foundation and piled up at the foot of the ladder to the new lighthouse.

In 1891, five years after he had rescued keeper Leander White, Walter S. Ames was named keeper of Whaleback Light, and during his tenure performed more rescues.

As an example of the tricks that seas and currents play here, Edward Rowe Snow—writer, historian, and the flying Santa Claus who, for forty years, dropped Christmas presents to lightkeepers along the New England coast told this story. He flew over Whaleback, dropped his Christmas package, saw that he had missed his target and the gifts had fallen into the sea. Snow made another pass in his plane and dropped another package. Six weeks later, a man walking the beaches of Cape Cod found the package Snow had dropped into the sea. It had floated ninety miles in almost a direct line across Massachusetts Bay.

Coming out from Kittery today, Whaleback Ledge Light rises on the northeast side of the harbor entrance. It seems puzzling to see a sort of double tower when the chart states only one. The base of the first tower still stands next to the newer one, making it seem as though the navigator is seeing double.

Nubble Light, Cape Neddick

To more than a hundred thousand summer visitors at the popular beach resorts at York, Wells, and Ogunquit, the spectacular lighthouse at Cape Neddick is the essence of handsome lighthouses on the coast of Maine. Nubble Light is easy to drive to, visitors are welcome, and the views from it in all directions have a memorable grandeur.

The light is relatively new, built in 1879. But the white man's history here goes back to twenty years before the arrival of the *Mayflower* and the Pilgrims at Plymouth Rock.

In 1602, the English explorer Captain Bartholomew Gosnold held a parlay here with Indians during his voyage along the coast of Maine. Gosnold named the place Savage Rock in memory of his meeting here with the "savages," as told in this account written by John Brereton, the historian aboard Gosnold's little ship:

> The fourteenth of May, 1602, about six in the morning ... we descried land that we called Savage Rock, because the savages first showed themselves there ... From said rock came towards us a Biscay shallop with sail and oars, having eight persons in it, whom we supposed at first to be Christians distressed. But approaching nearer we perceived them to be savages. Those coming within call, hailed us and we responded. Then after signs of peace, and a long speech one of them made, they came boldly aboard us, being all naked, saving about their shoulders certain loose deer skins, and near their wastes seal skins tied fast like Irish dimmie trowsers. One that seemed to be their commander wore a waistcoat of black work, a pair of breeches, cloth stockings, shoes, hat and band, one or two more had also a few things made by some Christians: these with a piece of chalk described the coast thereabouts, and could name the Placentia of Newfoundland; they spoke divers Christian words and seemed to understand much more than we, for want of language to comprehend. These people were in color swart, their hair long, their hair uptied with a knot ... They paint their bodies which are strong and well proportioned. These much desired our longer stay, but finding ourselves short of our purposed place, we set sail westward, leaving them and their coast.

This account implies there had been considerable interchange between whites and these Indians some years before 1602 and this

Gosnold meeting with them at Cape Neddick. Later, after settlements had been established here by whites, relations with the "savages" turned bloody. In 1676, Indians attacked the white settlement at Cape Neddick and killed or kidnapped all forty inhabitants.

The first official record of the need for a lighthouse hereabouts comes from the report of Captain Joseph Smith, who was on an inspection trip of the Maine coast in 1837. He urged that a light be built at the entrance to the York River. Others recommended one at Cape Neddick Nubble and this location got new impetus after the fabled wreck of the bark *Isidore*.

The *Isidore* set sail from Kennebunkport Harbor late in the morning of November 30, 1842, under the command of Captain Leander Foss, headed east. As she tacked down the bay, a snowstorm came on hard, with a strong breeze, and the sight of *Isidore* was lost to the hundreds of people who had gathered to see her off. The next morning, snow lay thick on the ground when the news came from down the coast at Ogunquit that the wreckage of a large vessel was strewn along that shore. The wreckage was of the *Isidore*, which had hit in the snowstorm off Savage Rock—whose name was by then Bald Head Cliffs—just north of Cape Neddick Nubble.

One of Maine's youngest lighthouses, Nubble Light, Cape Neddick, at York Beach was built in 1879. Though still an active aid to navigation, the lighthouse was automated in 1987. Courtesy of Philip Ziegler.

The story of the wreck of the *Isidore* became a fable told by many a Maine fireside because of the superstitious warnings surrounding its doomed departure from Kennebunkport. One crewman named Thomas King had a nightmare before sailing time that the *Isidore* would be wrecked and all aboard her lost at sea. He told his dream to Captain Foss and asked to be discharged from the crew because he was too frightened to sail with the *Isidore*. Foss laughed and told King to be on deck at departure, especially since he had already drawn a month's advance pay. But King hid out as the *Isidore* sailed and was briefly derided by his neighbors in Kennebunkport.

When the news of the wreck came from Ogunquit, his neighbors suddenly looked at King in awe. Another seaman had a similar nightmare the night before sailing. He told that he had dreamed of seven coffins, one of which was his. But his friends laughed at him and this seaman, shamed, decided to sail aboard the *Isidore*. His was one of the bodies recovered. Captain Foss's body was never recovered. The dead were buried in a common grave.

Fishermen near the Isles of Shoals say that they sometimes see the phantom bark *Isidore* manned by a crew with dripping-wet clothes still sailing through snowstorms.

There are happier memories of Nubble Light. Three weddings were celebrated in the lighthouse, one performed in the tower. Hattie E. Lewis, daughter of Brackett Lewis, keeper from 1885 to 1901, was married there. William M. Brooks, who succeeded Lewis as keeper, witnessed two of those weddings, and went on to be the oldest lighthouse keeper, before his death at ninety-six in December 1959. Keeper Brooks remembered the days when Cape Neddick was a cattle pasture and sightseers were ferried for ten cents round trip out to the light, and the keeper's wife took them through the light for a nickel each. Years later, in 1979, Coast Guard keeper David Winchester lived in the six-room keeper's house with three young children. His youngest daughter, Wendi Ann, came to live at the lighthouse when she was eight days old. When his oldest boy, Ricky, began school on the mainland, keeper Winchester rigged up a homemade kind of container in which he put Ricky and then hauled him by line to the mainland, where he jumped out of his personal breeches buoy and walked to the schoolhouse. Inspectors from the Coast Guard declared the contraption too risky and thereafter Ricky had to row, or be rowed, ashore.

After the wreck of the *Isidore* in 1842, Captain Joseph Smith's 1837 recommendation for a light at York River was dusted off and read again. Not until ten years after the *Isidore* disaster did Congress appropriate

$5,000 for a light. It was too little. So in 1874 and again in 1875, Congress upped the appropriation to $15,000. Yet no action was begun until 1879, when a light was quickly built—forty feet tall and ninety-two feet above the sea, and first lighted on July 1, 1879. The first keeper was a New Hampshire native, Nathaniel Ottersen, who served for six years at a salary of $500 a year. In 1877, a 1,226-pound bell was installed as a fog signal and it lasted until 1961, sounding for fifteen seconds out of every minute. It was replaced by a 255-pound bell. The old bell is on display at York Beach Park. Nubble Point, close to the lighthouse, was given to York Beach Village by its owner, Colonel William Sohier, and is now Sohier Park.

Boon Island Light

The nicest story about rough and isolated Boon Island is the story of how it won its name. For close to two hundred years, fishermen from York, eight miles away, packed emergency rations into a barrel and left it on the rocky island as a boon to shipwrecked sailors who might make it to this desolate shore, but need food to survive. The gruesome history of how shipwrecked and starving sailors survived by cannibalism led the York fishermen to put a boon of provisions on this perilous ledge.

In 1710, the English ship *Nottingham Galley* was shipwrecked on this unmarked ledge. Captain Deane and his crew were marooned here for weeks as never-ending storms beat upon them and prevented any passing ship from seeing their distress signals. Man by man, they began to starve to death or to die from madness. To keep themselves alive, survivors resorted to eating the flesh of their dead shipmates. (Their horror story was told by Maine author Kenneth Roberts, in his historical novel *Boon Island*.)

In 1799, General Benjamin Lincoln, superintendent of lighthouses for Massachusetts (which then included the Province of Maine), urged the government in Washington to build a beacon on Boon Island. By July 1800, the beacon was built—wooden and fifty feet high—at a cost of $600. The structure lasted through three winters, but the great storm of October 9, 1804, swept the island and washed away the beacon. The following July, a stronger beacon, made of stone this time, was built. When the job was done, a Captain John F. Williams arrived to take off the builders. On his return trip to the mainland, a squall upended the boat, drowning the contractor and two masons. Williams saved himself, bought another boat, and returned to take off the remaining workers, some of whom were hesitant about making the trip.

But the new stone beacon was not warning enough. In 1811, General Lincoln wrote to his top boss, Secretary of the Treasury Albert Gallatin, urging that a lighthouse be built on Boon Island. An invitation to bid on building this lighthouse appeared in Boston's *Independent Chronicle*. Contractor John Hill bid $14,000 to build a lighthouse, keeper's house, oil vault, and a cistern for water. He was hugely underbid by competi-

The present Boon Island Light, nine miles out to sea from York Beach, was built in 1812 and became unmanned in 1978. Courtesy of Philip Ziegler.

tors Noah Porter and Thomas Heath, who set their price at only $2,527. They won the contract, fulfilled it by winter, and the first keeper arrived. His stay was short. He quit after a few brief weeks on that desolate ledge, beaten by winter seas. On December 16, 1811, David Oliver, who had helped build the light, got the job as keeper. But soon Oliver also quit, and the job went to Thomas Hanna, who quit in May 1816. Commissioner Smith of the Treasury appointed Eliphalet Grover as keeper, even providing him with a boat as an inducement to stay on the job.

In 1831, another great storm swept away much of the lighthouse, and this time Simon Pleasonton of the Treasury authorized Seward Merrill to build a new light. The keeper's salary was raised to $600 a year.

Politics and patronage, as well as storms, bedeviled Boon Island Light during the 1840s. In June 1841, Mark Dennet quit as keeper and was replaced by Captain James Thompson. By September of 1843, Thompson was removed from his job so that John Kennard might get it as a political reward. Thompson wrote a protesting letter to President John Tyler:

> I have been a seaman from a boy—being now 60 years old, am poor, have a family to support, with little or no means. I voted for Your Excellency for Vice-president and intended to exert my feeble influence to promote another election for you as President—so why I am removed from my keeper's job, I am at a loss to know.

The letter did no immediate good for Thompson. John Kennard kept Thompson's job until Nathaniel Baker was given it, again for political reasons. Then politics gave the axe to Baker. Finally, in 1849, a fair political wind blew in Thompson's direction, and he got back his job as keeper.

The light—along with the keepers—was buffeted by many an ill wind, and threatened to topple. In 1852, Congress appropriated $25,000 to build a new lighthouse—almost twelve times the amount of money spent on the one built in 1811. The light was far bigger and stronger this time: 137 feet above sea level, 25 feet in diameter at the base, tapering to 12 feet in diameter at the top. It was finished in 1855 and looks today very much the same as it did then.

A tragic and heroic legend persists from those years in the middle of the 19th century. It concerns one keeper who brought his bride to live with him at this desolate light. The couple spent months in happiness together. Then, unexpectedly, the keeper fell gravely ill and died. That night a great storm lashed the light and the ledge on which it perilously stood.

The frantic young widow, alone with the body of her dead husband, climbed the 130 narrow, winding steps to the top of the tower to keep the five-wick lantern burning. In free moments she climbed down the stairs to stand watch over her dead husband. Night after night, day after day, the vicious storm kept raging, and the grief-stricken young widow would climb up and down between duty to light and to husband. The young widow finally lost her reason, and the light went out.

The next day the storm abated and fishermen from York Harbor came out to see why the light was extinguished. They found the demented girl grieving and mad, wandering the rocks. They took her and her husband, the living and the dead, home to the mainland.

A beacon or a light has stood on Boon Island since 1800. In the more than two hundred years since then, tragedy, grief, madness, fear, happiness, joy, and amazing gallantry have marked the lives of many keepers and their wives and families.

But no keeper spent more years on this desolate rock ledge than

William W. Williams, who spent twenty-seven years here, from the 1890s until World War I.

Boon Island is more ledge than island. It is only seven hundred feet long, and none of it is more than fourteen feet above the sea. Storms and waves sweep Boon Island, one of the roughest stations on the North Atlantic. It is barren, shrubless, treeless, and without natural soil anywhere. Yet this was home to Williams and his wife for more than a quarter-century. He lived past the age of ninety, and spoke of his memories as a keeper to another, younger keeper, Robert Thayer Sterling, who, in 1936, incorporated that interview into a book called *Lighthouses of the Maine Coast and the Men Who Kept Them*:

> "There were some days when I first went on station," remembered Williams when he was ninety and living in Kittery, "that I could not get away from the idea that I was locked up in a cell. All we had then was a little stone house and a rubblestone tower. When the rough weather came, seas swept the ledges clean. I was always thinking what I would do to save my life should the whole station be washed away ... I believe it is these things which gradually wear on the mind and finally upset the brain."

The men who kept the Boon Island Light in the earliest days of the 1800s, through the War of 1812, and up until the light was rebuilt in 1855, had an even worse time. All they had was a small stone tower and a funk hole dug into the rock for shelter when seas swept madly across the ledge, taking all with them.

Williams recalled two of the earliest of many wrecks he eyewitnessed. First was the schooner *J.H.&G. Perkins* out of Rockland, which was saved almost miraculously:

> She ran ashore slap bingo on the northwest breaker. We thought sure she was going to hang there but the backlash of the sea righted her and off she went again. When she flopped back on the starboard side, a gust of wind caught her sails and she stood off from the ledge pretty as a picture. In an east wind, she would have been wrecked.

Four years later, the same trick of God's weather saved the schooner *Pathfinder*: "There was no fog signal then and take thick weather a fellow had to just guess and begorry. If he hit, he hit, and if he went by, all well and good." *Pathfinder* hit in thick fog on the same northwest breaker and lay grounded until the next flood tide carried her off, sound and sailing. That was in summertime. But that November, just before Thanksgiving, the *City of Ellsworth*, a schooner laden with timber from Bangor and bound for Plymouth, Massachusetts, hit with no tide or wind to save her. She broke up, and was a total loss.

The mention of Thanksgiving triggers another story told by Captain Williams. The evening before a Thanksgiving holiday, Williams and his two fellow keepers were in the tower. It was storming and blowing hard outside, and they were busy keeping the lamps burning and complaining about the lean pickings they faced for Thanksgiving dinner. Supplies were down to bare subsistence level.

Then there was a tremendous thump on the lantern. Anxious to see what had caused it, Williams faced the storm and went outside. There on the deck outside the lantern room he found four pair of black ducks, dead as doornails. Below on the ground he found four more. Attracted by the light shining through the storm, they had flown into the lantern and killed themselves, fat and healthy though they were. Williams said he and his fellow keepers and families gave thanks to their Creator for providing an unexpectedly fine Thanksgiving dinner.

The most exciting time Williams had during his twenty-seven years on Boon Island was the rescue of the crew of the schooner *Goldhunter,* early one December—when the cold was down below zero:

> The schooner struck on Boon Island Ledge, about three miles from the light. The crew managed to get into their yawl boat and after a hard six-hour row reached the light station at 1:30 on the morning. We were roused by the barking of a dog. We got out our lanterns and climbed down over the icy rocks and made out the little boat just outside the big breakers. We yelled to the castaways to follow our lanterns around to the lee side of the island, and watched them, still guided by the glimmer of our lanterns, take their chance to run in on top of a sea. The dog leaped ashore, with the painter line in his mouth, and the three keepers grasped the boat rails and pulled the little craft up on the rocks, out of reach of the next sea.
>
> The crew was frozen to the thwarts and almost helpless. The keepers and their wives had a desperate task for the next few hours to resuscitate the almost lifeless men. One of the sufferers was a Negro boy 14 years old. Many, many years later I met this same boy and shook hands with him. The memory of that terrible night was still fresh in his mind.

Of course there was no telephone or radio link to the mainland in those days. Carrier pigeons brought news back and forth to the mainland in case of illness in the families ashore. One pigeon made the eight-mile trip in just ten minutes.

Keeper Williams had many narrow escapes from death during his years on Boon Island. One accident almost cost the lives of Williams and his family. He and his family were making the trip to the mainland in his small sailing craft, when a squall struck and capsized the boat, casting them all into the sea. Mrs. Williams was in the worst predicament.

She had been sitting in the lee, wrapped for warmth in an old sail. In the ocean the sail acted like an anchor, dragging her down. But their son managed to reach the dory that was always towed behind the sailboat. He whipped out his knife from his trouser pocket and cut the dory adrift, crawled into it, and rescued the four others who were floundering in the icy water.

There were few comforts on Boon Island. Up in the light tower, where the keepers stood watch, it was indeed a matter of standing. The only chair was an upturned soapbox. The wind howled around the tower, catching the braces of iron installed to strengthen it, and the weird sound was like mad music from an Aeolian harp.

To grow a few vegetables and raise a few flowers on the small barren rock, Williams and the other keepers used to bring out barrels of dirt from trips to the mainland. In a fine summer, the flowers and vegetables grew well. But if a storm blew up, waves would, in seconds, wash away all their labors of months.

The worst job on Boon Island was painting the cap on the lantern tower black.

> That job was truly scary and it rendered the most solemn moment of the island year. We threw a rope over the dome of the tower from the gallery rail and brought it around so as to make a loop held fast by the ball and lightning rod. Down below, you could see the anxious eyes of the wives and children watching the father who had volunteered to do the job. All work on the island ceased, to insure utter silence for the man who performed the duties of a steeplejack.

Boon Island Light was automated and unmanned in 1978, after keepers had lived for 167 years on this desolate, storm-beaten ledge.

Wood Island Light

The biggest, most popular beach in Maine is at Old Orchard. Standing out from Old Orchard Beach, eyed by tens of thousands of summer swimmers and sunbathers here, and at the army of summer trailers at Camp Ellis, stands the Wood Island Light. A few miles to the west, marking the entrance to Cape Porpoise Harbor, is Goat Island Light, built in 1833, by order of President Andrew Jackson. These are tourist meccas now—but once it was mackerel that schooled in Old Orchard Bay and Biddeford Pool. Fleets of seine boats chased them and waited for them. A few miles offshore lies Wood Island and at its eastern end, marking the south entrance to Wood Island Harbor, stands the light, ordered built by President Thomas Jefferson in 1808.

The tower was conical, made from granite blocks. As shipping multiplied, a better aid to navigation than the conical tower was needed, and under President James Buchanan the light was improved. Today it is further improved. The light sends out two 500,000-candlepower flashes every six seconds, stands seventy-one feet above the sea, and was one of the few island light stations along the Maine coast that was still manned, until its automation in 1986.

Stories of strange violence are a hallmark of the Wood Island Light. One is about a giant lobsterman who came to live a hermit's life on Wood Island. He was about thirty years old and had been a special policeman and part-time lobsterman at Biddeford Pool. He was so big and strong that he would heft his dory up onto his gargantuan shoulders and carry it from the low tide mark to beyond the high water mark on the shore, as though the boat weighed no more than a canoe. Then a younger squatter arrived, repaired a dilapidated henhouse, and set up housekeeping. He was about twenty-five years old, and though he lobstered off and on, his main occupation was taking off to the mainland to do some heavy drinking.

One day he arrived back, drunk, on the shore at Wood Island. He was carrying a rifle in his arms. The huge lobsterman was alarmed at the sight of his intoxicated neighbor lugging a rifle. He went up and tried to talk the young man into handing it over for safekeeping until he was sober again. He refused. So the giant lobsterman went back to his home, took out his special policeman's badge, and returned, this time to take the rifle into custody by force of law. As he approached, the drunken neighbor raised his rifle and shot the special policeman. The giant's wife rushed to her fallen husband's side, but he died quickly.

The drunken criminal then walked to the lighthouse and turned himself in as a murderer to the lightkeeper. The keeper told him to confess to the police and turned him away. The man walked back to his henhouse shack. There he shot himself through the head and died.

Some years later, another hermit-type came to Wood Island to live in one of the old henhouses and run some chickens of his own, as well as to set out a few lobster traps and do some fin-fishing. He kept the hens well, and made a garden and raised his vegetables. But the loneliness of his hermit's life soon began to turn his brain, and he could be seen pacing back and forth along the shore. One day he got into his boat, rowed ashore, and took a hotel room in Saco just to rest his mind. When the day arrived that he was due to return to his lonely life on Wood Island, he jumped out the window of his hotel room and was killed instantly.

Shipwrecks dot the history of Wood Island. One of the strangest happened in the 1870s, when, in fair weather one night, a schooner drove ashore on the rocks a few miles from the light. Seeing the vessel ashore near Fletcher's Neck, a group of fishermen from Biddeford Pool rowed out in a dory to lend a helping hand. As the dory bumped alongside the hull of the stranded ship, the captain heard the noise and came running up on deck. When he was told the fishermen had come to help him get off, the captain said, "My wife is below, sick to death with smallpox."

At that frightening news, most of the fishermen grabbed the oars and headed the dory for home. But three took a chance and went aboard to help the captain and his sick wife. They got the old lady off the ship and carried her to one of the shacks on shore, and then fetched a doctor for her from the mainland. After a spell of good nursing, the smallpox victim recovered. And none of the fishermen who had helped her caught the dreaded, highly infectious disease.

Another story is about a French bootlegger who set up his business at the west end of the island. He made most of his money selling liquor to the crews of boats out of Gloucester, up fishing in Maine waters. They would often anchor nearby, come ashore to buy their booze, and do some drinking on the island shore. One night the party got rough and the Gloucester crewmen, who had laid out so much money to the French bootlegger, got the idea that it would be great fun to burn down his shack. They set the place afire and the flames burned merrily until they reached the outbuilding where the booze was made.

When the flames hit this, the place exploded in fury and the night sky was brilliant with blue flames from the alcohol. Ships twenty miles away puzzled over the wild blue flames erupting out of the sea near Wood Island Light.

CASCO BAY

Two Lights, Cape Elizabeth

Two Lights at Cape Elizabeth is a landmark for landlubbers as well as seamen. On a fine summer weekend, thousands of visitors come to Two Lights by car. There is a handsome park, with picnic tables looking seaward and chain-link fences to prevent children from toppling over cliffs.

Artist Edward Hopper painted Two Lights in 1929, and it has become a vastly popular reproduction. The painting now hangs in the Metropolitan Museum of Art in New York City. It was issued on a postage stamp in 1970, the first lighthouse ever pictured on an American stamp. Today, the privately owned keeper's house has been renovated and remodeled. It no longer resembles the house Hopper immortalized in his painting.

This lighthouse was first built in 1811 on spectacular oceanfront land that the government bought for $80. On July 24, 1811, two Maine men, Edward Robinson and John P. Bartlett, signed a contract with the government to build an octagonal tower forty-five feet high, made from "the best kind of undressed stone, with a huge boulder as a capstone." In quick order, they finished their job by November and painted the lower half white and the top half black. This first tower, built on a cliff 125 feet above the sea, was a good mark for ships heading into Portland, but it was of no use in fog or darkness. Complaints poured in from the ever-increasing ship traffic bound for Portland, and in 1827, Stephen Pleasonton, the Treasury official in charge of building all lighthouses, decided to go ahead with plans for a better light.

The government bought twelve more acres of land, and in June 1828 contracted with Jeremiah Berry to erect not one but two towers for $4,250 and to demolish the old tower before he began work on the new twin towers. Berry was another fast worker, for he finished the twin towers by October. President John Quincy Adams appointed Elisha Jordan as the first keeper, at a salary of $450 a year and with strict instructions that this was a full-time job that required Jordan to live at the light.

In 1852, Congress appropriated money to put in a fog bell and in 1854, new Fresnel lenses were installed to increase the visibility of Two

Lights. But there was no money to paint the twin towers, and they stood a dingy and somewhat invisible brown. In 1880, Congress got together enough money to paint them white and to replace broken windows, but not enough to install a standby, second fog signal. Two years later, to save money, the Lighthouse Board ordered that the light in the western tower be extinguished. At this news, another hullabaloo of protest from Portland shipping reached Washington, and the order was rescinded. (This west light was finally and forever extinguished in 1924, after another hullabaloo of protests.)

Marcus Hanna was keeper during these years. Hanna took the job at Two Lights in 1873. He had fought in the Civil War as a sergeant and won the Congressional Medal of Honor in 1863, for outstanding gallantry in the Louisiana battles.

Hanna was awarded another high honor—the gold medal from the Life Saving Services—for his gallantry in the rescue of two men from the schooner *Australia*, which hit Dyer's Ledge below the fog signal at Two Lights, in a blizzard on January 28, 1885.

The *Australia*, out of Boothbay Harbor, was headed for Boston with a cargo of ice from the Kennebec in her hold, and 150 barrels of mackerel lashed on deck. She left Boothbay on the 27th of January and quickly ran into foul weather. Records show the temperature dropped below zero that night, and a heavy blizzard of snow cut visibility to almost zero. As soon as the *Australia* sailed past Halfway Rock, Captain John W. Lewis and his crew, Irving Pierce and Austin Kellar, decided to seek shelter from the worsening storm in Portland Harbor.

With no visibility, they strained their ears for sound signals. When they finally heard a whistle, they judged it was from the fog station at Two Lights. They were mistaken. What they heard was the whistle from the Boston steamer, and they set course to follow that track. But as the whistle from the steamer moved, the *Australia* began to weave an erratic course and soon Captain Lewis lost his bearings. Hopelessly lost now, he decided to "jog off and under reefed foresail until dawn." But in the extremely cold and stormy sea, spray from waves turned to ice as soon as it hit their ship. Deeply encrusted with heavy ice now, Lewis and his men were no longer able to tack or even properly steer their vessel. Fearing they might founder, the three started to hurl overboard all 150 barrels of mackerel.

While straining at this icy work, they heard the real fog signal blowing from Two Lights. Lewis decided to run toward the signal and run the risk of going aground in zero visibility, because if they hit, they would be closer to possible rescue.

Two Lights, Cape Elizabeth, was first built in 1829, and became automated in 1963. Today, a state park surrounds the light. Gannett file photo.

They almost made it. But just before daybreak, the *Australia* hit hard on Dyer's Ledge, close below Two Lights. The three men aboard clung desperately to the twin masts and soon they, too, were ice-coated by the raging blizzard.

As morning dawned, keeper Hanna lay sick in bed with a cold. But his wife spotted the wrecked ship and the frozen men clinging to the masts. Keeper Hanna leaped from his sickbed and went out into the blizzard, clambering through the snowdrifts, down the cliff, and over the rocks till he reached Dyer's Ledge. There, he and his assistant, Staples, tried a dozen times to hurl a line aboard, only to see it drop into the sea, blown back by the wind. Staples was too exhausted to keep on and stumbled back to the station. Finally, Hanna landed a line onto the battered vessel. On board the *Australia*, seaman Pierce bent the line around his waist and plunged overboard into the surf, as Hanna hauled on the other end to drag him to safety. Pierce was now totally blind from the ice spray freezing on his face. With Pierce ashore, Hanna again hurled his line and this time Kellar bent it around his waist and dropped overboard. But Hanna, spent, sick, and exhausted, doubted if he had strength enough to haul Kellar through the surf to safety. At this moment, Assistant Keeper Staples returned with two neighbors to help. The fresh hands then carried the two survivors, frozen stiff, to the station. They cut their clothes off them, wrapped them in blankets, thawed them out, and fed them hot soup. Within a few days they were right as rain.

But Captain Lewis, last to leave his sinking ship, was never rescued. He clung to the mast, frozen and despairing, waiting his turn as last man off. But while he waited, he lost his grip and was thrown into the icy waves and drowned. His vessel was pounded to pieces.

One of the biggest ships to be wrecked close by was the 286-ton bark *Tasmania*. Eighteen years before the wreck of the *Australia*, the *Tasmania* arrived in Portland from Liverpool, to take on supplies before heading for Nassau. Resupplied, *Tasmania* headed out from Portland on the evening of March 19, 1857, in calm seas. Captain Stickney eased his ship past Portland Head Light, heading toward Cape Elizabeth and straining to see Two Lights through the fog. He was pointed a mite more toward land than he should have been, and the big vessel hit at Broad Cove. The bark had her bottom torn out of her. She was dead where she lay, even though the seas were flat calm. Captain Stickney was able to save his crew and his cargo of iron and crockery from Liverpool, but his cargo of salt was ruined by the sea.

A year later, the schooner *Abigail* met her doom beneath the eastern tower of Two Lights. Sailing from the east in thick fog, she missed the entrance to Portland Harbor and struck on the ledges, where she quickly broke up. In 1861, the little schooner *Susan* hit and broke up on Dyer's Point.

In recent times, the worst wreck with the best outcome was the wreck of the coal collier *Oakley L. Alexander*, which broke in two on March 3, 1947, in a great gale eight miles out to sea. The entire 32-man crew clambered onto the stern of the vessel. The gales and seas carried the stern half onto the rocks near Cape Elizabeth's Two Lights.

Keeper Earle B. Drinkwater got all the station's rescue gear ready as he watched the gale blowing the stern toward shore. By the time she hit the rocks, Drinkwater had his Lyle gun set up, ready to fire. With the first shot, the hauling line reached the broken vessel and a breeches buoy was rigged.

The first to be rescued, at 8:07 a.m., was the young mess boy, David Rogers, who reported that all the crew was alive. Drinkwater brought all thirty-two men ashore by breeches buoy. It was a miracle none had been lost when the ship broke in two, eight miles off, and another miracle that all were hauled to safety.

Captain Frank L. Cotton, named head keeper in 1910, had more duty time at Two Lights than any keeper of his day. He shared some of his recollections in a 1925 interview with Robert Sterling:

> I came here to Two Lights 34 years ago. I was the junior man, third assistant keeper. I didn't expect to stay long, for as a young man I did not expect to like the Lighthouse Service. But I married young, and when a fellow marries he's got to have a more or less regular income. So I stuck for ten years and then, well, I was a lighthouse man for life.

After his first ten years as a junior at Two Lights, Cotton did a short stint at Spring Point Light, inside Portland Harbor, and then came a long, eight-year stretch of duty at Petit Manan, one of the hardest stations in the service.

> Think of it: four acres of the flattest kind of rocky upheaval, only sixteen feet above high-water level. All shoals and tide races. Couldn't have a garden. Nothing grows in those barren rocks. Lonesome? Well, any man who hasn't put in a good many years on one of those outside lights off the coast of Maine just can't appreciate what that life means. I have walked down to the shore, perhaps at dusk after I had the light going good but before it was really dark, and have looked off to the south where I knew Portland and civilization lay.
>
> I thought of the brilliant lighted streets and the theaters and the other life other folks of my age were enjoying—well, it did take some grit to stick it out if I do say it. I don't know what I would have done without Uncle Billy and Uncle Johnny over on Green Island, a few oar strokes away in a dory at high water. That's a little, small island just to the northward of Petit Manan—William Stewart and John Coombs, they were, from Milbridge, twelve miles off on the mainland and the nearest town of any size.
>
> They were lobstermen and they would come offshore to their little shanty early in the season and stay late. They were crackerjack lobstermen and they liked to play a friendly game of poker, too!

Portland Head Light

The light at Portland Head is the best-known, most visited, and most photographed light in Maine. And for good reasons.

First, Portland Head Light is historic—one of the oldest lighthouses in the nation. It was begun in 1787 by order of President George Washington. The man who paid the bill was Alexander Hamilton, Secretary of the Treasury. Second, the views from the tower are spectacular. All the myriad islands of Casco Bay and beyond are spread in a wondrous panorama: twelve other lighthouses can be seen, their beacons flashing through the night. Third, the light is very easy to get to from Portland, Maine's largest city, and visitors are welcome.

Fourth, this light is famed in American literature. Henry Longfellow walked here often, wrote about it frequently in his poetry, and often took a sunbath on the adjacent rocks. Elijah Kellogg in his once popular series of boys' books, the "Ellis Island" series, wrote about islands that could be seen from here; Harriet Beecher Stowe (of *Uncle Tom's Cabin* fame) wrote *The Pearl of Orr's Island*, and poet Edna St. Vincent Millay lived on Ragged Island, also in easy view from Portland Head Light.

Construction of the light first began in 1787 under supervision of the Commonwealth of Massachusetts, of which the District of Maine was then a part, and was taken over by the newly established federal government headed by George Washington. The local builders were Jonathan Bryant and John Nichols, who were given four years to finish it. Washington instructed them to use local materials and haul them to the site by oxen. The new government was poor, and this would save money. In a signed letter written January 7, 1791, Washington appointed Joseph Greenleaf as first keeper of Portland Head Light.

But the presidential appointment and letter were the only glorious things about the job, as far as Greenleaf was concerned. He got no pay for two years, although he could live rent-free in the keeper's little house. In July 1793 he got cash, too—a federal salary of $160 a year. But he didn't collect his money long, for two years later, Greenleaf died of a stroke while rowing his skiff across the Fore River.

He was succeeded by a blacksmith with the unlikely name of

Barzillai Delano, who had been in the running earlier for the job against Greenleaf. Delano, though a blacksmith rather than a mariner by training, did the job well and held it for twenty-five years, until he died on duty in 1820, the year Maine was set off as a state separate from Massachusetts. Despite his twenty-five-year tenure as keeper, Delano lived in a water-soaked house and tower for half of those years. Complaints about the damp came soon after the light had been built. General Benjamin Lincoln, superintendent of lighthouses for Massachusetts, urged improvements, but they were never made. However, his successor, General Henry Dearborn, came to the Portland Head Light in 1810, interviewed Delano, listened to his complaints, and ordered improvements made. When the carpenters arrived, they found that Delano had stored the whole year's supply of lantern oil in the room they were supposed to repair. Everyone had to wait until the oil was used up, and come back a year later to fix the leaks.

The light had its troubles. Not only was the keeper wet and cold, but sea captains complained that they could not see the light. They wrote to the top boss of lighthouses in the nation, Tench Coxe, Commissioner of Revenue, at the nation's capital in Philadelphia. The problem was that there was no proper ventilation in the lantern room, and the glass became heavily smudged by black smoke from the burning lamp wicks. The height of the original tower had been increased so the light would not be obscured by another headland. When they increased the height, the builders had to narrow the size of the lantern room, thereby reducing the available ventilation.

The glass and the lanterns were cleaned up, and complaints ceased—but a better solution was needed. So in 1850, thirteen new 21-inch reflectors and a new lantern were installed. They were no match, however, to the Fresnel lenses that were already being used in other New England lights.

The problem was made worse by the lightkeeper of the time—a newly appointed man called John F. Watts. The members of the new Lighthouse Board in Washington came to visit Watts and they Portland Head Light on July 5, 1852. They did not like what they saw. The lighthouse had hordes of rats living in, under, and around it. The reflectors on the lights, although only two years old, were already badly scratched.

But Watts himself shocked them. He said that when he was given the job as keeper, no one would show him how to operate the lights. So with his own money, he had to go out and hire an instructor. Even worse, Watts was blowing the fog signal only for the captains of those ships with whom he had made a money contract to provide the service. Others got no foghorn.

Authorized by President George Washington in 1787, Portland Head Light has been shining at Portland Harbor since 1791. Courtesy of Philip Ziegler.

Following the report of the Lighthouse Board, Portland Head received a new Fresnel lens in 1855 and a new fog bell that would ring for all ships. But the great gale of September 1869, which smashed twenty ships in Casco Bay, also tore the 2,000-pound fog bell from its house and threw it like a tennis ball down among the rocks. Workmen winched it back up and built a new bell tower in a safer location. But this was not enough to satisfy the ever-increasing ship traffic into Portland. So the Lighthouse Board brought in the old Daboll trumpet that had been used on Monhegan. It lasted from 1872 until 1887.

Meanwhile, the tower itself was having its ups and downs. During the raids on Portland Harbor in the Civil War, it was agreed that Portland Head Light should be made higher so it would be visible farther out to sea. The tower was heightened by eight feet in 1864, giving it an elevation of eighty feet above the sea. Later it was lowered twenty feet, only to be raised twenty feet the next year. No one satisfactorily explained these sudden changes. Finally in 1885, Portland Head Light was raised again, so it now stands 101 feet above the sea.

No keepers were more closely associated with Portland Head Light or more loved than the Strouts, father and son. Between them they kept the light for more than sixty-five years.

The father, Joshua Strout, had been an experienced sea captain. He had gone to sea first as a cabin boy, eleven years old. When he was eighteen, he became cook on a tug. In 1854, he took command of the brig *Scotland* and sailed her to South America and Cuba. Other vessels he skippered included the bark *B.F. Shaw*, schooners *Starlight, Nellie Chase, L.T. Knight, Hannah Westbrook,* and the barks *Arcadia* and *Andres*.

In an accident at sea, Captain Strout was thrown to the deck from the mainmast of the *Andres*, and this led to his retirement from command of ships and to his appointment as keeper of Portland Head. His salary in 1866 was $620 a year. His wife, May, received $480 a year as his assistant keeper. When sickness forced him to quit, his son, Joseph Strout, became keeper and served for half a century, till his retirement due to ill health in 1928.

"As a lighthouse man, Captain Joe belonged in a class by himself," wrote Robert T. Sterling, himself a keeper of Portland Head.

The ledges near Portland Head were the scene of terrible shipwrecks and some heroic rescues. On the night of February 22, 1864, the *Bohemian*—with 218 passengers and almost a hundred experienced crewmen aboard—hit Alden's Rock off Cape Elizabeth. Forty people died.

The *Bohemian*, a five-year-old iron ship belonging to the Montreal Ocean Line, had sailed from Liverpool on February 4. All the way across the Atlantic, she had suffered foul and stormy weather. By February 22, she was five days overdue in Portland, and a pilot boat was anchored a mile south of Portland Head, awaiting the *Bohemian*. About midnight, one of these pilots heard a gun firing from the direction of Cape Elizabeth. Since it was George Washington's birthday, he thought it was a gun being fired in celebration. A bit later, the pilots heard a steamer coming out from Portland, blowing her horn in thick fog.

She came alongside and hailed, asking if this was the pilot boat. The pilot recognized the vessel as the tug *Uncle Sam*. The skipper of the tug shouted that the *Bohemian* had hit off Broad Cove Rocks and been sighted there by the Boston boat, on her way home from Portland to Boston.

Pilot boat and tug set out for the scene. Once past Trundy's Reef, they got into their yawl boat and rowed toward the noise of a slamming iron door they heard by Broad Cove Rocks. It was the wreck of the *Bohemian*. She had shortly after 8 p.m. on the night of February 22, steaming through heavy seas and fog, feeling her way slowly toward Portland. The captain knew he had hit Alden's Rock. His vessel hit, then began to slide off and to sink with 313 souls aboard. The captain ordered "full ahead," hoping to ground her out. Apparently the ship got underway strongly enough to make another two miles—as far as the rocks outside Broad Cove. The captain ordered all hands to the lifeboats, knowing he was fast losing his ship. There were six lifeboats, each able to hold sixty-five people. Five boats reached shore safely, not two miles distant, saving the lives of two hundred seventy-three people. But the Number 2 lifeboat swamped as it was being launched, dumping forty people into the sea, where they drowned.

The women from Cape Elizabeth and all the islands of Casco Bay wore the fruits of the wreck. The *Bohemian* had sailed from the north of England with a cargo of bolts of wool, silks, and satins. That cargo was strewn along the shore and turned into finery by the time of the Easter parades.

Two years later, during a blizzard on Christmas Eve 1886, the *Annie C. Maguire* met disaster at Portland Head. She was a 34-year-old, British registered, three-masted bark, headed from Buenos Aires to Quebec. She had fifteen in crew, plus Captain Thomas O'Neil, his wife, and their young son, Thomas. The captain sought shelter from the storm in Portland Harbor. He thought he was headed for the main ship channel, but he was off on his bearings, and headed for the ledges under the Portland Head Light.

Weather bureau records seem to contradict the excuse of a blizzard, showing that Christmas Eve of 1886 was a balmy 49 degrees, with seas moderate and visibility excellent, and a light rain and southerly breeze blowing in from the sea.

Whatever the weather, the *Annie C. Maguire* hit the ledges so hard that the impact shook the lighthouse like an earthquake. Keeper Joshua Strout and his son Joseph raced from the family Christmas tree to the wreck. They rigged emergency lights and shone them on the still-filled sails of the ship and her frantic, scared crew. The Strouts hurled a line aboard, which the crew fastened to the cross trees, while the Strouts made their end fast to the base of the tower. Quickly they rigged a bosun's chair between the wreck and the lighthouse. The Strouts hauled the entire fifteen-man crew, the captain, and his wife and son ashore, as the *Annie C. Maguire* began to break up on the rocks below.

At daylight Christmas morning, they could see the huge hole stove in the hull. Seas poured through it and waves tore the frames asunder. The ship was so badly broken that when she was put on the auction block on December 29, the highest bid was $177.50. Before even those remnants could be salvaged, a storm on New Year's Day made matchwood of her carcass.

There is an odd end to the story of the *Annie C. Maguire*. Days before she hit at Portland Head, the sheriff had paid a visit to Keeper

Strout, advising him to keep an eye out for the *Maguire*. The Quebec company that owned her had failed, and American creditors were out to seize the ship before she was beyond their reach, safe in Canadian waters. So after the ship was wrecked, the sheriff was back at the lighthouse on Christmas Day to serve attachment papers. There was little left of the ship to attach; the sheriff searched the ship's sea chest for the essential papers of ownership—documentation, registry, and above all, the ship's cash.

The captain then discovered that the satchel with all the ship's money inside was missing. He whispered to his wife in frantic undertones. She whispered back, telling him to shut up and pretend that the money satchel had been lost in the wreck.

It turned out that the lady had the money and the ship's papers, well hidden. Just before getting into the bosun's chair to be roped ashore to safety, the shrewd woman had ransacked the strong box, taken the cash, and put it inside her hatbox. As she rode the bosun's chair, she—a woman leaving a shipwreck—carried her hatbox in her lap.

Letters painted in black on the sea wall below the lighthouse still commemorate the wreck and rescue.

In thick fog in the summer of 1914, the Boston-to-Portland steamer slid onto the rocks. Immediately she began blowing her shrill distress whistle. The revenue cutter *Androscoggin* rushed out from Portland and hauled her off before much damage was done. In a fog at 6:10 p.m. Tuesday evening, October 4, 1932, the schooner *Lochinvar*, with a load of forty thousand pounds of haddock, hit about a hundred feet from where the *Annie Maguire* had struck. The *Lochinvar* sank like a block of concrete. The men got off in the dories, but had a difficult time getting their skipper, Captain Frank Doughty, to leave his ship. This was Doughty's twenty-eighth year at sea and his first accident. He was a local man whose family had fished Casco Bay for generations. The boat belonged to the Willard-Daggett Company of Portland.

The light at Portland Head went out on June 27, 1942, extinguished lest it become a homing marker for German submarines operating in the area. The fog signal went silent on July 5. Both were shut down until after World War II.

Storms batter Portland Head Light as severely today as they did in years past. Petty Officer Robert Allen described the great storm of February 3, 1972, to the *Maine Sunday Telegram*:

About 2 a.m. Friday morning, three exceptionally big waves came up. They had to be twenty-five to thirty feet high to get up over the cliff below the light. The gale was blowing ninety-two miles an hour. It was too dangerous to go outside to see how much damage was being done, because of the flying debris. The waves tore a 2,000-pound bell from its house, ripped down 80 feet of steel guard fence which was rooted in concrete, pulled the steel handrail off the ladder to the foghorn, ripped shingles off the whistle house. The waves broke a window in the lighthouse twenty-five feet above the ground—over fifty feet above sea level. The keeper's house was a foot deep in mud and flotsam, including starfish.

Out at the *Portland* lightship, twenty-year-old Coast Guardsman William Marchant of Westbrook could not make it ashore to his own wedding to Brenda Bickford, age eighteen. "The waves at the lightship were twenty-six feet high, with winds gusting over sixty miles an hour. There was no way to get ashore."

"He better get ashore by Monday," said the bride-to-be, "because our blood tests run out then."

Just a week before this storm, another storm had washed young men to their death. Waldo D. Preston, eighteen years old, was swept into the wild ocean from a rock at Delano Park, near the light. His companion, John Maxwell, nineteen, was also swept into the sea. But happily, the waves washed him into a crevice between two rocks, from which he was able to scramble to safety. In another battering storm, on April 3, 1975, the officer-in-charge, Coast Guardsman Roy Cavanaugh, reported that seas and gales were so violent, they extinguished the light and shut down the foghorn. Cavanaugh said, "The south wall of the whistle house, made of brick and concrete, has been blown in. Waves are breaking over the office and the keeper's house."

The storm of March 23, 1977, put out the light. First, Portland's commercial power lines were downed. Then the Coast Guard's emergency generator burned out. The keeper's family, a wife and three small children, were evacuated to a motel. Waves broke open drums of diesel oil around the generator, which could not be restarted because of danger of fire.

The word flashed out to mariners at sea that the light and the horn at Portland Head were both out of commission. But the 200,000-candlepower light was soon back in operation, shining as a light had shone from Portland Head since the days when George Washington was president.

On August 7, 1989, the U.S. flag was struck for the last time at the decommissioning ceremony recognizing the automation of the lighthouse. In 1990, the Town of Cape Elizabeth leased the property. Three years later, through the efforts of U.S. Senator George Mitchell, of Maine, the property was deeded to the town. The United States Coast Guard still maintains the actual light and the fog signal, but the remainder of the property is managed by the Town of Cape Elizabeth.

Ram Island Ledge Light

Open the chart of Casco Bay, and you can count about a hundred aids to navigation. When I first came into Casco Bay from Down East on *Steer Clear*, the number of buoys and lights made the approaches to Portland look the way Times Square looks to a visitor from a small town in Kansas: scary.

These traffic signals of the sea are danger warnings. Accidents had taken their toll too often before these warning signals were in place. Every light along the coast of Maine was paid for dearly and in advance by the wrecks of ships and the drowning of sailors before that light was built.

Take Ram Island Ledge Light, for example. To incoming boats, this light is a checkpoint, a routine mark coming into Portland Harbor from the east. But it hasn't been there long by lighthouse standards. It was built in 1905, when Teddy Roosevelt was president, and is one of the last lighthouses built on the Maine coast.

The light is made from Maine granite and towers seventy-seven feet above the ledge. Its beam is visible seventeen miles away. The dangers it signals are the death-trap ledges that stretch out from Ram Island. At high water, these ledges are covered and invisible; without a light on the ledge, many a mariner had been tempted to pass too close to Ram Island, for it looked as though the water there was deep and safe. Many ships and men perished before the light was built.

On May 27, 1866, there were four disasters. The schooner *Laura Jane*, with four men aboard; the schooner *Hockomock*, with four in crew; the schooner *Eliza Crowell* and the schooner *Tizar*, both with five in crew. These were all Maine boats. Fortunately, the men aboard were all saved.

In a gale on November 12, 1872, the young cabin boy aboard the schooner *W.C. Wellington* was drowned when his schooner hit the west tip of nearby Bangs Island on her voyage out of Boston, bound for Brooklin, Maine. She was trying hard to find shelter when the gale from the southwest blew away all her sails—helpless, she struck.

The fishing vessel *Little Fanny,* the schooner *L.A. Johnson,* and others came to grief here, trying to make Portland Harbor.

On January 26, 1882, a British schooner bound from Nova Scotia to Boston tried to make it from the east into Portland Harbor. With a crew of eight aboard, she hit just beyond Ram Island Ledge on Bangs Island. The next day, a schooner from Georgetown, Maine, laden with ice for Baltimore, ran aground on Black Rocks in blinding rain and fog. On New Year's Day, 1884, the *Etna* sank, a total loss with her cargo of railroad iron out of Portland. Later that summer, another fishing boat bound from Rockland to Harpswell was wrecked on Ram Island.

So it went, year in and year out—good ships and good men lost trying to make it into Portland during foul weather and hard storms.

The spectacular grounding of the 400-foot transatlantic steamer *California* on the night of February 24, 1900 triggered the action long needed to get a light at Ram Island Ledge. The *California,* with a crew of ninety-six and twenty-one passengers aboard—plus a $300,000 cargo— left her berth at Grand Trunk just before midnight, bound for England. She steamed out from Portland in a northeast snowstorm, under the guidance of a harbor pilot. After the pilot left, the *California* fell off her course. She hit and stuck on Ram Island Ledge, her lights blazing and not a mile from the Cape Elizabeth shore and less than a mile from the houses on Cushing Island.

Crew and passengers were quickly rescued, with no loss of life. But six weeks passed before the steamer itself was freed from the ledges. Eventually she was patched up and returned to service.

Two years later on September 22, 1902, the British three-master *Glenrosa,* laden with 850 tons of coal for S.D. Warren paper company in Westbrook, hit the ledge in thick fog. A lucky wave pulled her off, then unlucky waves drove her back on, where she stuck and broke up. Fortunately, the crew got off in a lifeboat and rowed away—first to Ram Island and then into Portland. But the ship fared less well. The local wrecker, Captain Phil Doyen, refused to work on the *Glenrosa* the next day, because it was Sunday. So all day looters stole gear from the stranded ship. By Monday, seas were rough and the salvage crews could not get aboard. When they auctioned off what was left of her two weeks later, the hull fetched four dollars.

Three months later, a 95-foot fishing vessel, the *Cora & Lillian,* smashed into the ledge and became another total loss.

So many ships had been lost here that back in 1855, an iron spindle was erected on the ledge. Then in 1873, a bigger, 50-foot-high wooden triangle was built as a better warning. But that was useful only in daylight, and so battered by the seas that it washed away completely three times. Another wooden triangle was built, but it did nothing to save the *California*. Finally in June of 1902, Congress earmarked $166,000 for a lighthouse. Construction was delayed until the following year. During the delay, the *Glenrosa* and the *Cora & Lillian* were lost.

At last, in the spring of 1903, the government bought title for $500 to these ledges from two Cape Elizabeth families, and signed a contract with the Bodwell Granite Company to provide the blocks needed from its quarries on Vinalhaven. The Chebeague Island stone sloops, *M.M. Hamilton* and *Yankee Girl,* brought the huge granite blocks out to the ledge, numbered in the order in which they would be placed.

But first the ledge had to be flattened off to receive the first course of granite blocks. In July 1903, the first courses were laid in circular fashion, twenty blocks to a course, with each block weighing four tons. The work went fast, with crews of thirty to forty men on the job; and by the end of September, sixteen courses had been built and the tower stood thirty-two feet tall. Work stopped during the winter storms, but began again the next spring. By July 1904, 699 granite blocks had been laid in all, and the tower was complete. In September, the 26,000-pound lantern arrived on two railroad cars from Atlanta. A third-order Fresnel lens had been ordered in Paris and was on its way. But more delays followed, and the light was not lit as scheduled in December.

The delay, however, saved the lives of four sailors and the captain of *Leona*, a lime schooner out of Rockland. After the *Leona* passed Halfway Rock at midnight, fog closed in. She lost her bearings and in rough seas hit hard on Ram Island Ledge. Knowing the *Leona* would turn into a blazing inferno when the seawater ignited the lime in her holds, Captain L.S. Whitten and his four-man crew took to their little lifeboat and launched her into the teeth of the gale. For four hours, until dawn, the men rowed hard just to keep their lifeboat headed into the waves and wind. Their strength was down to almost nil. The captain fired the flares. By chance, some lighthouse workmen saw them, as they sheltered inside their shack on nearby Ram Island. They rescued the freezing and weakened crew—but the lime ship was an inferno and burned to the waterline.

On the night of April 10, 1905, the Ram Island Ledge Light was finally lit—more than five years after the transatlantic steamer *California* had gone aground and caused the outcry for a light. William C. Tapley was the first head keeper, a job he held for twenty-four years, until 1929.

Ram Island Ledge Light was electrified in 1958. Underwater cables from Portland Head Light supplied power for the new 20,000-candlepower beacon. On January 14, 1959, the light was unmanned and automated, controlled from Portland Head Light. Under the Maine Lights Program, coordinated by the Island Institute in Rockland, it was anticipated that Ram Island Ledge Light would become the property of some local organization, but, due to the lighthouse's relative inaccessibilit, none applied for ownership. In January 2001, the light was converted to solar power. The panels, mounted on the south side of the tower, supply two large batteries that provide power for the light and fog signal.

There has not been a major shipwreck on these ledges since the light went into operation in 1905. But one wonders why it took so long.

Ram Island Ledge Light in Casco Bay was built in 1905 and automated in 1959. Gannett file photo.

Portland Breakwater Light

Spring Point Light and the Portland Breakwater may be the unsung heroes of Casco Bay lighthouses compared to their more beautiful, powerful, and admired elder sisters—Two Lights and Portland Head Light. They have been admired and loved by mariners who have steered to safety thanks to these two guardians of Portland's inner harbor.

Portland Breakwater Light, conceived as the consequence of a devastating storm in 1831, was twenty-four long years getting born and built. Now affectionately nicknamed the "Bug Light," its lantern first shone in 1855. The first keeper, W.A. Dyer, lit the fixed red light atop the tiny white tower on August 1 and began earning his pay of $400 a year. This is the senior sister. Spring Point Light, one mile southeast, was not in service until forty-two years later. William A. Lane, the first head keeper, lit this light on May 24, 1897.

The storm that triggered the eventual creation of Portland Breakwater was the northeaster of November 22, 1831. Ships in the harbor were torn from their moorings, warehouses and wharves were splintered, part of Vaughan's Bridge was destroyed, and floodwaters undermined the banks of the important Cumberland & Oxford Canal. Portland marine interests demanded that the federal government provide some protection, and their voices were heard.

Within a year, Secretary of War Lewis Cass issued a directive that a plan for a seawall or breakwater be formulated. Within two weeks, Lieutenant Colonel John Anderson and his mapmaker, Lieutenant Poole, were on the job in Portland, surveying to decide where a breakwater could best be built and how much it would cost. Within a year, on October 19, 1833, their detailed report was on the desk of War Secretary Cass.

Their recommendation was for a big engineering job: a breakwater 2,500 feet long, built in seven sections, requiring 50,000 cubic yards of stone and rubble, which, they reported, could be obtained at nearby islands in Casco Bay. The price, including a pier and beacon on the outer end of the breakwater, was estimated precisely to the last penny: $44,417.08.

Two years went by before Congress acted, and then the appropriation was for only $10,000—enough to start building the first four hundred feet. Work began in July 1836, with a crew of thirty men under Freeman Bradford, resident engineer for the project. In the next two years, Congress appropriated another $51,000, and by November 1837 Bradford reported the breakwater was 1,765 feet long and that "the portion of the breakwater already constructed has been found efficacious in keeping off the heavy swell."

And there the work stopped, almost eight hundred feet short of the original design. Each year between 1837 and 1855, money was asked for and refused. Finally, in March 1855, the Lighthouse Board approved funds to build a lighthouse twenty-five feet above high water, octagonal in shape, and equipped with a sixth-order Fresnel lens. The job was finished in four months and W.A. Dyer lit the red lamp on the first night of August 1855.

But the construction was not up to the weather and the seas that buffeted it. Timbers began to rot and ironwork to rust. The keepers did not hold their jobs long. Dyer was succeeded by William L. Willard, who was followed briefly by Benjamin F. Willard in 1861, then Benjamin B. Watson in 1862, Len Strout in 1866, and Paul McKenny in 1867.

One reason for the fast turnover may have been the peril of getting out to the light. The breakwater had not been built high enough. At full tide, waves broke over it. In icy weather, the rubble rock was as slippery as a skating rink. In bad weather, keepers had to crawl the 1,765-foot length of the breakwater on their hands and knees, and get soaking wet in the bargain.

In 1865, a brilliant Army engineer named Colonel J.D. Graham persuaded Congress to appropriate $105,000 so he could extend the breakwater another four hundred feet and raise its level. Then, unhappily for Portland, Graham died. His successor, Brigadier General B.S. Alexander, threw out Graham's plans and drew up cheaper ideas of his own, which would cost only $60,000. All proposals were shelved, and, in true bureaucratic fashion, studies were begun. So no work was done for seven more years.

In 1872, the breakwater got another 2,750 tons of granite and was extended and the level raised. In 1874, an iron tower replaced the leaky wooden one. The new tower was and is a beauty in the classical Greek tradition. Exotically, the light tower on this Portland Breakwater was modeled after the Choragic Monument of Lysicrates, built in the year 300 B.C. The Breakwater Light stood just thirteen feet, two and a half inches high, and eleven feet, eight inches in diameter. Even the keepers benefited at last. Handrails were installed over the entire length from light tower to shore, so the walk was less life threatening.

In 1889, when Albus R. Angell was keeper, a two-room house for the keeper was built beside the tower. A strange dwelling it was, too, because its dimensions of eighteen by twenty feet meant that it far overhung the breakwater on either side! Within ten years, two more rooms and an attic were added, and the keeper had a substantial house overhanging Portland Harbor, 1,990 feet from shore. Wisely, two hundred tons of riprap stone were piled around the breakwater tower and house for protection from the seas.

In 1935, the light was electrified, automated, and controlled from Spring Point. There was no longer a need for the overhanging keeper's house, which was demolished.

Then came World War II, and the sudden development nearby of vast shipbuilding yards by Bath-Todd Corporation, where Liberty ships were turned out in record time and huge numbers. To make the basin-type building berths, the land around the Breakwater Light was extended far into the harbor. The contour of the shoreline was greatly altered. The new man-made land came out so far that the apparent length of the breakwater was cut in half. It was shortened further still in 1942 by the Navy's plan for a vast dry-dock area on the south side of the breakwater. After all of these changes, the Portland Breakwater Light stood less than a hundred feet out from dry land. The light was no longer needed. In June 1942, as a wartime measure, the light was extinguished. It was never lit again.

Yet its special beauty is neither gone nor forgotten. The light is now on the protected list of National Historic Places. And for its 108th anniversary party, the Portland Symphony staged a spectacular concert at Portland Breakwater Light—the beloved, unique Bug Light.

Spring Point Ledge Light

Don't be deceived by the way Spring Point Light in Portland Harbor looks today. This is a new look, acquired only in 1950. Until then, there was no breakwater at this light. For fifty-three years—from the time it was built in 1897 until the breakwater was added in 1950—the light stood alone, unlinked to the mainland, a caisson light marking the danger of the ledge, which had brought too many ships to their deaths. This ship-killing ledge runs from Fort Preble out to the main ship channel, and year after year, ships came to grief here.

Many managed to free themselves on the rising tide. But the *Nancy*, a lime coaster out of Rockland, hit here on September 7, 1832, and the sea poured in, igniting her cargo in the strange fashion by which water and lime, when combined, smolder in a fire that is often impossible to put out. The *Nancy* burned to the waterline in full sight of the population of Portland.

The public was outraged at this latest shipwreck in the inner harbor. But the lethargy of bureaucratic Washington was not aroused. The office workers there believed that the Portland Breakwater, a mile away, was enough for Portland Harbor. Reluctantly, they agreed to anchor a huge spar buoy at the point where Spring Point Ledge endangered the otherwise deep water at the edge of the main channel.

But a mere spar was of no use in foul weather. The accidents continued apace. The *Mazaltan*, the *Seguin*, the *Solomon Poole*, the *Smith Tuttle*, and other vessels hit hard aground.

Then came the spectacular wreck of the new 393-ton bark, *Harriet S. Jackson*. In the equinox gale of March 20–21, 1876, which caused havoc all along the New England coast, the *Harriet Jackson* hit hard on Spring Point Ledge at 1 a.m., in a howling gale, driving rain, and thick fog. When dawn broke, the crew saw they were practically on the beach at Fort Preble. They were so close that when the tide fell and the *Jackson* keeled over, they were able to lay a plank to the walls of Fort Preble and walk ashore. After six tries with various tugs over two days, the bark, severely damaged, was pulled off, towed into the Dyer yard, and repaired. She put to sea again for twenty-two years before she was lost off Cape Cod in 1898.

This accident bestirred Washington only a mite. But stronger political forces put the pressure on the federal government. In 1891, seven steamship companies joined forces and presented a report to the Lighthouse Board, urgently demanding a light to mark the danger of Spring Point Ledge. The shipping lines stated that between them, their vessels carried more than half a million passengers a year past this dangerous ledge, and that the lack of a light was endangering a multitude of lives. (Their report gives a vivid picture of the volume of passenger ship traffic in and out of Portland. More than a hundred years ago, more people were arriving in and departing from Portland by ship than do by air from Portland International Jetport today.)

The Lighthouse Board agreed. But Congress refused for two more years to appropriate the minor sum of $45,000 to build a light. Finally in 1895, four years after the steamship lines had made their urgent case, Congress appropriated $20,000 to begin construction of a fifth-order light and fog station, with the proviso that the total cost not exceed $45,000. Thomas Dyer of New York City won the contract to build a

The caisson-style Spring Point Ledge Light was built in Portland Harbor in 1896. It was automated in 1960. Courtesy of Philip Ziegler.

cast-iron cylinder twenty-five feet in diameter, forty feet high, composed of forty-eight sections. One end of the cylinder was to be bolted into the ledge in fourteen feet of water, and this section was to be filled with concrete. The upper compartments would house oil, coal, watchroom quarters, and the lantern tower.

From the start, construction went badly. Storms delayed work and spoiled what work had been done. Then government inspectors rejected the entire job because poor-quality cement had been used. Finally a compromise was agreed upon and work started again, with crews at double strength working around the clock. Spring Point Ledge Light went into operation May 24, 1897, with William A. Lane as the first keeper.

It had been a long fight. Automated in the 1960s, today the 200,000-candlepower white flash beams forth once every five seconds in a seven-degree arc. Beyond this small arc, the flash is red. Inbound vessels follow the white flash into the safety of the inner harbor. Supertankers laden with oil from far corners of the globe come in on the light, heading to the Portland Pipeline, and fishing boats use it.

But the Spring Point breakwater had been on the drawing boards for a hundred years; it was not built until 1951. The Army Engineers had been authorized to build a 900-foot breakwater in 1946, but a preoccupied Congress failed to appropriate $255,000 to begin the project until 1949. The breakwater was built of granite blocks, each weighing between three and five tons. By June 7, 1951, the job was done. Fifty thousand tons of stone had been laid at a cost of $200,000.

Halfway Rock Light

Halfway Rock gets its name from its position halfway between the light at Seguin and Portland Head Light. In clear weather, the distance seems short; but in fog or gale, it seems to take forever to make passage from Seguin to Halfway Rock.

Coming from the east in *Steer Clear* during recent years, I have made that passage once in thick fog and once in a southwest gale, with fourteen-foot seas, and worried if I'd ever live to see Halfway Rock again. The memory of those passages spoils my feelings toward Halfway Rock, which in most people's eyes is one of the handsomest sea lights along the Maine coast, rising seventy-six feet up from a barren acre of lonely rock, just out from the islands of Casco Bay.

Local demand for a light here started thirty-six years before a light shone from Halfway Rock. That demand in 1835 was ignored for thirty years. Then during Abraham Lincoln's time in the White House, new wrecks revived it; plans for a light were approved by his successor, President Andrew Johnson, and the light first flashed when Ulysses S. Grant headed our nation.

It was the usual story: wrecks and lost lives triggered local demand for a light, which finally reached ears in Washington, followed by a too-small appropriation from Congress to build it, more delays in construction when those funds ran out, more appropriations, then more delays due to weather and shortage of labor, and, at last, a completed light. The elapsed time in this case was thirty-six years, from 1835 to 1871. Here is how it all began.

At twilight on June 19, 1835, the Maine coast was being battered by a nasty southeast gale. The brig *Samuel* rounded Cape Elizabeth, running for her home port of Bath, after a trip to Providence, Rhode Island. Captain George W. Small knew well how those southeasterly gales turn the coast of Maine into a dangerous lee-shore. So as darkness came, Small sent his crew up to reef the top mainsail and the boat *Samuel* battled the gale under a close-reefed fore-topsail.

Despite the precautions, the brig hit hard at 10 p.m. on Halfway Rock. In the rush to save his ship just before it hit, Captain Small and his steward were struck by a rogue wave as they wrestled with the jib boom. They were washed overboard and lost.

Hard aground on Halfway Rock, the leaderless crew abandoned their disintegrating vessel and sought safety behind the ledges of the wave-swept island. Fishermen on Hope Island saw their distress signals, although Hope lies northwest a full five miles from Halfway Rock, and Jewell and Cliff islands lie between Hope and Halfway Rock. When morning dawned, the men from Hope Island rowed to the rescue of the survivors.

This was the loss that triggered local outcry for a light and led Captain Joseph Smith of the revenue service to write his Washington headquarters in 1837: "I respectfully recommend the erection of a stone monument on this rock and the cost of it I estimate at $3,000." Of course, the "monument" he had in mind was not a memorial but a warning device. But for twenty-six years, no one in Washington paid any heed—until after another wreck cost more lives.

On February 12, 1861, masses of wreckage began washing up on Jewell and Inner Green Islands, three miles inshore from Halfway Rock. And that was all the evidence there was that another ship had gone to its death on Halfway Rock. Searchers on Jewell found deck planking, knees, spars, and a smashed medicine chest with the name "Boadicea" barely visible on it.

Boadicea was a British bark that had cleared New Orleans on December 2, 1860, bound for Glasgow, Scotland. The ship had smashed so hard and without warning onto Halfway Rock that all aboard were drowned on February 12, 1861. This disaster pushed Washington into slow-motion action on the forgotten plea for a navigation aid on Halfway Rock, made by Captain Smith back in 1837.

Eight years after the wreck of the *Boadicea*, on March 3, 1869, Congress finally authorized $50,000 to build a light at Halfway Rock. Four months later, preparation of the one-acre, rough rock surface to receive a foundation was finished. Vessels laden with granite blocks from other Maine islands began to arrive and unload into smaller boats. Then funds ran out before the job was done, and another delay ensued, until another Congress and another president, Ulysses Grant, earmarked more money for Halfway Rock. But now labor was scarce. Finally, workmen who had been building federal gunsites on other Casco Bay islands were sent to do masonry work on the new light. Thus it was not until August 15, 1871 that the light on Halfway Rock was lit for the first time—thirty-six years after the *Samuel* had met its death on those ledges.

The first keeper was Captain John T. Sterling. Sterlings, like Strouts, were Maine lightkeepers for more than a century. Scores of terrible

Halfway Rock Light, in outer Casco Bay, lies halfway between Seguin Island Light and Portland Head Light. First built in 1871, it stands 65 feet high and was automated in 1976. Courtesy of Philip Ziegler.

storms battered keepers of Halfway Rock for more than 105 years, until the light was automated and keeperless in the 1970s.

During the great gale of December 1887, when the schooner *D.W. Hammond* was driven onto Portland Head, seas inundated Halfway Rock to a depth of eight feet. Three years later, the oil house was washed away in another great storm. So noisy were the great seas battering the rock that the fog bell could not be heard. So in 1903, it was replaced with a Daboll trumpet, followed later by newer devices. The original lantern of the second order was replaced with a first-order Fresnel lens.

Civilian keepers gave place to young Coast Guardsmen, three of whom at a time kept the light—though in greater comfort, with electricity, radios, and eventually, even a telephone, television, and helicopter pad—until the light was unmanned. But they, too, had their hardships. In October 1962, the living quarters were under water and practically washed away while Coast Guard keepers sought safety atop the seventy-six-foot light tower. That storm ripped out the railway for the boat-launching ramp. In June and July of 1972, fog closed the coast. The keepers at Halfway Rock lived with the blasting of their enormous foghorn in the eardrums every fifty-one seconds, day and night, for more than two weeks without letup. In 1975, the light was automated and the Coast Guardsmen were taken off forever.

The magnificent Fresnel lens, which stood almost seven feet tall and five feet in diameter and was housed in a rich brass case, was dismantled. In a romantic departure from the rock where it had functioned for more than a hundred years, the lens was taken aboard the famed Coast Guard sailing bark, the *Eagle*, and sent to the Coast Guard Museum in New London, Connecticut. It was replaced with an airport beacon.

Mark Island Monument Light

Mark Island Monument is known to every vessel entering or leaving Casco Bay, coming west or going east. This stone obelisk stands tall. The monument itself is about sixty-five feet high, and Little Mark Island, the rocky ledge on which it stands, is ten feet out of the sea. So the full elevation is seventy-five feet, visible from many miles away.

It was not built as a lighthouse, nor properly considered one, although there is a light on it flashing every four seconds. The monument was built in 1827 as a mark from which mariners could take their bearings. The monument is almost exactly in the middle of the mouth of Casco Bay, lying about three and a half miles directly inside Halfway Rock Light. It stands out to sea from Harpswell Neck and Bailey Island.

The monument, however, was not built to mark the best entrance into Casco Bay. Far from it, as there are tricky ledges here, and though it is well buoyed, this is not a preferred course into the bay. A safer course is to head in, passing outside the red buoy just west of Eagle Island.

The monument was built on Little Mark Island instead of Eagle Island because it was cheaper, due to the amount of available loose stone for making the obelisk. The base of the monument is eighteen feet square, and the walls are three feet thick. This makes a room twelve by twelve feet inside the base.

There is a kindly story that a thoughtful government made this room for the shelter of shipwrecked sailors. But the fact is that it's there simply because it saved building material to leave this space open rather than fill it with stone. Today the room is used to house storage batteries for the blinking light at the top.

The top of the monument does not come to a point, as it looks from a boat, but rather to a four-foot-square platform where the light sits. An iron railing runs around this platform, and the way to reach it is by an iron ladder that runs straight up the side of the sixty-foot-tall monument. Deliberately, it has been made hard to get onto that iron ladder. The first rung is eight feet above the ground, a discouragement to vandals or curious explorers who want to climb to the top.

The ledge called Little Mark Island supports no vegetation now, though at one time sheep were set out here during the summer months.

Out to sea from Harpswell Neck and Bailey Island is the automated monument light on Little Mark Island. Gannett file photo.

MIDCOAST MAINE

Seguin Island Light
Kennebec and Sheepscot River Lights
Hendricks Head Light

Boothbay Region Lights
    The Cuckolds
    Ram Island Light
    Burnt Island Light
Pemaquid Light
Franklin Island Light
Marshall Point Light
Tenants Harbor Light, Southern Island
Two Bush Island Light
Monhegan Island Light
Monhegan Light Museum
Whitehead Light
Owls Head Light
Matinicus Island Light

Smaller Lights, Midcoast Maine
    Lowell Rock Light, Rockport
    Rockland Breakwater Light
    Curtis Island Light
    Grindel Point Light
    Fort Point Light, Searsport
    Dice Head Light, Castine
    Pumpkin Island Light
    Heron Neck Light and Green Ledge Light

Seguin Island Light

Treat Seguin with respect. It is one of the oldest sea lights on the Atlantic coast. George Washington ordered the building of Seguin Light in 1795, late in his second term as president. The cost was $6,300.

Furthermore, Seguin is one of the foggiest places on the coast of Maine. One foggy year, the fog signal blew more than 30 percent of the time, for a total of 2,734 hours. The sea can be rough and nasty here, especially when the tide is running fast down the Kennebec River and the wind is blowing hard from the ocean, so wind and tide are coming from opposite directions. The Indians in their canoes suffered from that beastly chop. The Indian name from which Seguin derives—*sutquin*—means "the place where the sea vomits." Another hazard for navigators is the magnetic disturbance just north of Seguin, around Ellingwood Rock, which can send the compass spinning.

The first white colonists to settle on the mainland of North America knew Seguin. On Wednesday night, August 12, 1607, the ships *Gift of God* and *Mary and John*, commanded by Captain George Popham and Captain Raleigh Gilbert, hit rough water and a storm off Seguin as they tried to sail into the Kennebec River. They found shelter for the next few days at Stage Island. Finally, on August 19, the entire company of more than a hundred sailors and colonists went ashore at the place now called Popham, and began building the first colony, a full thirteen years before the *Mayflower* arrived at Plymouth.

After a year of hardship and disaster, they gave up and sailed home to England. Nevertheless, by Seguin, at the mouth of the Kennebec, was the first effort to establish a colonized settlement by the English in North America.

The tower on the lighthouse at Seguin is the highest in Maine, standing 186 feet above the sea and throwing a beam that can be seen forty miles away on a clear night. The reason the tower stands so tall is not because the tower itself is high, but because Seguin—a barren, 22-acre rock—rises 150 feet out of the sea. Seguin was not always barren. It was once heavily wooded, providing an ample supply of firewood for the early keepers; and its soil was considered rich enough to grow crops and raise hay for the cattle. The benefits available from the woods and arable land was the reason why the first keeper of Seguin Light was paid only two hundred dollars a year.

The first keeper of Seguin was a colorful character named Count John Polereczky, who had been born in Alsace. He left Europe for the New World and fought in the American Revolution as Major John Polereczky from Pownalboro, Maine. As a reward for his military service, he was named first keeper of Seguin Light in 1796, at a two-hundred-dollar annual salary. He may have been glad to get the job, but he was far from pleased with his salary and his standing. On May 12, 1796, the ex-major unburdened his complaints in a letter to his former commander, General Benjamin Lincoln, who was now district superintendent of lighthouses:

> You know my dear General all the difficulties and expense a light at Seguin involves ... The first three years will cost me money out of my own pocket. There is no feed on the island, and I must carry two cows for my family and keep them on hay, summer and winter, which I must purchase and carry to the island, with the greatest difficulty. I must also keep a horse ... I must purchase a good boat. I must purchase each individual necessity for my family till I can raise it. I must build some sort of small barn for my cattle and hay. I must hire one man in case of sickness ... Now my dear General I must request you to assist an old soldier ... If the time of my tending the light could be ascertained for five or six years ...

Eager to help an old comrade from the battlefields, General Lincoln sought the good offices of the Commissioner of Revenue, who headed the Lighthouse Department. The commissioner was not impressed and answered General Lincoln impatiently:

> In the case of Major Polereczky, there are advantages of plenty of fuel, without expense ... the opportunity to fish for his family use, or even for sale ... there is land for tillage and grass, and a plentiful garden ... It is plain that the duties of a light keeper are not in their nature adapted to the standing of a field officer, or a Major of Brigade.

Polereczky had financial losses. Storm after storm hit Seguin, making it a poor spot to earn money by farming and fishing. The storms also smashed Polereczky's boats; in the first year, he lost a twenty-five dollar boat, a canoe, and a bigger boat worth three hundred dollars. Boatless, Polereczky was marooned for months. Death finally relieved him of his troubles as the first keeper of the light on Seguin, which was more than his superiors had done for him.

The original wooden light tower had gone to pieces and, in 1819, Congress earmarked $2,500 to replace it with a new stone tower. Storms demolished this one, too. In 1857, Congress appropriated $35,000 to build a new tower. Much improved and modernized, this basic tower stands today with a fully automated light.

However, after automation, the future of Seguin Island Light was uncertain. In 1986, real estate broker Anne Webster led some concerned citizens to create the Friends of Seguin Island in 1986. They received a ten-year lease on the property from the Coast Guard in 1989. And in February 1998, under the Maine Lights Program, the group was granted ownership of the property.

Also that February, the Coast Guard announced plans to replace Seguin's first-order Fresnel lens with a modern solar-powered plastic optic. It was too expensive to maintain the 17,000-foot underwater cable necessary to run the light inside the large lens, so the Coast Guard would save taxpayers' dollars by replacing it.

The Friends of Seguin Island wanted the lens to remain in the lighthouse. The Coast Guard did offer an alternative: leaving the lens in place but inactive, replacing it with a solar-powered light mounted on a nearby mast.

The Friends of Seguin Island mounted a petition drive to convince the Coast Guard to leave the historic lens in operation. They collected more than 7,200 signatures, and, in March 2000, Senator Olympia Snowe of Maine announced that the Coast Guard had agreed to leave the lens in operation. It is the last operating first-order Fresnel lens north of Rhode Island.

Seguin Island Light, off the mouth of the Kennebec River. A wooden tower was built first in 1795, followed by a stone tower in 1819; which was rebuilt in 1857 and still stands today. Gannett file photo.

Kennebec and Sheepscot River Lights

Tens of thousands of vessels have turned north from Seguin into the Kennebec and Sheepscot rivers, bound for local harbors or the once-busy ports of Bath and Augusta. Now there are river lights to guide them: Pond Island Light, Perkins Island Light, Squirrel Point Light, Doubling Point Range Lights on the Kennebec, and Goose Rocks Passage Light and Hendricks Head Light on the Sheepscot.

Steer Clear often heads up the Kennebec and Sheepscot, especially when the weather out on the ocean is cold, rough, or foggy. These are beautiful and historic rivers, brimming with hundreds of years of Maine history; they are filled with lovely islands, snug, small harbors, and remarkable hideaways for a quiet night on anchor, such as the Oven's Mouth, approached by the fjord-like passage through Cross River off the Sheepscot.

On most weekdays, even in summer, these rivers are not crowded with other boats. A game I play in my mind is to picture them as they used to be—crowded, bristling, and busy with an amazing variety of ships.

In one of my log books aboard, I have quotes from two small news items taken from the *Bath Daily Times* more than a hundred years ago, which I like to show to shipmates as we cruise, almost alone, upriver. Here is one from July 1880, reporting on the river traffic between Augusta and Bath:

> Yesterday on the passenger steamer *Henry Morrison*, we counted 27 schooners at Bath, 13 more between Bath and Richmond, 55 more between Richmond and Hallowell, and two more docking at Augusta.

That reporter had counted ninety-seven vessels on a summer day in 1880, loading and unloading cargoes and passengers in that short stretch of the Kennebec. The other clipping reports on the ship traffic farther downriver, at the mouth of the Kennebec. Taken from the *Bath Daily Times* of April 7, 1884, it reports:

> In the month since the tug *Seguin* was launched, the in-and-out traffic on the Kennebec was 892 vessels ... 755 schooners, 86 steamers, 39 sloops, 7 barks, 3 brigs.

Today, if you turn into the Kennebec from Seguin Light, the first light you come to is Pond Island Light, which stands off from the grand sandy Popham Beach—not far from Fort Popham, where in 1607 the first one hundred and twenty sailors and settlers tried for a year to establish the first English-speaking colony in North America, a baker's dozen years before the arrival of the *Mayflower*.

The fort at Popham, however, was built as a defense against Confederate raiders in the Civil War. A flashing beacon now marks Fort Popham.

White explorers from Europe were here in the Kennebec even earlier. David Ingram, who said he walked from Florida to New Brunswick, said he was on this peninsula in 1582; his report was quoted in the first edition of Hakluyt's Voyages.

In 1605, the French explorer Champlain made the turn at Seguin, sailed up the Kennebec and circled back down on the Sasanoa and Sheepscot rivers. The next year, 1606, explorer Martin Pring was back charting the Maine coast and wrote such glowing reports about the Kennebec River and this Popham Beach area that Sir Ferdinando Gorges sent his two ships and one hundred and twenty men here in 1607 to try and establish that first colony.

About a mile farther up the Kennebec in mid-channel is the next river light: Perkins Island Light, an octagonal tower built into the keeper's house.

Another two miles upriver, the channel winds by Arrowsic Island. The next light, Squirrel Point Light, was built there on the southwestern tip of the island in 1898. Arrowsic was one of the first and largest early settlements. As early as 1670, more than fifty families were settled here and across the river at Parker Head. But on a harrowing night in August 1676, Indians sneaked past sentries at the stockade gate and massacred nine Arrowsic families.

There is a clear run upriver, past the flasher on Ram Island in mid-channel, until the sharp turn at Doubling Point. Here, dead ahead from the bend by Fiddler Reach, are the two beacons or range lights at Doubling Point, the only range lights now in existence in the First Naval District. After making this turn, Doubling Point Light lies on the right, still a part of Arrowsic Island. This small, handsome light is a white octagonal tower set on a stone pier and connected to Arrowsic by a footbridge. It was built in 1898, the same year as Squirrel Point Light.

This sharp double bend in the river is not hard to navigate for most boats. But it can be a trial and tribulation for ships more than six hundred feet long, built nearby at the Bath Iron Works and on their first trials. It gives pilot, helmsman, and rudders a healthy first test. The light has long since been automated and unmanned. Its best-known, most-liked keeper was Captain Harry L. Nye, an old deepwater skipper who retired from the sea to become keeper in the 1920s, first of Seguin Light and then the light at Doubling Point.

"Skipper" Nye made several rescues of crews of stranded boats that had come to grief on nearby rocks. On December 28, 1928, Nye made a rare kind of rescue. He rescued four young men who had been fooling around on the big ice floes on the Sasanoa River, a mile or so upstream, opposite the city of Bath. The ice floe broke loose and a strong outgoing tide carried it swiftly downriver with the four men on it, heading toward the sea. Nye manned his boat, made it out in time to intercept them, and took them off to safety.

In 1981, Doubling Point Light began to be monitored again from the Kennebec River Range Lights (Doubling Point Range Lights) Station. It was the responsibility of one keeper to tend the Range Lights, Doubling Point Light, and Squirrel Point Light, as well as their fog signals. For a few years this job was done by Coast Guard Bo'sun's Mate Karen McLean, one of a small number of female Coast Guard lighthouse keepers. Married to a Coast Guardsman stationed in Boothbay, McLean and her two children lived at the keeper's house at the Range Lights. The lighthouse was automated in 1988.

Doubling Point Light on the Kennebec River. It was built in 1898 at Bath. Note the cranes from Bath Iron Works in the background. Gannett file photo.

For a time, Squirrel Point Light and its fog signal were operated by the keeper of the Kennebec River Range Light Station. In 1979, however, the light was automated, and its fifth-order Fresnel lens was removed and replaced by a modern optic. The original lens is on display in the Museum at Portland Head Light.

Mike Trenholm, a semi-retired real estate dealer from Yarmouth, Maine, first saw Squirrel Point Light while cruising on the Kennebec River in 1993. Three years later he formed the non-profit organization, Squirrel Point Light Associates, Inc., and the Coast Guard transferred ownership of the five-acre station to Trenholm.

He has since made several improvements to the property, including installing new wiring, heating, and plumbing in the keeper's house. His ultimate goal is to establish an educational facility at the light station.

Automated in 1959, Perkins Island Light still serves as an aid to navigation. Unfortunately, the Victorian-style keeper's house has fallen into disrepair. In May 2000, the lighthouse was leased to the American Lighthouse Foundation and later that year the bell tower was restored, funded by the Maine Department of Conservation and a grant administered by the Maine Historic Preservation Commission. Local resident Joshua Bate was the project foreman and volunteers from all around the state helped with the restoration.

Hendricks Head Light

Going east past Seguin Light and before The Cuckolds lies Sheepscot Bay, wide mouth of the handsome Sheepscot River. Two miles upriver, with Southport Island on the right, is the light at Hendricks Head. The light is no longer in operation, though it is an excellent daymark.

Hendricks Head Light, which stands out from the sheltered, landlocked Cozy Harbor on Southport Island, six miles from Boothbay, was first built in 1829. It was rebuilt as a square tower in 1875.

In January 1978, a ferocious storm destroyed the boathouse at Hendricks Head Light as well as the walkway that had connected the lighthouse to the fog-bell tower. The next year the tower's fifth-order Fresnel lens was replaced by a modern optic. Ben and Luanne Russell of Alabama bought the $4^1/2$-acre property, and completely restored all of the structures. The buildings are in beautiful condition and the fixed white light with red sectors still operates as an active aid to navigation.

Hendricks Head Light, Southport Island on the Sheepscot River. It was first built in 1829 and, though automated in 1975, is no longer operating. Absent are the bell tower and its footbridge connecting it to the main structure. These were demolished by a storm in 1978, but have since been rebuilt by the current owners. Gannett file photo.

The story of an amazing rescue of an infant from a shipwreck more than a hundred years ago was retold in this century by Edward Rowe Snow in his 1945 book, *The Lighthouses of New England.*

During a wicked March gale in the 1870s, the keeper saw a vessel driven aground on a ledge half a mile from his light. As the ship began to founder and break up, the people aboard climbed into the rigging for safety and to escape the torrents of icy waves pouring across the deck. But the freezing spray that drenched them turned to winding shrouds of ice, which locked them onto the rigging.

The keeper wanted to launch his dory to try and get out to rescue them. But the seas were pounding in fifteen feet high and it would have been certain, swift death to the keeper and his boat. To give hope to the freezing people aboard the stranded, foundering vessel, the keeper and his wife lit a big bonfire on shore, as a signal that they knew the vessel was there and would come to the rescue as soon as they could.

As he stood on shore, feeding the fire, the keeper spotted a big box or bundle being blown and swept toward shore. Thinking it might be wreckage, he grabbed a boathook, rigged a safety line around his waist, and waded into the breakers to grab it. Breaking out the bundle on shore, the keeper found he had rescued two feather beds, tied together and soaking wet. He ripped them apart. Inside was a box, and inside the box was a baby girl, yelling for dear life. He rushed the infant into the warmth of his house and the care of his wife. Inside the blankets in which the infant was wrapped, he found a locket and a message from the mother, commending her baby to God.

The keeper ran back to the bonfire, hoping to make a signal that would indicate he had rescued the baby. But all sign of the vessel was gone. The storm had smashed the ship and all aboard to eternity. The keeper and his wife had recently buried their own child. They shortly adopted the baby delivered to them from the sea.

Snow also tells the story of the suicide of a stranger. This death happened between World War I and II, when Charles L. Knight was keeper. One night, walking to the post office on Southport, he passed a dignified woman walking silently in the opposite direction. The postmaster had seen the stranger, too. Strangers are conversation pieces when they show up after dark on a remote road on Southport Island. The next day, her body, weighted down with a flatiron, was found on the shore at Hendricks Head. No one ever learned her name, but she was buried decently in Southport. Some people say that she still walks the rocky beach at night, alone and sad.

———————— Boothbay Region Lights ————————

The Cuckolds

Why the name The Cuckolds?

Odd names, revealing names, abound on Maine's coast—Drunkard's Ledge, Bailey's Mistake, Hen and Chickens—but The Cuckolds outside Boothbay Harbor? Does its name carry echoes of an unfortunate local fisherman, cuckolded while out tending his traps?

Apparently not. The cuckolding has royal roots reaching back to England and King John. King John bedded the wife of a Londoner and soothed the anger of the injured husband by giving him a point of land on the banks of the Thames River. The local fishermen there nicknamed the point The Cuckolds and built a marker on it in the shape of a pair of cuckold horns. Centuries after King John had signed the famous Magna Carta with his angry barons, whose rights he had usurped, a transplant colonist from the Thames to the Boothbay region remembered the seamark called The Cuckolds and gave the name to these ledges outside Boothbay Harbor.

The Cuckolds began as a fog-signal station and not as a lighthouse. Benjamin Harrison, in his final year as president, signed the appropriation bill in 1892, which allocated money to build a fog signal and keeper's house on The Cuckolds. Until then, only a tripod had warned mariners of the treacherous shoals. For the next fifteen years, the wail of this horn was the warning that helped ships entering and leaving Boothbay, then one of the busiest fishing harbors along the coast of Maine.

The station was poorly built. The keeper's house and fog-signal engine room were often awash with water from stormy seas. Worse, on many nights when the weather was clear, ships had no warning of these dangerous shoals as they made course into Boothbay Harbor. Demand increased for a light. Finally in 1907, when Theodore Roosevelt was president, Congress appropriated money to build a light here, thanks in large part to a strong and vociferous delegation from Maine.

Because the land area of The Cuckolds was small, there was not room enough to erect a separate lighthouse. So a white octagonal tower was built atop the keeper's dwelling and the light was installed in it. And that is the way it looks today. Storms continued to wreak havoc on the keeper's house.

When Mr. Seavey was the assistant keeper, the giant seas of the January 1933 storms swept through his dwelling and destroyed household effects. He filed a claim for damages to his sofa, bed, easy chair, and Hawaiian guitar. The Department of Commerce paid his claim in total, even to the guitar.

The Cuckolds Light was automated and unmanned in 1975, and the Blizzard of 1978 destroyed the keeper's dwelling along with outbuildings and the boat ramp. The light remained in service, however, and still flashes a white light as an active aid to navigation. It can be seen from many of the excursion boats out of Boothbay Harbor and from a public-landing pier in Newagen. Even so, it looks like a tempting place to make into a special summer home on the outskirts of popular Boothbay Harbor.

The fourth-order lens from the original light is on display at The Shore Village Museum, Rockland, where it is operating and rotating as it did on The Cuckolds. It is a most unusual lens as it is American-made, manufactured by The MacBeth Glass Company in Pittsburgh, Pennsylvania. Museum officials are certain this is the only lens made by MacBeth on display anywhere.

The Cuckolds lighthouse, drawn before the Blizzard of '78 demolished the boathouse and boat ramp. Courtesy of Philip Ziegler.

Ram Island Light

Until recently, Ram Island Light was a sad and tattered affair, at the entrance to Boothbay Harbor. After its automation in 1965, the station soon fell victim to vandals. The house was damaged, and in 1975 the fourth-order Fresnel lens was stolen. (The lens was eventually recovered and is now at the museum of the Boothbay Region Historical Society.) This fall to vandalism and decay was tragic because the origins of Ram Island Light were so simple, so brave, and so close to the lives of Boothbay fishermen, helping each other to reach home harbor safely.

In 1983 the keeper's house was scheduled to be destroyed when the Grand Banks Schooner Museum Trust, associated with the Boothbay Railway Museum, stepped in and took charge of the station, except for the tower. Under the Maine Lights Program, the property was transferred to the Museum Trust in 1998. The Ram Island Preservation Society has restored the house, and they hope to reconstruct the walkway to the tower. Caretakers live on the island in summer.

About a hundred years ago, before lobsterboats had engines, a local lobsterman was sailing home after dark, and almost met his death when he came suddenly perilously close to the rocks of Ram Island. Grateful for his narrow escape, he appointed himself to the job of setting out and keeping a warning light burning. Late each afternoon, he set out a lantern to burn through the night and guide fellow sailors. He did this lone duty faithfully for years until he moved away.

On the last night he tended his lantern, another fisherman was saved from shipwreck because he spotted the lantern's warning gleam through the fog. This fisherman took on the self-appointed job. He rigged a box to protect the oil lamp from being blown out by the night wind. He made glass on all sides of the box, so the lantern's rays could shine as a warning to others. Each evening as he sailed home from lobstering, he stopped at Ram Island and lit his lantern. Eventually he, too, moved away.

Yet a third fisherman took on the job. He used a different method: He anchored an old dory and rigged a lantern in its bow. The last fisherman who sailed by at sunset on his way home from hauling would stop at the dory and light the lantern, as a guide for those not yet in harbor. It was a nice system, but it did not last after a bad easterly tore the dory from its anchor and dashed the boat to pieces on the rocks.

Now a fourth man took over. He was a hermit fisherman who lived alone on close-by Fisherman's Island, and he agreed to light a lantern on foggy or stormy nights. But it was so weak, a mere flicker, that it was visible from only fifty feet. Wrecks became frequent. One stormy night, the hermit saw a dismasted schooner being blown hard down onto the rocks close to shore. The gale was too fierce to allow him to launch his own small dory and get out to the rescue, though the schooner was only a few yards offshore. So he tied a line around his waist, made one end fast to an iron ring on shore, and waded out until he was able to hurl a line to men on deck. A rescue line was rigged and all the crew managed to haul themselves safely ashore by this lifeline.

Soon after this rescue, the hermit fisherman saw only the sad aftermath of another doomed ship. He looked one morning across the narrow gut of water that separates Fisherman's Island from Ram Island and saw a lone figure stumbling along the Ram Island shore. He rowed across and found bodies and wreckage washed up on the weed-covered ledges. He tied up his skiff and went to the man stumbling in circles at the edge of the island. The sole survivor was insane, and could not remember his own name or the names of his drowned shipmates. The hermit flagged down a passing boat that afternoon and the sole crazed survivor was taken to a hospital in Boothbay, where he shortly died.

Then there was no one to light a warning lantern. But stories are told in Boothbay today by fishermen whose fathers told the stories to them as boys—that ghosts and spirits took on the job. There is the story that tells of one night of howling gale and pitch dark, a sailor aboard a ship in peril saw a woman dressed all in white waving a flaming torch from the shore of Ram Island, warning off the ship.

Another lone fisherman running for home through dense fog lost his course and was almost onto the ledges when he saw a ship burning on Ram Island and veered off. Next day he went back but could find no trace at all of a burned boat. Yet another skipper was coming close by Ram Island in a blinding snowstorm when he was warned off by the sound of a whistle—but there was no whistle on Ram Island.

Finally in 1883, the government built a lighthouse and keeper's dwelling on Ram Island. For the next three-quarters of a century, a fine light and well-kept keeper's house stood there, a handsome entrance to Boothbay Harbor. The light was built far out on the rocks on the south side of Ram Island. A solid, well-painted walkway connected it to Ram Island, where stood the keeper's handsome home, commanding splendid views to sea, to the eastern and western stretches of the coast, and into Boothbay Harbor. The boathouse and launching ramp were built on the north side, facing onto the narrow gut between Ram and Fisherman's, and two strong moorings were set there for Coast Guard boats.

Ram Island Light was unmanned and automated in 1965. About this time, *Steer Clear* began coming into Fisherman's Passage and picking up one of the Coast Guard moorings there for a lunch stop or an afternoon of rowing onto Ram Island or Fisherman's to explore their peace and beauty. The keeper's house was boarded up, but the fields abounded in sweet fern and wildflowers. Birds nested in the high grass. Moles and mice found sweet sanctuary there. It was a grand spot for boatmen to stretch their legs or lie out in the sun with solid ground beneath them for a change. The little island became a popular picnic spot.

The town of Boothbay had a chance to buy the house and island from the Coast Guard after the keeper's house was no longer needed following automation of the light. But ownership carried with it responsibilities for policing, maintenance, and care, which the town was unable or unwilling to fulfill. Vandals got the upper hand. The keeper's house became a hangout. Next the walkway from the island to the light fell into disrepair. Planks rotted and weather weakened the handrails, which made the walkway an inviting but dangerous hazard; it was ordered to be destroyed.

Now there is no way to walk out to the light, but the light still stands, an automated and needed beacon. The house has been restored, and there is hope that the walkway will be, as well. And, of course, little Ram Island stands and the wildflowers still grow. Of a summer day, it is still a joy to row ashore and stretch your legs on the speck of an island that has so long been a guardian to handsome Boothbay Harbor.

Burnt Island Light

Running into Boothbay Harbor, leaving Southport Island close to the west, lies Burnt Island, about four miles inshore from the Ram Island Light. Here in 1821 was built Burnt Island Light, a manned station until 1989, when it became automated.

In 1962, Burnt Island Light became the last lighthouse in New England to be converted from kerosene to electricity, then in 1989 it became one of the last Maine lights to be automated. Today's light is from a modern 300mm lens. In 1969, two Fresnel lenses from the light at Burnt Island were moved to the Rockland Coast Guard base; they are now on display at the Shore Village Museum in Rockland.

The light and automatic fog signal remain active aids to navigation.

In February 1998, the Maine Lighthouse Selection Committee approved the transfer of Burnt Island Light to the Maine Department of Marine Resources as part of the Maine Lights Program. The "Burnt Island Living Lighthouse" will provide maritime history programs as well as programs in navigation, ecosystems, fisheries, art, literature, and music. The programs will be aimed at children as well as the general public.

Boothbay Harbor is one of the prettiest, biggest, and most popular yachting centers along the coast of Maine. More sailing yachts, says the Coast Guard, pass Burnt Island Light than any small light on the East Coast.

One of the greatest sights in summer is to drop anchor near this light and watch the handsome windjammer fleet sail into Boothbay Harbor for Windjammer Day. The big vessels, under a full suit of canvas, bespeak the great days of Maine shipbuilding. Some of these handsome windjammers were indeed coasting schooners a hundred years ago, now restored and modernized to accommodate passengers for an unforgettable week of sailing the Maine coast.

Watching the fleet arrive in the year of 1985, I sat on *Steer Clear* and found it easy to conjure up pictures of how this splendid harbor, with The Cuckolds, Ram Island, and Squirrel and Southport Islands, looked when a hundred and more ships of sail made men and made fortunes in these same waters.

Pemaquid Point Light

Pemaquid is my favorite light, by sea and by land. By land, Pemaquid is at the tip of the peninsula where I lived for twenty-one years in Damariscotta. There is a small and good art gallery at Pemaquid, where area artists show paintings of the region and sculptures of herons and porcupines, otters and owls. Here at the summertime show, visitors buy local paintings of local Maine scenes. There is an interesting Fisherman's Museum open to visitors in summer, in the old keeper's living quarters. The museum is run by volunteers from the town of Bristol, Maine, where the lighthouse is officially located.

In winter storms, scores of local residents head for Pemaquid Light to watch the enormous fury of the sea. Magnificent and overwhelming as this spectacle is, it can be dangerous to go close to the edge of the rocks, for freak waves suddenly reach far up and can sweep an innocent onlooker to death by drowning. On Easter Sunday, sunrise services are held beside Pemaquid Light. Often the weather is cold and windy. But the view across the water toward Monhegan in the east and to the White Islands, Outer Heron, and Fisherman's Island in the west, with early morning lobsterboats bobbing and hauling in between, gives a deep sense of timelessness, stability, peace, and gradual purpose to the world. The words of the Easter service and the music of Easter hymns are imbued with special qualities when they are heard on the Pemaquid cliffs at sunrise.

By sea, Pemaquid Light has been my homecoming beacon, heading in from either east or west. With Pemaquid Light off my bow, I knew my home harbor was just around the corner, and shortly *Steer Clear* would be back again on her mooring, safe and seaworthy, in her homeport of New Harbor.

Pemaquid Light was a luxury post for any keeper who had done duty on Seguin, Boon Island, Matinicus, or Mount Desert Rock lights. The light has been automated since 1934, and the keeper's house has, in years past, been rented to artists who have had the world's finest seascapes at their doorstep.

Pemaquid Light was first built under President John Quincy Adams in 1827 for $4,000. Isaac Dunham from Bath was the first keeper, and he farmed the land around his light. During his stint, Dunham built several barns on the property. When Dunham was transferred to become first keeper at Minot's Ledge Light, reputedly one of the most dangerous lighthouses in America, lying off the Cohasset, Massachusetts shore, Dunham asked for and received $1,100 from his successor, Nathaniel Gamage, for the improvements he had built.

This proved a poor investment for Gamage because, in 1841, politics cost Gamage his job. New President Benjamin Harrison fired Gamage to make way for a local Harrison supporter, J.P. Means. Means refused to pay a lump sum to Gamage for the farm and barns and offered to pay rent instead. But all Gamage got over two years was twenty-six dollars. Gamage appealed for payment or for his old job back as keeper. Neither President Harrison nor his successor, President John Tyler, gave Gamage the justice he sought. Poor Gamage got no money for his farm buildings and no reinstatement as keeper of Pemaquid Light.

Pemaquid Point has had its share of shipwrecks and history. In August of 1635, the famous *Angel Gabriel* struck on ledges, five people lost their lives, and all the belongings of a hundred colonists from England were lost. Shipwrecks continued through the centuries. In the twentieth-century storm of September 16 and 17, 1903, when Captain Clarence Marr, a lifesaving hero of many spectacular rescues, was keeper, the fishing vessel *George F. Edmunds* ran from the gale at sea and made course for Pemaquid Light. The gale's fury increased so much that a mile or so from the light, the skipper, Captain Willard Poole, reefed the mainsail and steered for John's Bay, hoping for snug harbor behind South Bristol. But he made a mistake of eight hundred feet in his calculations of drift, and came hard on the rocks in Lighthouse Cove. Captain Poole and thirteen of his crew were drowned. Two were rescued, but the vessel was smashed to pieces.

A smaller mackerel seiner, the *Sadie and Lillie*, had run for shelter alongside the *George F. Edmunds*. Captain Poole of the Edmunds told Captain William S. Harding of the *Sadie and Lillie* to follow him to South Bristol Harbor. Harding's boat hit, too. But one of the keepers, Weston Curtis, saw the disaster and managed to get a line to the boat. He rescued two men, but when it was Captain Harding's turn to leave the sinking ship last, the lines jammed and he drowned.

Here on the Pemaquid peninsula, down John's Bay from the light, lies Pemaquid Harbor, a fountainhead of early American history. When Raleigh Gilbert in the ship *Mary and John* sailed into these waters in 1607, a few days before he helped establish the first American colony at Popham, he came to Pemaquid to meet with Indian leaders. His guide was the Indian Skidwarres, one of the native Indians kidnapped a few years earlier by Weymouth and taken to England. Skidwarres was returning to his home territory. He led Gilbert to Pemaquid to meet with the chief there. The Indian chief turned out to be none other than Nahanta, another of Weymouth's kidnapped Indians. The meeting was not cordial, but Nahanta let the colonist proceed peacefully to the Kennebec River by boat.

The Duke of York established the first custom house early in the seventeenth century, and built fortifications at Pemaquid. Excavations have uncovered the foundations, cellars, roadways, and many artifacts of this early settlement. These are now on display in the Pemaquid Museum. The Fort at Pemaquid has been under the command of three nations—England, France, and the newly independent United States. Now restored, it is open to the public.

I'd like to give special treatment to my home light of Pemaquid, because it was my regular landmark for my first twenty-one years of cruising Maine waters, when *Steer Clear I* and *Steer Clear II* were home-ported at nearby Round Pond and then New Harbor, and partly because I knew so many fishermen and their families in this area.

In 1972, Hilda Libby, an important member of the fishing community, organized the Fisherman's Museum in the former keeper's house. She also wrote a pamphlet about the light, especially its early construction. I'd like to quote from her history:

> In 1826, Samuel and Sarah Martin sold to the federal government a few acres at Pemaquid Point for $90. Congress appropriated $4,000 to build a light at Pemaquid Point in the same year. In 1827, Isaac Ilsley, superintendent of lighthouses for the state of Maine, contracted with Jeremiah Berry, bricklayer of Thomaston, to build, finish, and complete a lighthouse and dwelling house at Pemaquid Point.
>
> The contract specified that "the tower was to be built of suitable split, undressed stone: the form round, the foundation to be sunk as deep as may be necessary to make the whole fabric secure; all to be laid in good lime mortar. The base of the tower to be eighteen feet, and at the top, ten feet. The walls were to be three and one-half feet thick, and to be uniformly graduated to two feet at the top, where an arch was to be turned, on which there was to be a dish of soapstone eleven and a half feet in diameter, five inches thick, fitted with a 'scuttle' by which to enter the lantern, the glassed-in section that housed the light itself. There was to be a circular stair of hard pine, clear of sap, seasoned and planed, with an iron ladder at the top reaching to the 'scuttle.'"
>
> On the same day that Mr. Ilsley contracted with Jeremiah Berry to build the tower, he also entered into a contract with Captain Winslow Lewis, of Boston, to "fit up the Light House at Pemaquid with ten patent lamps and sixteen inch reflectors" at a cost of $500. Other equipment

included in this contract was "six double X tin butts, to hold ninety gallons each and painted three coats, and six wooden horses, two spare lamps, one lantern canister and iron trivet and double tin wick box and one double tin tube box, one oil carrier, one glazier's diamond, one hand lantern and lamp, two pairs scissors, two files, two tube cleaners, one stove funnel, one oil feeder and all other apparatus, in the same manner as Light-Houses have been fitted by said Lewis, with the addition of Black's apparatus for conducting the heat to the lamps to the oil therein."

Within the detailed contract with bricklayer Berry were instructions to build a dwelling house of stone, thirty-four feet by twenty feet, one story, eight feet in the clear and the walls eighteen inches thick. Instructions called for two rooms, with a chimney in the middle and a fireplace in each room, together with closets and shelves "back of the chimney." Stairs were to lead into the chambers which were to be partitioned off, with all rooms to be lathed and plastered with double floors "well nailed."

Attached to the house was to be a porch or kitchen ten feet by twelve, the walls to be the same as in the dwelling house. There was to be a chimney built in the kitchen "with an iron crane, trammel and hooks; on one side an oven of middling size with an iron door, on the other side a sink with a gutter to lead through the wall, out of the house." The roof of the house and the kitchen was to be covered with good, seasoned boards and shingles. The price agreed upon for the tower and the house: $2,000.

Here was a contract, written in 1827, that could be a lesson in clarity and detail for those in the federal government who today write those jaw-breaking, incomprehensible, legalistic contracts.

However, much went wrong in the fulfillment. The stone tower began disintegrating eight years after it was built. So in 1835, John Chandler, who had succeeded Isaac Ilsley as superintendent of lighthouses in Maine, drew a new contract, this time with Joseph Berry, mason of Georgetown, "to rebuild, finish, and complete the Tower at Pemaquid Point."

Specifications were identical in most ways with the earlier contract, except for one or two curious directives. For example: "The whole to be laid in the best lime mortar; the same to be used never to have met with salt water; the mortar to be mixed with fresh water." And: "It is hereby stipulated...that the walls of the Tower are to be built solid with Stone and Mortar, in a single wall, or where there is more than one thickness of stone, the walls are to be carried up solid and bound together, and not done by building two walls, and filling in, in the middle, and all stones are to be laid so the upper side of the stone will not incline downward on the inside, and thereby tend to convey the water through the wall."

The price for this new tower, for which Joseph Berry was authorized to use "existing materials," was $1,395.

There is a postscript, later added to the contract, that suggests either that an outstanding job was done or that this Berry wanted full protection against any future comebacks for sloppy work. The postscript, in the handwriting of Isaac Dunham, first keeper of the Pemaquid Light, states: "This may Certify that Captain Berry has completed the Light House in a good workmanlike manner and according to the Contract in every way—and I will venture to say, a better tower and lantern never was built in the State. Also the lamps reflectors and apparatus is according to Contract."

Despite these glowing words, the same kind of deterioration bedeviled the new construction. For in 1857, thirty years after it was finished, a new keeper's dwelling had to be built, this time of wood. That dwelling still stands today beside the light, and has now been transformed into the Fisherman's Museum; it looks much as it did in an early photograph from 1857.

Pemaquid Light, automated in 1934, is only a fourth-order light; the distance from the light to the center of the lens is only $9^8/_{10}$ inches. (In a first-order light, this distance is $51^3/_{10}$ inches.) Its white light flashes every six seconds during darkness, with 9,950 candlepower, and a visibility up to fourteen miles. A sun relay system turns the light on and off at dusk and dawn.

The tower stands thirty feet above the ground, and the iron lantern housing the light is forty-eight feet above the ground. Since the ground here is seventy-eight feet above sea level, the lantern itself shines from 127 feet above the sea.

Inside the Fresnel lens is a 250-watt light bulb, especially made for lighthouses. It is fixed into a four-bulb lamp changer that turns automatically when a bulb is burned out. A series of batteries at the foot of the tower is equipped with a trip mechanism worked by a mercury switch whenever there is a power failure. Otherwise, the light is connected to the regular electrical system serving the Pemaquid area.

Still standing on the south side of the tower (though badly damaged and since repaired from waves hitting it in a giant storm in the late 1970s) is a small brick house built in 1897 for the hand-operated fog bell. This was replaced after one year with duplicate Shipman oil-burning steam engines to ring it. This lasted only one year, too, and in 1899 was replaced by a Stevens striking machine and the close-by wooden triangle, built to house the clock-weights.

The lightkeeper, at the onset of fog, would wind up the Stevens machine, which caused the weights to travel to the top of the triangle tower. Then for the next eight hours, the bell would be struck at set intervals,

Pemaquid Point Light, built in 1827. In 1934, it became the first light in Maine to be automated. The keeper's house is now a fisherman's museum. Courtesy of Philip Ziegler.

the weights slowly descending as in a cuckoo clock. If fog persisted after the eight hours, the lightkeeper again wound up the Stevens striking machine.

In September 1940, six years after the light was automated, the Coast Guard sold the adjoining land to the town for perpetual use as a park. An art gallery for Pemaquid area artists has also been added to the Fisherman's Museum.

Pemaquid keepers in order of tenure were: Isaac Dunham, 1827; Nathaniel Gamage, Jr., 1837; Jeremiah S. Means, 1841; Ephraim Tibbetts, 1845; Robert Curtis, 1849; Samuel C. Tibbetts, 1853; John Fossett, 1858; Joseph Laler, 1861 (his daughter Susie, born June 10, 1868, is the only child born at the lighthouse); Marcus A. Hanna, 1869; William L. Sartell, 1873; Charles A. Dolliver, 1883; Clarence E. Marr, 1899; and Herbert Robinson, 1922 (his daughter, Edith, was married on the porch of the lightkeeper's house). In 1934, the light was automated.

Pemaquid Light is one of the most-visited, best-loved lights on the Maine coast. The spectacular views of the coast and an array of islands to the east and west, especially famed Monhegan Island, attract crowds in summer and natives in winter storms. There is ample room for parking, a fascinating Fisherman's Museum, an art gallery, and the Bradley Inn is close by for accommodations and food. Also close is the museum at the Pemaquid Fort Restoration and a good swimming beach. Only a mile or so away is busy, picturesque New Harbor and Back Cove, each filled with working lobsterboats and with two restaurants with open decks overlooking the harbor scene.

Franklin Island Light

Franklin Island Light deserves lots of respect as the third-oldest workhorse light in Maine—but Franklin gets little love or admiration.

Franklin was built by order of President Thomas Jefferson, almost two hundred years ago. Started in 1803, the light has been flashing across Muscongus Bay since it was finished in 1807. Only Portland Head Light (1791) and Seguin (1795) are older than Franklin. It is a testimony of how important the shipping trade that sailed through the general area of Monhegan, Friendship, Port Clyde, and Pemaquid was to our young nation.

The light at Monhegan was not built until 1824, and the light at Pemaquid was not started until 1827. Two other Maine lights, the nearby light at Whitehead (1804) and the light at West Quoddy Head, close to the border with Canada (1808), are of the same vintage as Franklin Light. And in 1855, when Franklin Pierce—the Bowdoin graduate—was president, Franklin Light was improved and rebuilt.

Twenty-seven of Maine's lights were not built until after Franklin had been rebuilt. These facts indicate how busy coastal shipping was in this part of midcoast Maine, and how great a danger were the myriad ledges around Franklin. For these reasons, Franklin merits respect. Keepers manned this light for 160 years, until it was automated in 1967.

These days, Franklin Light gets little attention or admiration, perhaps because it has no beauty either as a light or as an island. Franklin is surrounded by some of the most beautiful and historic islands and coastline in Maine. Monhegan, one of the most famous and beautiful islands, rises like a whale out of the sea only a few miles to the southeast. A short distance due east from Franklin is the snug Georges Harbor, beside Allen Island, where Weymouth landed in 1607 and held the first Protestant church service in North America, with a granite cross marking the spot today. Inland lie Cushing, made so famous by Andrew Wyeth's paintings; Friendship, home of the famed Friendship sloops; and Port Clyde, where one can plainly see the grooves left ten thousand years ago by Maine's last Ice Age, and where one catches the mailboat today going out to Monhegan.

I have set my course by Franklin Light hundreds of times. Going east from New Harbor, our homeport for twenty years, Franklin Light has been my first seamark.

Yet I have been ashore there only twice, and briefly at that. There is no inviting spot to anchor, and no enticing cove in which to land a dinghy. I have been afraid to walk out of sight of the dinghy, and if this scruffy-looking island has hidden charms, I have not explored it enough to find them. *Steer Clear* most often cruises past Franklin through the rather narrow passage, filled with lobster-trap buoys, that separates Franklin from Crane and Harbor islands (where my old friends and neighbors, Leverett and Eugenie Davis, live most of the summer). Harbor Island has since been deeded to the Maine Coast Heritage Trust.

Lev Davis, once a minister and teacher, sailed around the world as a young man aboard the famous *Yankee*. He and his artist wife live in a whitewashed stone cottage, which has a sad but sweet love story as part of its history. It was built long ago by a fisherman from Ireland who came here to make money enough to go back to Ireland, marry his childhood sweetheart, and bring her to Maine. He built this cottage in the Irish croft style for his bride-to-be. But the poor fellow took too long to make his nest egg. When he had his money salted away, he went home to Ireland only to discover that his love had married another man in his long absence in the New World. The bereft fellow let the cottage he had built go to wrack and ruin. It became a decrepit shanty, used by lobstermen from Friendship and Port Clyde as a place to store gear. But in recent years, Lev and Eugenie Davis have made it into a simple, plain yet beautiful small home, surrounded by fields of wildflowers on Harbor Island. *Steer Clear* has too seldom put into Harbor Island in recent years for a visit, but instead has gone by to anchor for the night, and sometimes for days on end, in the favorite little cove on the south side of close-by Otter Island. From that tight anchorage, we watch the light flashing from Franklin, where a light has been flashing for almost two hundred years.

Franklin Island Light, in Muscongus Bay. Gannett file photo.

Marshall Point Light

Located in Port Clyde, Marshall Point Light—the first light inland from Franklin Island—is a beauty. But as a historic seamark, Marshall Point is younger and less important. It is more loved, and more photographed and painted than plain and isolated Franklin. From a keeper's point of view, this was a sought-after mainland light, whereas Franklin was an unpopular station.

Marshall Point Light was built in 1832, during the presidency of Andrew "Stonewall" Jackson, and enlarged and remodeled in 1858. The United States Weather Bureau maintained a station here until the mid-1920s. The Coast Guard kept a lifeboat station on Burnt Island, five miles south out to sea from here, just over halfway out to Monhegan Island.

A loran "A" transmitting station was linked to Marshall Point Light in 1972, until the light was automated in 1980. The fifth-order lens was on display at the Coast Guard station in Rockland. It was stolen in 1974 and never found.

The mailboat and ferry to Monhegan Island is also located in Port Clyde, and provides Monhegan's official link to the mainland. A few miles to the east is Southern Island Light, at the entrance to Tenants Harbor, and just beyond that is famous Whitehead Light, built in 1807, at the entrance to Muscle Ridge Channel. Another lifesaving station was maintained there for many years, along with another weather station (see later section on Whitehead). Thus, Marshall Point Light is part of a cluster of lights, bunched within a few miles of each other: Pemaquid, Franklin, Monhegan, Southern Island, Matinicus Rock Light, Whitehead, and Two Bush, which marks the outer Two Bush Channel, paralleling the inner Muscle Ridge Channel.

The light at Marshall Point is a thirty-foot white tower built on an outcrop ledge and joined to the land by a long walkway. The keeper's spacious house and outbuildings are built in an open field near the start of the walkway, and the whole scene has attracted many artists to paint it. The light shines out over Herring Gut—the name once given to this Port Clyde waterfront when it was a center of the sardine industry, much used by the fleet from Gloucester, Massachusetts. Though not as great a fishing center as it was, and though the granite quarries are silent now, the harbor has allowed Port Clyde to remain a commercial fishing port.

Marshall Point Light in Port Clyde awaits repair to its footbridge. First built in 1832, the light was automated in 1980. Gannett file photo.

—— Tenants Harbor Light, Southern Island ——

The use of Tenants Harbor Light was discontinued by the government in 1934 and sold at auction. Bought by a Rockland resident, the lighthouse passed through several hands until it was bought in 1978 by artist Andrew Wyeth and his wife Betsy James Wyeth.

The Wyeths spent a number of summers on Southern Island. "I love everything about this house," Betsy Wyeth told *Architectural Digest* in 1986. "Just walking into it refreshes me. It's like being on a ship—the brass polished, everything swept clean. I love the patterns of our life here."

Since 1990, Betsy and Andrew's son, artist Jamie Wyeth, has lived on the island with his wife, Phyllis Mills Wyeth, "It's like living in an Andrew Wyeth painting," Jamie Wyeth told *National Geographic*. The pyramidal bell tower is actually a studio built by the Wyeths. The family has done a wonderful job maintaining the buildings and grounds.

In March of 1993, Jamie Wyeth weathered a blizzard at Southern Island, spending most of the storm in the lighthouse. "It really blew a gale. There are vents in the lighthouse tower, and when the wind came screaming through it sounded like fifty metroliners."

Tenants Harbor Light has appeared in several Wyeth paintings, including Andrew's "Signal Flags" and Jamie's "Iris at Sea," painted to raise funds for the Island Institute in Rockland.

Painters Andrew, and his son, Jamie, who lived for many years in nearby Cushing, have become island enthusiasts. Jamie Wyeth lived and painted great work on Monhegan. Around 1975, Jamie bought Burnt Island, which lies between Port Clyde and Monhegan. He has restored the big white Coast Guard station house and its long wooden dock. The snug harbor is a much-used overnight anchorage for the whaleboats from the Outward Bound camp on Hurricane Island. "When I bought the island, people told me I'd run out of things to paint," Jamie Wyeth told *Down East* magazine. "I think I could spend two lifetimes here and not run out of subjects."

Betsy Wyeth more recently bought historic Allen Island, just west of Burnt Island. She cut the scrub trees that had long overgrown the northern tip of Allen and turned it into sheep pasture and started a herd. Allen Island is located off Port Clyde and is about fifty acres smaller than its southern neighbor, Monhegan Island.

In conjunction with the Island Institute of Rockland, the Wyeth family's Up East Foundation has allowed the University of Maine access to Allen Island to study sea life.

The light on Southern Island no longer operates, but the tower is a splendid daymark for boats crossing West Penobscot Bay, between Whitehead and Port Clyde.

Two Bush Island Light

Two Bush was one of the last lights built on the Maine coast. It was built in 1897, which makes it by far the youngest sea light along midcoast Maine. Only the light at the entrance to the Isle au Haut Thorofare, built in 1907, came later than Two Bush.

Before Two Bush, shipping either gave a wide berth to the dangerous shores of the score of islands lying close to Two Bush, or chose to take the inside passage and be guided by the light at Whitehead (1804) and Owls Head (1826) through the Muscle Ridge Channel.

Only on clear days with lots of daylight hours ahead does *Steer Clear* take this outside course, which cuts the distance to Isle au Haut.

Two Bush Island is a rough and barren spot. The name is a misnomer today, for there is no visible bush on the island. But once two tall pines stood here, and that is how it got the name. The sixty-five-foot tower was a manned light from 1897 until it became automated in 1964. Since no state agency, town, or private buyer was interested in acquiring the keeper's house, it was blown up by in a demolition exercise by U.S. Army Special Forces.

I have been on Two Bush only once—and that was by helicopter. An acquaintance, Freddie Vahlsing, who had made big news stories with his multi-million-dollar white elephant of a sugar beet plant in Aroostook, flew from New Jersey and landed in the meadow by my house in Damariscotta on a Sunday afternoon, wanting to talk news business. As a kind of sweetener for spoiling my Sunday, Vahlsing offered to take me flying in his Bell jet helicopter along the coast, so I could hover over my favorite islands and see them for a new perspective.

While we were flying around my favorite islands along the Muscle Ridge Channel, Vahlsing hovered low over Two Bush, fascinated by the light tower. Then he spotted the old concrete foundation on which the keeper's house had stood. He chose to use it as a helipad, and we landed and walked around. It seemed a risky thing to do even at the time, and in retrospect, it seems downright stupid. I have never chosen to return, either from sea or air. And I pity the poor keepers who lived there through sixty-seven winters.

One keeper—Captain Norton—owned a dog that was more than a good companion. The mutt, called Spot, saved the lives of two shipwrecked fishermen only a few years after the light was first lit. Aboard the *Clara Bella*, Captain Pulk and his mate George Samuels were working the fishing grounds near Green Island Ledges, inside Matinicus Island, when a nor'easter storm of wind and snow blew up suddenly and overtook them before they could find shelter. Their boat had been seen by other fishermen and then was seen no more—for three days and nights—by anyone except keeper Norton and his dog Spot.

The *Clara Bella* had lost her steering and her bearings in the storm, and smashed hard and started breaking up fast on a ledge that neither man knew. They took to their dory and rowed away fast to seek shelter in quieter seas in the lee of one of the islands. From eleven o'clock that night until two the next morning, they rowed through the blackness and violent seas, with sea water icing up over them, their hands, their faces—and worst of all, their boat—which was badly weighted down and losing buoyancy.

Suddenly over the roar of wind and seas, they heard the sound of a barking dog. "It sounded to us like the voice of an angel," said Pulk a few days later.

The barking of Spot alerted Keeper Norton that something was wrong just off the ledge. Norton followed the dog, who was running wildly back and forth, to the edge of the cliff, and there he could hear two men shouting for help. Using his lantern as a signal to them, Norton guided the men toward the boat slip. But a wave took them by surprise, capsizing the boat and throwing the two men into the wild sea. Norton had left the light with a long coil of rope. He hurled one end to the men in the surf and hauled them out to safety.

The dog leaped with joy all over the half-drowned and frozen fishermen, licking their faces as though they were his long-lost friends. When they had recovered, the rescued men tried to buy the dog that had saved their lives. Keeper Norton refused, wanting to keep his good companion on this isolated and brutal station.

Monhegan Island Light

Through the fog, Monhegan Light flashes a welcome, reassuring beam that looks yellowish on the white fog.

The first Monhegan light was built for three thousand dollars during the administration of President James Monroe, and for 178 years a light from Monhegan Island has been guiding sailors, since the day Thomas B. Seavey lit the first lanterns here on July 2, 1824. Seavey burned sperm oil for his ten lanterns. Their flickering light was magnified by sixteen-inch reflectors, which produced a red and white flash at each revolution.

Today, the light at Monhegan is automated. From the tower 180 feet above the sea, it flashes a 170,000-candlepower beam.

Across the fog, the island's diaphragm horn explodes with two terrific blasts every minute. But this fog signal, wailing over the invisible sea, comes not from Monhegan but from Manana Island, the treeless hump on the west side of Monhegan Harbor.

The first fog signal installed here was operated by Sylvester Davis. It was a 2,500-pound bell, cast in Boston in 1832 and brought here in 1854, paid for by an appropriation of $3,500 during the presidency of Franklin Pierce. President Pierce, incidentally, had Maine ties. He was a Bowdoin College graduate, a classmate of Henry Wadsworth Longfellow. A native of Concord, New Hampshire, Pierce first served in his state legislature, then was elected to the House of Representatives, later became Senator from New Hampshire, and finally, president of the United States.

While President Pierce had no direct ties to Monhegan, he may have warmed to fond memories of the Maine coast when he approved the $3,500 for the bell at Monhegan. When that bell was installed in 1854, the keeper had to ring its vast clapper by hand to warn ships off the death-trap rocks. But when the wind was blowing, sailors could not hear it. So in 1870, a ten-inch Daboll trumpet operated by an Ericsson engine replaced the giant hand-rung bell. This trumpet was installed across the harbor on Manana Island. But even the trumpet could not always be heard—a severe handicap to trans-Atlantic ships that made Monhegan their landfall, as well as to coastal and local vessels.

A steam whistle was installed, back beside the lighthouse on Monhegan. But this worked no better. So in 1877, a new, first-class Daboll trumpet was located across the harbor, again on Manana, with Frank E. Adams in charge of it.

The problem now was that the fog signal and the lighthouse were half a mile apart, separated by the harbor. The solution was to string a telegraph line linking the lighthouse keeper, atop the highest point on Monhegan, to the fog-signal keeper lower down and far away on Manana. When Betty Humphrey, the famous woman lightkeeper, spotted a fog bank far at sea while in her lookout atop the lighthouse, she pushed a button. The button set off a loud electric gong in the bedroom of Fog Signal Keeper Frank Adams over on Manana, who would leap from his bed or armchair and start sounding his Daboll trumpet. This trumpet lasted until 1912, when an air siren took its place. There were more replacements during the next fifty years, until the arrival of the loud diaphone horn that now stands on Manana, sending two terrific blasts every minute out through the fog. The last civilian keeper was Henley C. Day, who retired in 1956.

Landsmen—even sailors—seldom realize how often expensive replacements and improvements have been made to lights and fog signals. The fog-signal changes at Manana and Monhegan add up to lots of money and effort. More money and work were spent on improving lights and fog signals than on improving roads, docks, and water systems on Monhegan itself. These days when we sail by Monhegan, we've got so much help in finding our way that I wonder whether any modern-day sailor could match the navigators who found their way to Monhegan almost five hundred years ago. Here and on other islands on the Maine coast is where America really began.

Most of us forget that this is historic ground when we sail out to Monhegan today, and go ashore and see the island crowded with summer visitors. But the Monhegan story may go back more than a thousand years. Some believe the runes you can see today by the Coast Guard station on Manana were carved by Vikings around 1000 A.D. Whether that is true or not, it is certain that more than five hundred years ago, fishermen from England sailed to Monhegan, and caught and salted cod for European markets on these island shores. Men and ships perished on the rocks here hundreds of years ago, not far from the spots on our charts named Dead Man's Cove, Washerwoman Ledge, and Pulpit Rock.

The native Indians used Monhegan as a fishing station; the name Monhegan, translated from their language, means The Island. After white men settled here, the Indians returned to raid and burn the settlement and forced the white families to flee and leave the island uninhabited.

The French explorer Samuel de Champlain called the island Le Nef, because he thought that from a distance it looked like a ship. Captain John Smith, of Pocahontas fame, came ashore at Monhegan in May 1614 and gave the island a name which never stuck: Barties.

James Rosier, the reporter who kept the ship's diary on Captain Weymouth's voyages to New England, first saw Monhegan in May 1605 and wrote this description:

> We descried the land, which bare from us North-North-East, but because it blew a great gale of winde, the sea very high and neere night, not fit to come upon an unknown coast, we stood offe till two a clocke in the morning, being Saturday ... It appeared a meane high lande, as we after found it, being but an Iland six miles in compasse, but I hope the most fortunate ever discoured ... This Iland is woody, gruen with Firre, Birch, Oke and Beeche, as farre as we saw along the shore; and so likely to be within.

Since ships began sailing to the New World, Monhegan has been a landfall for seamen from the Old World. To understand why Monhegan was so important to early navigators, it is necessary to see it from far at sea rather than from the Maine coast. Coming in from the sea approach, it is possible to see the tree-crested outline of Monhegan from forty miles away, rising almost two hundred feet above sea level.

The early trans-Atlantic navigators set their course for the Maine coast because Maine is three hundred miles closer to Europe than any other part of the United States, and Monhegan rises high out of the sea nine miles before the Maine coast.

There is a legend that the Irish came to Monhegan even before the Vikings, Leif and Thorwold, sons of Eric the Red, sailed to the island from Iceland in about 1000 A.D., looking for trees to cut into lumber to build houses on treeless Iceland.

The Irish legend is that in about 565 A.D. an Irish monk named Brendan and a band of seventeen followers sailed here in a reed boat. The monks supposedly found wild sheep on an island and captured a lamb to roast in celebration of Easter. They built a rough altar on a barren ledge and started a fire. To their amazement, the ledge began to move through the ocean. The monks realized they had set their fire on the back of a giant whale ("Jasconius is his name").

John Cabot in his explorations in 1494, made his landfall at Monhegan, according to some historians. Others say his landfall was at Newfoundland.

Monhegan Island Light was built in 1824 and automated in 1959. The keeper's house is now an island museum open to the public in summer. U.S. Gannett file photo.

There is stronger evidence that explorer Giovanni da Verrazano (for whom the bridge in New York Harbor is named) inspected Monhegan when he was mapping these parts for the French king, in his vessel *La Dauphine*. The English explorer Martin Pring, with his two ships *Discoverer* and *Speedwell*, dropped anchor at Monhegan in 1603, a full seventeen years before the *Mayflower* dropped anchor off Plymouth Rock. Pring's log gives an accurate description of Monhegan and pinpoints its exact latitude, 43.5 degrees north.

But it was the irrepressible adventurer Captain John Smith who put Monhegan into the public spotlight with his description of it:

In the month of April, 1614, with two ships from London, I chanced to arrive in New Englande, a parte of Ameryca, at the Ile of Monhegan in the 43.5 of Northerly latitude; our plot was there to take Whales and made tryalls of a Myne of Gold and Copper ... We found this Whale-fishing a costly conclusion; we saw many and spent much time chasing them, but could not kill any ... For our Golde, it was more the Master's device to get a voyage that projected it, than any knowledge he had of any such matter. Fish and furres are now our gold ... Of dry fish we made about 4,000. Of cor fish about 7,000. While our saylors fished, myselfe with nine others ranged the coast in a small boat and got for trifles near

1,100 Beaver skins, 100 Martine, and near as many Otters ... With these furres and the cor fish I returned to England in the Bark: where within six months of our departure we arrived safe back. The best of the fishe was solde for five pounds the hundredth, the rest by ill visage betwixt three and four pounds. The other ship staied to fit herself for Spaine with the dried fish.

The other ship, captained by Thomas Hunt, did lasting harm by capturing twenty-seven Indians at Cape Cod, chaining them in the hold, and then trying to sell them for slaves in Spain—unsuccessfully.

Largely as a result of Captain Smith's reports, three more London ships came to Monhegan in 1615. The Plymouth Company sent out four ships in 1616 and eight privately owned ships also arrived. By 1618, two years before the Pilgrims set foot on Plymouth Rock, Monhegan had a year-round settlement. Governor Bradford, leader of the Plymouth Colony, reported buying four hundred pounds sterling in supplies from the Monhegan settlement in 1626. That trade indicates how much more advanced the settlement at Monhegan was than the settlement at Plymouth.

Tragedy lay ahead for Monhegan settlers through no fault of their own. This Maine island suffered because in Europe the king of England suddenly became friendly with the king of France: the two became allies against Spain. In a gesture of friendship, England gave back to France the contested lands in Acadia and Nova Scotia. With this foothold, the French began to expand their ambitions and staged raids against the Maine coast, especially the settlement at Monhegan. (The French later captured the fort at Pemaquid.)

By 1635, the settlers on Monhegan fled for safety from French and Indian raids, and the island was deserted for the next twenty years, used only as a summertime fishing station.

Slowly, the Monhegan settlement came back to prosperity, until it was the most heavily taxed settlement in Maine, according to court records in the 1670s.

Again turbulence in Europe disturbed the peace on Monhegan. In 1688, King James II of England was dethroned to make way for Prince William of Orange. King James fled to France and stirred up the French by urging them to make war against the English Colonies in North America.

The French Baron Castine sailed out from his fort at Castine to attack Pemaquid and Monhegan. He had a personal vendetta against these two settlements because they had earlier seized a ship laden with wine and spirits for him. He lost eight hundred gallons of Malaga wine and one hundred and thirty gallons of brandy.

Using Indians as his raiding parties, Baron Castine destroyed the settlement at Monhegan in October 1689. With their island plagued by Indian raids and destruction, the Davidson family of Boston, who had owned Monhegan for ninety years, sold out.

In 1749, Shem Drowne, a Boston tinsmith, got a real bargain. He bought Monhegan and all its 440 acres for only ten pounds, thirteen shillings. Drowne was the artist who made the famous golden grasshopper still seen above Faneuil Hall in Boston. Drowne's son, Thomas, sold Monhegan for a handsome profit to the Bickford family of Salem, Massachusetts. They paid 160 pounds sterling for it in 1770. Seven years later, during the American Revolution, the Bickfords sold Monhegan to Henry Trefethren, a cabinetmaker from Kittery, who paid 300 pounds for it. The population of Monhegan, which had been over a hundred, was down to forty-eight in 1810, and by 1820 had increased slowly to sixty-eight year-round residents.

Monhegan was an important harbor during the War of 1812. Privateers sought safe shelter there, secure against the British sloops of war, the *Rattler* and the *Bream*, which burned many a Maine vessel between Monhegan and Castine. During this war, the spectacular and famous battle between the *Boxer* and the *Enterprise* was fought not far from this island, with both captains slain, but the Americans winning the day.

The importance of Monhegan as a landfall was getting greater as shipping between Europe and the United States increased and as coastal traffic grew. In 1824, four years after Maine became a state, splitting away from Massachusetts, Congress appropriated three thousand dollars to build the lighthouse tower on Monhegan. Monhegan, though geographically part of Lincoln County, has been and still is a self-governing, independent plantation. Its first plantation meeting was held April 27, 1840. Sixty dollars was voted for schools and fourteen dollars for roads. For a couple of generations, each man on Monhegan had to take his turn sailing in to Port Clyde on the mainland to fetch the mail. In 1883, Captain William S. Humphrey was named sea-going mailman and received a yearly salary of $336 for making two mail runs a week in his sloop, the *Goldsmith Maid*.

But the most famous Humphrey in Monhegan history is Betty Morrow Humphrey, the woman who was keeper of the Monhegan Light from 1862 until 1880.

Her husband, John F. Humphrey, had been named keeper in March 1861, two weeks before the outbreak of the Civil War. Their two sons, Albert and Edward, immediately enlisted and left Monhegan for the battlefields. In December 1861, Humphrey became sick and died. The capable widow was named keeper in his place at a salary of $820 a year. She got the sad news in 1864 that her youngest son, Albert, who had enlisted at seventeen, had been killed. Edward was wounded and disabled, and came home to help at the lighthouse as much as he was able. But Lightkeeper Betty was in charge for eighteen years, even though the money-strapped federal government forced her to take a pay cut from $820 down to $700 a year.

Over the 178 years that the Monhegan Light has been burning, there have been many wrecks, many rescues, and many drownings. A recent event happened on the stormy night of February 2, 1981. During an icy gale, the light went out. Coast Guardsmen William Spencer and Mark Wilson got the bad news as they were standing duty across the harbor in the Coast Guard building on Manana. They launched their sixteen-foot outboard into the teeth of the gale and set out across the harbor to repair the light atop Monhegan. But halfway across the harbor, their outboard quit and their boat capsized. The forty-knot winds swept the two men, clinging to their capsized boat, onto the ledges at Smuttynose.

Drenched and freezing, they scrambled ashore and used their portable radio to reach their fellow Coast Guardsmen back on Manana, who in turn relayed their plea for rescue to the Coast Guard station in Boothbay Harbor, fifteen miles away. For Boothbay to get a rescue boat through the storm and out to Monhegan waters would take hours.

So at 3:00 a.m. on Monhegan, Selectman Sherman Stanley and harbor master Steve Rollins were awakened by a call from the Boothbay Coast Guard, asking if they would try rescuing the men stranded and freezing on Smuttynose. Stanley and Rollins went out into the raging winter storm. They knew the seas and winds had already wrecked one outboard motor, so they rowed the three hundred yards in a small skiff to Smuttynose and rescued the two freezing Coast Guardsmen. Later, the Coast Guard honored them with medals. The Monhegan Light was repaired the next day. Its beam is shining now, as it has through 178 years.

Monhegan Light Museum

The lightkeeper's house on Monhegan has been saved and turned into a fascinating local museum, saved from the bad fate too many other keepers' houses have met—being demolished or sold to the highest bidder.

In 1959 the lighthouse was automated. The old kerosene Welsbach lanterns were replaced by an electric light, powered by a generator at the fog station on Manana. The new light was operated by remote control from the Coast Guard quarters on Manana. This meant there was no longer need for the lightkeeper's house on Monhegan; under law, the Coast Guard had to demolish it or sell it.

Monhegan Associates polled the residents and summer colony, and their overwhelming choice was to buy it and make it into an island museum. By sealed bid on June 1, 1962, Monhegan Associates acquired the keeper's house and outbuildings. Unhappily, they were not able to get the old lens and lanterns, which had been taken off. But they did get the chance to obtain the old and heavy fog-signal bell. The problem was, it weighed twenty-five-hundred pounds and was across the harbor on Manana. It was up to the association to transport it across to Monhegan and install it high on the hill by the keeper's house. How to do it? There was risk and danger in getting it downhill on Manana to the shore, in loading it aboard a boat, in getting it across the harbor, unloading it, and then somehow transporting the huge dead weight up to the keeper's house.

The Coast Guard wanted it out of the way. In 1969, the Coast Guard said the bell had to be moved or it would be destroyed. The bell was now widely famous, having been captured by Jamie Wyeth in his painting called "Bronze Age."

Finally, a way was found, though it took years to find it. In 1972, the Monhegan Water Company needed a heavy new water tower. The only way to get it to the island from Thomaston was by a heavy-duty helicopter. So a deal was struck: After the helicopter delivered the water tower, it would fly over to Manana, lift the 2,500-pound bell, fly it across, and ease it down onto a platform that had been built near the keeper's house to receive it. On May 1, 1972, the deed was done.

Today, the old fog bell stands by the new museum. The museum has grown year after year, and is open to the public every afternoon between July 1 and Labor Day.

"Will people spoil Monhegan?" That question has been raised every summer for the twenty years I have been cruising to Monhegan. I hope, and believe, that only one part of the answer is "Yes." On a hot weekend in August—when day-tourist boats from Boothbay Harbor, New Harbor, and Port Clyde disgorge hundreds of visitors—too many people do spoil Monhegan to some extent. But between the start of school in September and the Fourth of July, the answer is, to all but mossbacks, "No." Too many people are not spoiling Monhegan year-round. About a hundred men, women, and children live year-round here, on an island that is $1^3/4$ miles long and $3/4$ mile wide.

Monhegan changes people more than people change Monhegan. First, Monhegan's roots run deep. Second, life year-round on Monhegan is not easy; in fact, it is right only for very few. Third, Monhegan is protecting itself. Strict limits have been set upon the number of people who may live on the island—the number being governed by the available supply of water, which dictates how many houses can be built. The limit has just about been reached.

Monhegan also has hard and fast rules that prohibit overnight camping, and those rules are enforced. If a person lands in summer on Monhegan without a place to stay, he or she must be aboard the last boat for the mainland. Another important safeguard is that much of Monhegan is owned by an association that will permit no structures to be built on most of the eastern part of the island. Monhegan Associates was established in 1956, spearheaded by the family of Thomas Edison, the inventor (who had summered here); they bought control of almost half the island. To lobster fishermen, Monhegan is as attractive a fishing ground as it is a summer destination for vacationers. But here again, Monhegan has protected itself and has maintained its own guidelines for lobster fishing.

There is no lobstering on Monhegan from June through December. The result is that the lobstering is extra good in winter and spring, when lobsters elsewhere are scarce and prices are highest. Then comes Trap Day in January. It is equivalent to a national holiday on Monhegan. Trap Day ranks right up with Christmas, Easter, George Washington's Birthday, and New Year's Day.

Trap Day is that day in December or January, chosen by the fishermen in a meeting around the potbellied stove in the general store, when everyone will set their traps. They pick the day and the hour and no one tries to jump the gun. The days and nights before Trap Day, the island is a hive of busy preparations. Marker buoys are freshly painted, new pot warp and new bait bags are readied, and traps are piled eight feet high along both sides of the island wharf. By dawn on Trap Day, men are loading traps onto their boats and racing out to sea to set them where they think the lobsters are.

Monhegan and the Atlantic for two miles around the island is privileged—even sovereign—territory, belonging only to Monhegan fishermen, of which there are only a few. No lobsterman from the mainland or other islands in the bay is fool enough to set traps inside Monhegan waters, winter or summer.

Monhegan people are a breed apart: a self-reliant, friendly, gentle people who know who they are and like it. But they are full of surprises.

Monhegan may have had the only road worker, David Boynton, who was a nuclear scientist from MIT. Two lobstermen, Bill and Duggie Boynton, graduated from Wesleyan University, in political science, and from Trinity College, in Chinese studies. Monhegan may be the only place that had a doctor who also served as town clerk, director of civil defense, registrar of voters, school physician, prime political lobbyist for Monhegan's telephone link (where Monhegan beat New England Telephone), and also worked as a newspaper correspondent. She was Dr. Alta Ashley.

In summer, Monhegan's population jumps to several hundred. Summer houses are crowded with families and visiting friends who have been coming to this special place for generations. Artists have long flourished here. Robert Henri came to paint here in 1903, and told his pupil, Rockwell Kent, about the island. In 1905, at age twenty-three, Kent came to the island and lobstered, carpentered, and became accepted by the islanders as much as the stormy, womanizing, rebellious Kent was ever accepted anywhere. He did much of his best work on Monhegan. Henri also sent the prolific George Bellows here to paint in 1911, 1913, and 1914. Jay Connaway, Arthur Winter, Ernest Fiene, Joseph de Martini, Leo Meissner, Ernest Hekking, Reuben Tam, Zero Mostel—and most notably in recent years, Jamie Wyeth—have all lived and painted on Monhegan.

But at bottom, Monhegan is a fisherman's island, and the island belongs to the sea around it. Monhegan is today, as it was hundreds of years ago, a beacon to mariners. This is why the Monhegan Light and the fog signal and radio beacon on Manana are seamarks famous to sailors everywhere.

Whitehead Light

The good guardian at the western entrance to Muscle Ridge Channel is the light at Whitehead. Standing bold on a barren headland, Whitehead has an illustrious history, is handsome, performs well—yet I cannot muster for Whitehead the affection and warmth I feel toward Owls Head, at the eastern end of the Muscle Ridge Channel.

Whitehead is a mark I have often rejoiced to see and hear, especially when fog has shut down as we have been coming from the east through Muscle Ridge, or when fog has caught us heading across the bay from Monhegan. The fault is mine, but no sailor loves all lighthouses equally.

Whitehead's ancestry is impeccable. Thomas Jefferson himself ordered the erection of this light, which began operation with a scandal— one of the first oil scandals in our history. As oil scandals go, the Whitehead one may also be the smallest in history: Ellis Dolph, first keeper here, apparently lined his own pockets by selling some of the oil meant for his light.

This sideline business of Dolph's was uncovered in 1807, probably because he ran a good thing into the ground. Dolph kept ordering more frequent and larger supplies of oil from the lighthouse supply ship. This roused suspicions, and an inspector was sent from Boston to investigate.

The inspector poked around the communities of Thomaston and St. George, and obtained a written statement from Deacon Elisha Snow, Jr., to the effect that in the fall of 1805, he had bought a barrel of spermaceti oil from Ellis Dolph, keeper of the light. Hezekiah Prince, citizen of St. George, gave a statement to the same effect to the inspector. Prince alleged that over the past two years, he had seen Dolph sell two hundred gallons of oil to people in Thomaston. Joseph Coombs and his wife, storekeepers in Thomaston, had bought barrels of oil from the lightkeeper. When the inspector got back to his office in Boston with the evidence, Keeper Dolph was dishonorably discharged from his duties.

Scarcely six years after this scandal had subsided, another broke. In 1813, Winslow Lewis, making an inspection of Whitehead, reported that Keeper Ebenezer Otis was derelict in his duties and urged that he be dismissed. Otis answered that his spirit was willing, but his flesh was weak.

He had been ill, he said, and pleaded for another chance. Otis managed to hold his job, but not his good health; he died in July 1816.

Whitehead has the unhappy reputation of having more fog than any other spot in Maine. The average amount of fog along the Maine coast is reported as 874 hours a year. Translated into days, that amounts to five weeks of fog. But Whitehead Light gets 1,920 hours of fog a year, which translates into eighty days, or more than eleven weeks of fog per year. In comparison, Portland averages forty-two foggy days a year, and Boston just eleven days. But the curse is also a blessing of sorts. Because it is foremost for fog, Whitehead has been in the forefront of experiments with fog signals.

Perhaps because West Quoddy Head is the easternmost light in the United States, it got the first fog bell in 1820. The keeper who had to ring it complained about the extra work it took to ring the bell. So in 1827, a special act of Congress provided that "the keeper of the Quoddy Head Lighthouse, in the state of Maine, shall be allowed, in addition to his present salary, the sum of sixty dollars a year, for ringing the bell connected with said lighthouse."

At Whitehead, the records show that Luther Whitman put up a fog bell in 1830. But the bell apparently was not much help to mariners. There is a laconic record that the bell "from some cause ... had ceased to sound its warning note to mariners."

There were so many complaints that in 1837, Congress acted on the urgings of Army engineer Colonel Loammi Baldwin and appropriated money for erecting a new bell "at the entrance to Penobscot Bay on Whitehead, to be rung by the power of the tide," based on a new design by Andrew Morse, Jr.

The design sounds like a Rube Goldberg contraption, but it apparently worked well for a few years. Here is a description of it, taken from a letter signed by John Ruggles and Sullivan Dwight:

> The power which rings the bell is obtained by the rise and fall of the tide and the swells, which at that place are constant and unceasing. One end of a large stick of timber, nearly 30 feet long, projects out upon the water, the other end being confined by chains and braces to the middle of another stout timber, some 20 feet long, which lies along the shore, hinged at each end of a projecting rock, both together forming a T. From their point of junction, a small timber rises vertically to a height of 18 or 20 feet, being well braced to its position; to the upper part of this mast is attached a chain, which with a continuous rod of iron, extends up to the bellhouse, a distance of about 140 feet. The chain receives the vibrations from the outer end of the long timber, and a "take-up weight" in the bellhouse gets a constant reciprocating motion, which, acting upon the

machinery in the bellhouse, winds up the heavy weight of about 2,000 pounds, that drives both the regulating and the striking part of the apparatus ... Bell is struck four times a minute by 15-pound hammers. Object sought has been fully and successfully accomplished by it, and that for such a purpose is a valuable invention.

That is an engineer's cumbersome description of a cumbersome way to ring a fog bell. But mariners praised it and wrote enthusiastic letters to the inventor, Andrew Morse, Jr. Thomas Howes, commander of the steamer *North America*, wrote:

Sir: Having been repeatedly guided in my course by the sound of your "Perpetual Fog-Bell" now in successful operation at Whitehead on the coast of Maine, and being fully satisfied that your invention is invaluable to the commercial interest generally, I can cheerfully give my testimony in favor of it ...

That letter was dated December 3, 1840. The next day another letter, from another Captain S.H. Howes, commander of the famous steamer the *Bangor*, wrote:

Sir: I consider this bell as the only completely successful attempt which has ever been made to navigate our waters in dense fogs. I am master of the steamboat Bangor which plies between Boston and Bangor, by way of Portland. For the last two seasons I have been able to run my boat into and out of Penobscot Bay in the thick fogs which frequently occur, by the aid of one of Mr. Morse's fog-bells, situated on Whitehead ... Without the assistance of this bell I should have been compelled very frequently to have stopped my passage ... I sincerely hope these bells will be placed all along this dangerous coast.

These may have been sincere, unsolicited letters from different ship captains with the same last name, who wrote them within twenty-four hours of each other. Yet reading them today, I sniff a scent of collusion, a slight aroma that inventor Andrew Morse may have been out soliciting testimonials and endorsements of his product in hopes of getting a big order for more bells.

The bell and the keeper at Whitehead both got black marks from an inspector of lighthouses, the dour Mr. I.W.P. Lewis in 1842, two years after the glowing testimonials from the two captains. Inspector Lewis reported that the tide-bell had failed entirely, being several times damaged by the surf. Lewis gave demerits to the keeper, reporting that "the keeper of this place adopted the novel experiment of attaching a line to the clapper of the bell, the other end of which leads through a hole in the window of his bell chamber, and amuses himself after retiring for the night with tolling an hour or two."

Most keepers get sick and tired of the sound of a fog signal ringing through their lives. But this one, according to Lewis, would lie in bed and toll the fog bell for his own amusement, hours on end.

Fog bells were still rare. By 1843, there were only four on the Maine coast.

Thomas Jefferson, third president of the United States, ordered the light at Whitehead built in 1803. Millard Fillmore, thirteenth president, ordered it rebuilt and modernized in 1852.

For most of the next three-quarters of a century, Whitehead operated from those buildings and with aging equipment. It served well in the busiest days of local shipping, when hundreds of heavily laden vessels carried cargoes of cut granite from the islands along the Muscle Ridge Channel and from Penobscot Bay. There were big and boisterous cargoes of men over the weekends, when granite workers by the thousand shipped into the waterfront taverns and sporting houses of Rockland, with money burning holes in their pockets and thirst gripping their throats, and the need for a woman's company pumping in their loins.

Then in the Depression of 1933, under the 32nd president, Franklin D. Roosevelt, Whitehead was at last modernized to twentieth-century standards. New diesel engines, new compressors, new generators, new lenses, and new foghorns were put into service. One large diaphone horn pointed south, out to sea, and another pointed northeast for vessels coming along the Muscle Ridge Channel.

When the old steam whistles were taken from Whitehead, there was only one steam fog whistle left along the coast—at West Quoddy—and that was converted the next year.

Two never-to-be-known men have been silent witnesses to every change at Whitehead. Two unknown sailors from long ago are buried at the light. Some time before 1805, two shipwrecked seamen froze to death on the shores of Whitehead. Their bodies are buried together there in a common grave.

Whitehead Light, first built in 1804, was automated and unmanned in 1982. But the lens used on this light and the one-room schoolhouse that was once part of the cluster of buildings near the light are preserved and can be seen at the Shore Village Museum in Rockland. This lens was made by the famous French glass-making firm of L. Sauter in Paris, and was installed at Whitehead in 1857. It is so big that a person can stand inside of it—and today, children often do. Ken Black, the curator of the Shore Village Museum and former warrant officer in the Coast Guard, obtained the beautiful old lens, reassembled its parts, and today encourages visitors to the museum to walk inside of this remarkable, huge lens. The modern replacement for it is a small, mundane acrylic cover for a 250-watt bulb, which burns continuously.

In December 1997, the Maine Lighthouse Selection Committee tranferred ownership of Whitehead Light from the Coast Guard to Pine Island Camp, a historic boys' camp situated on Pine Island in Great Pond of the Belgrade Lakes. In 1956, the owners of Pine Island Camp, the Swan family, had bought 70 acres of Whitehead Island, and campers have been visiting the island ever since. Under a new work program, campers at Pine Island will help restore the lighthouse and keeper's dwelling.

Owls Head Light

"Which is your favorite lighthouse on the Maine coast?" I don't know. It is as hard to answer that question as it is to name a favorite book, a favorite dog, or a favorite piece of music. Humans are fickle; our favorites change as we change, and our memories and encounters enlarge.

But Owls Head is always close to first on my list, partly because it is so handsome and beautifully situated, and partly because I am always so happy to see it. The light stands on a tree-studded cliff a hundred feet above the sea, commanding West Penobscot Bay, Muscle Ridge Channel, and scores of lovely islands.

If I am headed down east on a fine day, passing Owls Head means I have a lovely trip coming up across West Penobscot Bay, heading for Browns Light on the Fox Islands Thorofare or maybe putting into Camden.

Coming from the west, I look forward to running past Owls Head to the Ash Island can, then along the Muscle Ridge Channel, past my small beloved islands—Dix, High, Beech, and a score more where I like to anchor, swim, picnic, or spend a night.

If the weather is foul or thick, I am even more glad to see Owls Head Light. Memories are all too vivid of tense trips in thick fog, poking across the bay from Vinalhaven, yearning to hear the horn from Owls Head. The distance is short, no more than six miles or so, but too often this has been a draining journey for me in *Steer Clear*.

Then, suddenly, there is Owls Head Light, towering above us, dead ahead.

Lord, how beautiful Owls Head Light looks! Yes, Owls Head is one of my favorite lights on the Maine coast.

Why is it called Owls Head? (Nautical charts use no apostrophes.) Some say it is the English translation of the old Indian name *Medadacut*—and that the promontory looks like an owl. A simple, good reason, but I have not yet been able to decipher an owl. True believers say they can see the owl's head depicted by the cavelike hollows, which make the eyes, and a ridge, which makes the nose, and that the rocks on either side form two owl's ears. Maybe.

But there is no doubt that the high flat plateau behind the light was the scene of bitter fighting between Indians and whites. The worst battle was fought on June 7, 1757, when American forces under Captain Joseph Cox reversed tradition: They scalped two Indians.

It was the busy trade in lime, quarried at Thomaston soon after the Revolution, that led to the building of a light at Owls Head. In 1822, the price of Maine lime was from eighty-four cents to a dollar a barrel. Because building was booming in the fast-growing cities of Boston, New York, and Philadelphia, there was a huge demand for Rockland and Thomaston lime. A little armada of tramp ships laden with lime was constantly departing Rockland harbor, bound for these cities and for Europe.

Too many were getting wrecked in Penobscot Bay fog, and demand grew for a lighthouse and fog signal. The high ground at Owls Head was chosen for the site, because it towered eighty-two feet above the sea near the entrance to Rockland. Construction began under President John Quincy Adams. The light has never been rebuilt. By 1825, the light was ready, needing only a keeper, and there was political competition for the post. Stephen Pleasonton, fifth auditor of the Treasury and the bureaucrat in charge of lighthouses, wrote urging the appointment of Captain Joseph P. Chandler to the job, which paid $350 a year. But within three weeks, Pleasonton received word from higher up the political ladder that the president had instead chosen Isaac Stearns for the post. (Three months later, canny bureaucrat Pleasonton finagled his man Chandler the job of keeper of the light at Plum Island, Massachusetts.)

Stearns worked as keeper of Owls Head for the next thirteen years, retiring in 1838. He was followed by William Masters for three years. Masters was removed in 1844, replaced by Perley Haines, who was reappointed in 1845. Haines, looking to sea from his lighthouse tower, may have been the last local man to see the brig *Maine* as she sailed out of Rockland on November 9, 1844, on her maiden voyage, bound for New Orleans with a cargo of lime and nine men aboard.

That was the last that was seen or heard of the *Maine* for three long years. Then a ship's atlas, a mahogany chest, and a navigation book belonging to the *Maine* showed up on a vessel that put into Rockland. The articles had been left behind by a trio of Portuguese sailors who had jumped ship at Vera Cruz. The gear was recognized as belonging to Captain Thorndike of the *Maine*, and his mates Abenezer Coombs and George Cooper. No other trace was ever found of the *Maine* or her crew.

A close-up of the light deck and lens at Owls Head Light. Gannett file photo.

Six years later, in the terrible gale of December 22, 1850, when Henry Achorn was keeper, Owls Head was the scene of one of the eeriest wrecks and rescues ever to happen along the coast of Maine.

That night was a killer, with waves so high and winds so violent that five ships were driven ashore in the eight-mile stretch between Owls Head and Spruce Head. So bitter was the cold on that third night before Christmas, that the gale-driven spray turned to ice as it blew over the wrecked ships, quickly encrusting them in shrouds of ice inches thick.

A small coasting schooner was riding out the storm on anchor off Jameson's Point in Rockland harbor. The mate, his bride-to-be, and a deckhand were aboard, asleep below decks; the captain had gone ashore. Near midnight, the raging gale snapped the anchor lines and the schooner blew like an exploding cork out of Rockland harbor. The gales blew her fast past Owls Head and smashed her hard aground between two ledges. There she stuck, jammed hard, while water poured in below the water line.

The mate, his bride-to-be, and the deckhand sought safety up on deck. They dragged up blankets and wrapped themselves inside them. But coats of ice built up as each wave-spray swept across them. Soon all three were wrapped in ice like mummies. The deckhand used his knife and fists to punch a breathing hole through the ice shroud. By the first light of dawn he saw the mate and his girl encased in ice, motionless and seemingly frozen dead inside the ice.

The deckhand, using his sheath knife like an auger and his fists as battering rams, broke out of the thick ice that imprisoned him. He determined to get help somehow. He struggled across the wave-lashed, ice-coated decks, jumped to the ice-covered ledges that gripped the boat, and set out through the storm toward the lights shining from the keeper's house at Owls Head. Halfway along the dirt road, he collapsed.

Peering through the storm, the keeper saw the body and went to his rescue. When the deckhand was revived in the warmth of the kitchen, he told of the mate and girl still frozen in ice aboard the schooner. A rescue party was organized, reached the schooner, and cut the bodies out of the ice, even though all agreed the pair must already have frozen to death. They manhandled the stiff bodies ashore to the warmth of the keeper's house and poured cold water over the ice sheath. Gradually they increased the water temperature to fifty-five degrees, and the two bodies were freed of all ice, stripped naked, and wrapped in fresh blankets. Inch by inch, the rescuers began to manipulate the hands and feet of the unconscious couple, and then to rub and massage their bodies. Although there seemed to be no hope, the rescuers kept at their task. After two hours, the unconscious girl stirred; an hour later, the mate showed signs of life and opened his eyes. Weeks later they were able to walk. Six months later, in June 1851, they were married. But the man never fully recovered.

A dog who loved ships is buried close to the fog signal at Owls Head. The dog, a springer spaniel named Spot, belonged to the last keeper in the old Lighthouse Service who kept the Owls Head Light, veteran Augustus R. Hamor, who kept the light from 1930 until World War II.

Spot's life centered around the fog bell and the ships passing below. From watching his master, Spot learned how to pull the rope that rang the old fog bell. When he saw a ship getting near, Spot would run over to the rope on the fog bell, grab it in his teeth, and pull until the bell was pealing out to the ship below. When the captain aboard had had enough, he would blow his fog horn in a return signal to Spot. Then Spot would rush down to the water and bark joyously until the boat was out of earshot.

Life was neighborly in those days. Mrs. Stuart Ames, wife of the skipper on the mailboat running from Rockland to Matinicus, would sometimes telephone the light station to ask whether they had seen her husband going by, so she'd know whether to start his dinner. One stormy night, Mrs. Ames phoned to say her husband was several hours overdue and to ask if he had been seen coming by Owls Head. The keeper said that there had been no sight nor sound from the Matinicus boat, but that it was snowing heavily and blowing hard and he might have missed it.

The frantic Mrs. Ames told the keeper that her husband had often told her about the dog Spot, who never missed welcoming the mailboat as it passed. She asked the keeper if he would let Spot outside to listen. The keeper agreed and Spot went out into the storm, but came back wet and dejected in a half hour, and curled up beside the fire to dry and sleep. Suddenly the dog woke, and went to the door and scratched to get out. He had heard the whistle from the mailboat. The keeper let out the dog, who went plunging through the snow to find the rope on the fog bell to pull it. Because of the deep snow, the dog never found the rope, but went shouldering his way through snowdrifts to the water's edge, and stood there barking at the mailboat he knew was somewhere close by in the storm. Then came the sound of the mailboat whistle, which Keeper Hamor could now hear. Spot's frantic barking got louder, more persistent. Then came three blasts on the mailboat whistle, a signal that Captain Ames had heard the barking dog and was holding a safe course now for Rockland. Two hours later, a grateful Mrs. Ames called to say that her husband had made it home, thanks to help from Spot.

The dog was buried near the fog bell he loved.

Matinicus Rock Light

If you want to see puffins, this is the place. These parrot-like, colorful clowns love Matinicus Rock and for many years have made this thirty-nine-acre island of volcanic rock a favorite breeding and nesting place. Here, too, are huge colonies of Arctic terns, guillemots, Leach's petrels, and gulls of every kind.

Carl W. Buchheister, a longtime president of the National Audubon Society, and his wife, Harriet, were the world's most loving experts on this strange and wondrous island, and the birds that populate it. The Buchheisters served as volunteer Audubon Wardens on the Rock from 1936 to 1981. They hunkered down on wooden floors, huddled against stormy, cold weather in sleeping bags. They knew generations of Coast Guardsmen who manned the light. They were experts on the Rock's history as well as its birdlife. Consequently, they were protective about it.

Access to the island is very limited today. The island is owned by the U.S. Fish and Wildlife Service and managed by the Audubon Society, which conducts research there. The Society uses the historic lighthouse and its associated buildings as its research center. The light and fog warning still serve as active aids to navigation; the power for the light station and the research center is provided by solar panels. The only way to see puffins today—other than by volunteering at the island—is to take a boat cruise and enjoy them from the water.

Matinicus Rock is twenty-five miles into the Atlantic from Rockland harbor and is part of a chain of eight small islands: Matinicus, Tenpound Island, Ragged Island (also known as Criehaven), No Man's Land, Two Bush Island, Wooden Ball, and Seal Island. It has been marked on marine charts since men first sailed into the Gulf of Maine. Captain John Smith, reputed lover of the Indian princess Pocahontas, wrote in his ship's log in 1614 about "three isles and the rock of Mattinack."

Jutting high out of the ocean, Matinicus Rock has for centuries been a landmark for sailors headed into Penobscot Bay or along the coast of Maine. It stands out halfway between Monhegan Island and Mount Desert Island Rock. The lighthouses on these three islands are a vital series of marks to all sea traffic.

So Matinicus Rock is where the federal government decided to put a lighthouse in 1827, when John Quincy Adams was president. Surprisingly, President Adams had to choose between half a dozen eager competitors for the job of first keeper of remote Matinicus Rock Light. On June 8, 1827, President Adams got the following letter from Stephen Pleasonton, his man in charge of federal lighthouses:

> Sir, I have the honor to enclose the recommendations of the following persons to be Keeper of the Light on Matinicus Rock in the State of Maine, viz: John A. Shaw, Isaac Tolman, Samuel Holmes, John Wales, William Dyer, William Young, and Esias Preble.
> The appointment of John A. Shaw is respectfully submitted, and that his salary be fixed at four hundred and fifty dollars per annum.

Shaw got the job on June 26, 1827. I was amazed to find he was sixty-five years old when he became keeper. Sixty-five is a common retirement age today; back in 1827, when life expectancy was far shorter, it was a very ripe age for John A. Shaw and his wife to begin keeping the light at a new station twenty-five miles offshore.

Shaw and his wife may have had a hard first day, even getting ashore, because landing is hard except in flat calm. Waiting for them was a stone building with a wooden tower at either end, in which the lanterns were hung. Two fixed white lights were forty feet apart, each illuminated by fourteen lamps with 21-inch reflectors. Shaw took one look at the wooden towers and wondered how long they would last.

They didn't last long. No sooner were Shaw and his wife half settled in when the gales of September began to blow hard. He and his wife kept a logbook, in which these laconic entries were written:

> 3 Sept. 1829—heavy gail of wind to NW.
> 31 Oct.—a saver (severe) gail Broak over rock.
> 9 Nov.—a bad storm
> 25 Jan. 1830—a vilent Snow Storm
> 30 Jan.—A Sataday night Very cold
> 9 Feb.—trim wicks. Set up All night
> 21 Feb.—1 schooner passed near today
> 23 May—The keeper very sick
> June—The keeper is Beter and he aught to be.

The entries stop on Sunday, March 20, 1831, the day Shaw was taken off the island to the mainland because he was too sick to endure any longer on the Rock. He died in a Portland hospital a month later, at the age of 69. His years on the Rock, hit by storms, with flimsy wooden towers to house his lights, must have been dangerous and busy for Shaw and his wife.

Twenty-five miles out to sea from Rockland, Matinicus Rock Light was first built in 1827. Automated in 1983, it is now an Audubon Society research center for studying puffins and other seabirds. Gannett file photo.

Their log makes no mention of birds, puffins, or visitors.

Abner Knowles came out as keeper in May 1831 and reported "all in good order." But he soon left, and was succeeded by Phineas Spear, who was also taken sick and carried back to the mainland, where he died in April 1834. There were four more keepers, each of whom lasted only a year or two. None of the six men who had sought the job along with Shaw was ever named to succeed him.

The light itself was not performing well, and the buildings were not standing up to the weather. Inspector I.W.P. Lewis reported in 1833 that the lights could not be seen anywhere near the fourteen-mile visibility they were supposed to have. He urged more powerful lights be installed and that stronger towers be built for them. By 1846, nineteen years after Shaw first lit the light, a bigger, stronger granite house with towers at either end was built, and stronger lights installed.

But poor Matinicus could not seem to get its twin lights, its light-keeper, or its foghorn in very good shape. One major problem was that the twin lights seemed to blend into a single light from a short distance away, causing severe problems for mariners looking for twin lights.

Furthermore, Matinicus was shrouded in fog 1,718 hours a year, but had no fog signal worth its name. In 1855, the Lighthouse Board installed a fog bell, which proved useless. The next year a steam fog signal was installed and the bell relegated as a standby for emergency use.

Matinicus was a constant worry to the Lighthouse Board, which requested $35,000 for building a new single tower and a new keeper's house. The plan was to change from twin towers and twin lights to a single tower with a single light.

But the bureaucracy had second thoughts about this plan. In 1857, the two granite towers, which were only eleven years old—practically brand new by lighthouse standards—were cut down to the height of the keeper's house, and two completely new towers of cut granite were built. They were some distance from his house and far apart from each other. The keeper had to walk the 180 feet that separated the towers—no pleasure in gales, subzero weather, or heavy snowstorms. For some reason, one tower was five feet shorter than its twin.

Fresnel lenses (third order) were installed to improve the power of the beams. In 1867, the fog signal got some improvements: a new actuating machine and a new bell tower.

But Matinicus Rock Light was still not satisfactory in fog, and the fog was thick 20 percent of the time. A second fog signal was installed, and a brick engine house was built to house it. There was also urgent need for a reliable water supply, so the old keeper's house was torn down and a large brick cistern to catch rainwater was built in the cellar hole of the old stone house. Meanwhile the parapets on the towers had sprung leaks and cracked, so these had to be replaced with cast iron.

If all this sounds like a lot of costly repair, the destructive forces of pounding seas and strong gales had caused most of the damage. Matinicus catches severe weather. An idea of how much the station must have endured can be read from this fact from the lighthouse record: the brick fog-signal house, fourteen feet wide and thirty-two feet long, was entirely swept away during one storm in November of 1888.

Debate continued over the lights. Change to a single light? Stay with two white lights? This time around, the one-light contingent won the battle; on July 1, 1883, the light in the north tower was extinguished and the light in the south tower was changed from a fixed white light to a fixed red light.

It was a bad decision. The changeover to red hugely reduced the light's power. No other primary seacoast light on the Atlantic coast uses a fixed red light. Some use red flashes in combination with a white light, but only Matinicus tried using a fixed red light. It took five years for the authorities to admit their mistake and change back, on July 1, 1888, to two towers, each showing a fixed white light as before.

This lasted until the 1920s, when the ancient twin light versus single light controversy flared anew. Once again the light in the north tower was extinguished and the characteristic of the light in the south tower was changed to alternate single and double white flashes every fifteen seconds.

What was it like on Matinicus Rock over a hundred years ago? The annual report of the Lighthouse Board, usually a dry bit of literature, gave a fair description in 1891:

> There is neither tree nor shrub, and hardly a blade of grass on the rock. The surface is rough and irregular and resembles a confused pile of loose stone. Portions of the rock are frequently swept over by waves which move the huge boulders into new positions ... The lightkeeper effects a landing by steering his boat through the breakers on top of a wave so that it will land on the boat ways, where his assistants stand ready to receive him, and draw his boat up so far on the ways that a receding wave cannot carry it back to the sea ... The rock is half a mile long and of irregular width, nowhere exceeding one-eighth of a mile, and the highest part is not over fifty feet above the sea on a calm day.

More than two dozen men and women have kept the light. Harriet Buchheister's research records show the following names and dates:

John Shaw 1827–31
Abner Knowles 1831–32
Phineas Spear 1832–34
Unknown keeper 1834–37
Thomas McKellar 1837
Samuel Abbott 1840 to unknown date
William Young from unknown date to 1853
Samuel Burgess 1853–61
Captain John F. Grant 1861–90, assisted by sons, wives, children
William G. Grant 1890–1900
James E. Hall 1900–04
James E. Hall 1904–08
(whether the son or a reappointment of the same keeper is not clear)
Merton Tolman 1908–11
Charles G. Dyer 1911–16
Arthur B. Mitchell 1916–19
Frank O. Hilt 1919–34
Alvah Robinson 1934–36
Roscoe Fletcher 1936–42

When World War II started, the Navy took charge of all lighthouses.

Many keepers were local men with long family ties to the Maine islands. For example, James E. Hall, assistant keeper under William Grant and then head keeper, was a descendant of Ebenezer Hall, who was killed by the Indians on Matinicus in 1757. Keeper Hall died a violent death, too. In 1916, he was killed in an explosion while blasting rock at Grindel Point Light on Isleboro.

The man who followed Hall was Merton E. Tolman, part of the

Tolman family from Matinicus Island. In 1913, Frank O. Hilt, a giant from St. George on the Cushing peninsula, was assistant keeper to Charles G. Dyer. In 1919, Hilt was named head keeper, and stayed on the Rock until he was transferred to Portland Head Light.

All keepers kept logbooks, but they were men of very few words. For example, the Rock suffered a terrible storm on January 27, 1839. The entry in Thomas McKellar's log is "Lighthouse tore down by sea." No light shone for two days thereafter. But by January 29, the keeper had rigged a makeshift light to warn ships from the killer ledges.

A young girl, Abbie Burgess, left the most vivid description of a bad storm on the Rock. Abbie Burgess will live forever as one of the great heroines of seafaring Maine. She came to the Rock as a girl of fourteen when her father was named keeper in the spring of 1853. She was to act as keeper in emergencies as a child, to marry on the Rock, bear children on the Rock, and bury one infant there. In all, she spent forty years of her life in lighthouses.

Keeper Samuel Burgess sailed to his job with his invalid wife, four daughters, and a son. The boy soon left to become a fisherman in New Brunswick, leaving Abbie as the only child old enough to help her father with the light, and help her invalid mother with the chores of managing the family. Before long, her mother became bedridden, leaving Abbie to take care of her, her father, and the younger sisters. After she had put her young sisters to bed, Abbie would help her father with his evening duties at the twin light towers, trimming and tending the twenty-eight lamps with such efficiency that her father soon called Abbie his assistant keeper. To supplement his salary of $50 a year, Samuel Burgess would catch lobsters and sail to the mainland twenty-five miles away to sell them, and buy medicine for his sick wife, along with replenishing food supplies.

In these times, Abbie would keep the lights as well as manage the household. On the rough and barren Rock, Abbie kept five hens, who became her friends and pets, as well as an egg supply for the family.

On cold winter nights, Abbie and her father would often take turns sitting up in the towers, nursing along the feeble wicks fed by thin summer oil, which burnt poorly. On long nights like these, Abbie would take down and read the old logbooks, wherein former keepers gave brief accounts of their troubles and the storms they lived through. She read how waves thirty and forty feet high had swept across the Rock seven times in the past ten years, invading the keeper's house and the light towers. She read about the great storm of January 27, 1839, when huge waves demolished the keeper's house and forced his family to flee for their lives.

If a bad storm hit, Abbie knew she could not move her invalid mother to safety, take care of the younger children, the hens, the house, and help her father with the lights—all at the same time. So in that November of 1855, Abbie moved her mother out of the old, weak building into a stronger, safer room behind the lighthouse towers.

The next month a great storm swept the Rock and seas poured into the old building where her mother had been. Only spray drenched the windows of her mother's new bedroom. A month later, in January 1856, food and medicine supplies were practically exhausted. The supply ship had failed to make its scheduled stop in September. Burgess dared not risk winter on the Rock without a store of provisions. He had to make an emergency trip to Rockland.

That night a northeast storm trapped Burgess ashore. For three days and nights the storm blew. In the wee hours of January 19, 1856, on the fourth day, the dreaded waves swept across the Rock. The dwelling where her mother had been living was destroyed and swept away.

Abbie, seventeen, kept her family safe and the lights burning for a week. The next year another storm stranded her father ashore again. This time, however, Abbie's brother was on the Rock to help. During a respite from the gale, her brother rowed six miles to Matinicus Island to get food. For the next twenty-one days, neither father nor brother could get back. The storm raged every day and night for four weeks. Abbie thought they had both drowned. Food on the Rock was almost gone. Abbie put the family on a tight ration of one cup of corn meal mush and one egg a day. And she kept the lights burning.

In a letter to a friend, Abbie Burgess gives her own account of those scary times:

> Early in the day, as the tide rose, the sea made a complete breach over the Rock, washing every movable thing away, and of the old dwelling not one stone was left. The new dwelling was flooded, and the windows had to be secured to prevent the violence of the spray from breaking them in. As the tide came, the sea rose higher and higher, till the only endurable places were the light towers. If they stood, we were saved, otherwise our fate was only too certain. But for some reason, I know not why, I had no misgivings and went on with my work as usual.
>
> For four weeks, owing to rough weather, no landing could be effected on the Rock. During this time we were without the assistance of any male member of our family. Though at times greatly exhausted with my labors, not once did the lights fail. Under God, I was able to perform all my accustomed duties as well as my father's.
>
> You know the hens are our only companions. Becoming convinced, as the gale increased, that unless they were brought into the house they would be lost, I said to Mother: "I must try to save them." She advised me

not to attempt it. The thought, however, of parting with them without an effort was not to be endured, so seizing a basket, I ran out a few yards after the rollers had passed and the sea fell off a little, with the water knee deep, to the coop and rescued all but one.

It was the work of a moment, and I was back at the house, with the door fastened, but I was none too quick, for at that instant, my little sister, standing at the window, exclaimed: "Oh look! Look there! The worst sea is coming!" That wave destroyed the old dwelling and swept the Rock.

Keeping a light, even a light as tough, lonely, and dangerous as Matinicus Rock, was considered a political plum, a patronage post. So because of a change in Washington politics, Samuel Burgess lost his job.

In 1861, President Abraham Lincoln fired Burgess. One might think that Burgess and his family—especially daughter Abbie—would be glad to get off the Rock. Not so. After Lincoln named John Grant to replace Burgess, Burgess stayed on to show the ropes to the new keeper and his family. Abbie stayed, too. And before the year was out, Abbie had fallen in love with Isaac Grant, strapping son of the new keeper. The couple was married and Isaac Grant was named assistant keeper to his father. This meant Abbie stayed on the Rock with him. Over the next years, four children were born to them, all born on the Rock.

After fourteen years on the Rock as a wife, plus the eight years as a daughter, Abbie Burgess Grant and her husband finally left. But they did not leave the Lighthouse Service. Isaac was named keeper of Whitehead Light on Muscle Ridge Channel, virtually a shore-based station. His father, old John Grant, kept the Matinicus Rock Light burning for thirty years in all. In 1890, he was succeeded as keeper by his grandson, William G. Grant, the boy who had been born on the Rock.

This Grant kept a cow called Daisy. The animal had been ferried over in a small boat from Matinicus Island, six miles away. A journalist named Gustav Kebbe, writing in *The Century Magazine* in 1897, recounted:

[He] had often seen Daisy standing on that mass of barren rock, the only living thing in view, the wind furrowing up her hide. She would gaze out at the waste of wild waters with a driven, lonely look, the pathos of which was almost human ... Often the cow looks over in the direction of Matinicus Island and moos pathetically ... She formerly found some companionship in a rabbit, with which she was accustomed to play at dusk; but the rabbit died.

Just before Christmas 1983, the Coast Guard unmanned Matinicus Rock Light. The light, which keepers and their families had manned for more than 156 years, was automated.

The last two men to man the Rock, twenty-five miles to sea, were First Class Bo'sun's Mate Joseph Michaels, a career petty officer with twelve years' service, and Fireman Donald LeCours, from Eustis, Maine, who had been assigned to the Rock right out of Coast Guard school. Their duty tours were four weeks on the Rock, one week ashore, and the tour lasted one year. They were taken off by helicopter—a far cry from the sailboat on which the first keeper arrived.

The new automated light was a far cry, too, from the first oil-fed lanterns. The new light was small compared to the beautiful twelve-foot lens that had worked so long on the Rock, and that would cost more than $6 million to duplicate today. The new automated light was nothing but a pair of 24-inch airway beacons, similar to those in use at most airports. These new beacons consisted of 1,000-watt bulbs powered by regular 110-volt AC household current. The new light is visible twenty-four miles away, a one-mile improvement over the old lens. The flash signal, however, was different: a flashing white light every ten seconds. The old light had a finer rhythm: a 5.8-second flash, followed by darkness; then a 2.8-second flash, followed by darkness; and then a 5.8-second flash again.

But the old light from Matinicus Rock is still in Maine, thanks to the devoted efforts of retired Coast Guardsman Warrant Officer Kenneth Black. Black has the light lens on show at his Shore Village Museum in Rockland.

But there is still a touch of loving, human sentiment on the Rock. A gravestone now marks the resting place of two-year-old Bessie Grant, who died there in 1881—the only person buried on Matinicus Rock. At the time of her death, the best that could be done for her burial was for the Grants to scrape together a few handfuls of soil, make a wooden cross, and bury the child between rock ledges. Almost a hundred years later, Harriet and Carl Buchheister hired marble mason George R. Perry of Rockland to carve a headstone. The Coast Guard helped to erect it over Bessie's grave. Long believed to be the daughter of Abbie and Isaac, Bessie was actually the daughter of Isaac's brother, John Francis Grant, and his wife Samantha.

Even with the loss of her niece, Bessie, Abbie Burgess Grant was not embittered toward the Rock. A letter she wrote in 1891, when her husband was keeper of the Whitehead Light, and sixteen years after they had left the Rock, reveals her love for lighthouses:

> Sometimes I think the time is not far distant when I shall climb these lighthouse stairs no more. It has almost seemed to me that the light was part of myself. When we had care of the old lard-oil lamps on Matinicus

Rock, they were more difficult to tend than these at Whitehead.

Many nights I have watched the lights my part of the night, and then could not sleep the rest of the night, thinking nervously what might happen should the lights fail.

In all these years I always put the lamps in order in the morning and I lit them at sunset. These old lamps ... on Matinicus Rock ... I often dream of them. When I dream of them it always seems to me that I have been away a long while, and I am hurrying toward the Rock to light the lamps there before sunset ... I feel a great deal more worried in my dreams than when I am awake.

I wonder if the care of the lighthouse will follow my soul after it has left this worn-out body! If ever I have a gravestone, I would like it in the form of a lighthouse or beacon.

Many years after Abbie Burgess Grant was dead and buried, her hope came true. A replica of a lighthouse beacon was placed over her grave in St. George by Edward Rowe Snow. The 1,800-pound fog bell from Matinicus Rock and a ten-foot-long trumpet from the old diaphone fog signal and one of the old red lamp chimneys are on display today at the Shore Village Museum in Rockland.

Smaller Lights of the Mid-Coast

When you need it, every light is important, no matter its size or history. Along the Maine coast are many lesser light—lesser only because some mark the entrance to a comparatively small harbor and as a result are small in size. Others are small in history, largely because they are relatively new. They may be small in adventure or shipwreck stories, though local residents may have many an enthralling tale to tell about them.

Lowell Rock Light, Rockport

Coming into Rockport Harbor, the best and most visible daytime mark is the old lighthouse structure on Indian Island. This light has been abandoned by the Coast Guard and is now privately owned, so it shows no flash after dark.

It has been replaced by the automated light beacon close by on Lowell Rock. This stands twenty-five feet high and flashes red every ten seconds. The harbor at Rockport is handsome and spacious, and there is a good dock, restaurant, and art gallery in the hilly village. But if you plan to sleep aboard on a mooring or at anchor, be prepared for a lot of rolling, especially at ebb tide.

Rockland Breakwater Light

During the 19th century, Rockland Harbor served as a major port for shipping lime rock. Beginning in 1881, a mile-long granite breakwater was built to protect the wide harbor. It took eighteen years to construct, and in 1902, a lighthouse was erected at the end of the breakwater. The initial cost was $30,000. The light was automated in 1965 and today the breakwater and lighthouse are the property of the Town of Rockland, though they are maintained by the Friends of Rockland Breakwater Lighthouse. The breakwater itself is a popular tourist

The Rockland Breakwater Light was built in 1902 at the end of a mile-long granite breakwater. It was automated in 1964, but remains a popular tourist attraction.

attraction and it's a pleasant walk out to the lighthouse on a nice day. The lighthouse is being restored by the Friends in the hope of creating a living history museum.

Curtis Island Light

Curtis Island Light stands fifty-two feet above the sea at the entrance to Camden Harbor, one of the real jewels on the Maine coast. The light is an old one, first built in 1832 under President Andrew Jackson and rebuilt in 1896, in the second term of President Grover Cleveland.

Curtis is the recent name for this island. For centuries it was called Negro Island. The story goes that when an early settler sailed into Camden Harbor he had a African-American deckhand aboard. The deckhand, said the white man, could have the mainland, but he wanted that little island—and so it was called Negro Island.

The name change came about to honor Cyrus H.K. Curtis, the Maine-born boy who made millions as publisher of the *Saturday Evening Post, Ladies Home Journal,* and other magazines. Curtis had an oceanfront summer estate here, and kept his magnificent steam yacht

Lyndonia here. This luxury yacht, built in 1922, was taken over by the Navy in World War II. Her days ended far from home, in November 1945, when she went down in a typhoon in the China Seas and sank in forty fathoms of water off Okinawa.

Cyrus Curtis gave the town of Camden the waterfront land and building that is now the Camden Yacht Club, and in his honor the name Negro Island was changed to Curtis Island.

When the Coast Guard automated the light in 1972, it had no further use for the land and keeper's house, and title to both was acquired by the Town of Camden, which has made the lovely island into a public park.

Grindel Point Light

Grindel Point is one of the all-too-few decommissioned lights that have been saved by the local community they served. When the government announced Grindel Point Light was being discarded and that they had no further use for the tower, there was an outcry of fear from Islesboro natives and summer people lest the beloved light be dismantled or sold to some stranger. They banded together and petitioned the government to allow them to keep the light as a monument to the sons of Islesboro who had sailed ships. So today the light stands at the pier where the ferry from the mainland (Lincolnville Beach) docks.

The light was first built in 1850, when Franklin Pierce was president, and rebuilt and improved under President Ulysses S. Grant in 1874. It was unmanned in 1934.

It is one of the early generations of lights built with a square white tower, with the lantern room at the top of the keeper's house. The Grindel Point Light shone from a modern modular skeleton tower right next to the old light from 1934 to 1987. At the request of local citizens, the Coast Guard moved the light back into the old tower in 1987, and removed the modern tower.

Fort Point Light

Fort Point marks the entrance to the historic Penobscot River, which winds twenty-four miles up to Bangor, once the busiest lumber port in the world. More than three thousand ships sailed up to Bangor in a year to load with lumber. Since the river was frozen solid three months or more, the ship traffic was intense.

Built in 1850, Grindel Point Light stands today as a monument to the "sons of Islesboro" who went to sea. Courtesy of Philip Ziegler.

The light was built in 1836, during the presidency of Andrew Jackson. This, like the light at Grindel Point across the bay on Islesboro, was built as a square white tower, with the lantern room on top.

In the year the light was built, the great Bangor land boom was in full swing. Land speculators from Boston were crowding every boat headed to Bangor. Land auctions in Bangor began at 8 a.m., with free champagne flowing for all in attendance.

In a single day, the same parcels of forestland might be sold several times, with the price doubling and redoubling in a few hours. The short-lived bubble burst within two years, in the crash of 1837, when banks in Bangor and across the nation went broke, failed, and closed.

But if Bangor's land boom was over, the great lumber boom was just beginning, and this would last for fifty years. Population had been twelve hundred when Maine won statehood in 1820. By 1846, Thoreau reported that twelve thousand were living in Bangor, and, by 1860, the figure was almost seventeen thousand.

In a peak year for lumber, the rivermen drove 216 million board feet to the 410 sawmills around Bangor, and their output was stupendous. For example, just one mill at Orono, in one year (1854) turned out 62 million feet of lumber; 2.2 million clapboards; 2 million shingles; 500,000 pickets; 20,000 barrels; 60,000 oars; and 40,000 staves. All of this and much, much more went out by boat.

In 1860, when Ephraim Lansill was captain of Bangor port, his record showed 3,376 vessels arriving—and all of them entered the Penobscot River by the light at Fort Point.

This was key ground in early American history. In 1759, Governor Pownall of Massachusetts and five hundred Massachusetts men built the fort here, that bears his name. Traces of it can be seen near the light. Forty years later, on August 14, 1799, this river was the site of America's first day of naval infamy, equivalent to Pearl Harbor in the 20th century. This was the day when forty-three American ships were lost, and one thousand American soldiers fled from the enemy. Colonel Paul Revere, in charge of the artillery, and Commodore of the Fleet Dudley Saltonstall, were the scapegoats and cowards in 1799, when they were defeated and routed by a far smaller force of British ships and troops that scattered and sunk them all over this part of Penobscot Bay.

Fort Point Light, standing eighty-eight feet high above the sea, was manned from its first lighting in 1836 until it was automated in 1988. There were happy, long-term keepers at this handsome light, with its comfortable house and spectacular views, for more than 150 years.

Today, the lighthouse is part of Fort Point State Park. The pyramidal bell tower is one of the few left in New England and is listed on the National Register of Historic Places. The bell, replaced by a fog horn, hangs outside the tower, but the lighthouse's 1857 Fresnel lens remains in use.

Dice Head Light

A short five miles down the bay from Fort Point, handsome Dice Head Light marks the entrance to Castine Harbor. This light was built in 1829, when Andrew Jackson was president, and it was enlarged and improved in 1858 under President James Buchanan because of the ever-increasing amount of shipping.

The light was unmanned in 1935. It is only a very handsome tower and keeper's house now, long unused as a light. That job is done now by a tower below, close to the water, that stands twenty-seven feet tall and flashes a white light every six seconds.

Castine is replete with early history. The town has the finest markers in Maine that relate what happened at each historic site. French traders were the first to settle here in 1614. Then it was occupied in 1629 by fur traders from Plymouth Colony, led by Thomas Allerton. Ownership seesawed with wars. The French took over again in 1635, then the English drove them out again in 1654. In 1674, a Dutch or Flemish corsair captured the garrison. About 1676, Baron de St. Castine took possession and made the town peaceful and prosperous for a long period, thanks in part to his marriage to the daughter of the Indian chief Madocawando, who held sway over the tribes in this region.

Pumpkin Island Light

Cruise another seven lovely miles or so from Castine, past Cape Rosier, then head toward Little Deer Isle, and at the head of Eggemoggin Reach, you will see the handsome light and keeper's house on the tiny island rightly called Pumpkin.

This light was built during the Mexican War, under President Franklin Pierce in 1854. For a hundred years it flashed, first for the lumber vessels, and later the pleasure yachts heading into Eggemoggin Reach. Then in 1934, it was discontinued and sold at auction to a private buyer. The acre or so on which it stands is a private home today. A dry-ledge beacon nearby does the light duty automatically.

Heron Neck Light and Green Ledge Light

Heading east across Penobscot Bay from Two Bush Light to Vinalhaven, a distance of about ten miles, you pick up Heron Neck Light on Green Island and then make for the newer solar-powered light on Green Ledge to guide you into Carvers Harbor, the fishing port of Vinalhaven.

Heron Neck Light was built in 1854, the same year as the light at Pumpkin Island in the Eggemoggin Reach, and one year before the Portland Breakwater. It was unmanned and automated in 1982.

Down East Maine

Browns Head and Goose Rocks Lights
Saddleback Ledge and Isle au Haut Lights
Eagle Island Light
Mark Island Light, Deer Island Thorofare
Burnt Coat Harbor Light
Great Duck Island Light
Libby Island Light
Petit Manan Light
Nash Island and Moose Peak Lights
West Quoddy Head Light
Avery Rock Light
St. Croix Light
Mount Desert Rock Light
Little River Light

Lesser Lights Down East
Baker Island Light
Bear Island Light
Egg Rock Light
Winter Harbor Light
Prospect Harbor Point Light
Emms Rock Light
Dog Island Light
Lubec Channel Light
Whitlock's Mill Light

Browns Head and Goose Rocks Lights

I sailed *Steer Clear* into the Fox Islands Thorofare for more than eighteen summers. We never cruised through, direct from Browns Head Light to Goose Rock Light at the other end, then out into Penobscot Bay and across to Stonington and Deer Isle. Instead, we always stopped at J.O. Brown's dock for a talk with Jim, and to top our fuel tanks. But it wasn't the best place to fill water tanks. The water was brown. So was the ice, if it had been frozen from local water—even Jim called it "swamp ice." Then we restocked food supplies from Waterman's, the general store close to Brown's wharf. Franklin Waterman was the butcher there, and it would be hard to find better meat anywhere. Gordon Peters did the books from an upstairs office for many years. His wife, Irma, presided over the cash register on the main floor and knew everyone by name, and every bit of news.

Frequently we'd mosey across the Thorofare after these pleasant chores were done and spend the night tucked inside Perry's Creek, one of the most protected anchorages and best sleeping grounds along the island route down east.

Many a summer we spent several days and nights on anchor or a mooring there—either because it was just so beautiful and quiet, with good bird-watching, good walks along the wooded shore, and interesting rows over the mud-and-mussel bar up into the creek—or because it was thick fog outside. A cruising boat could spend a week or two simply enjoying the coves and anchorages and old quarries on North Haven and Vinalhaven.

Browns Head Light, at the west entrance to the Thorofare, was built in 1832, by order of President Andrew Jackson, and rebuilt in 1857 at the order of President James Buchanan.

It is a handsome light, joined to the keeper's house by a covered walkway that offers protection from the weather. The house, the view, and the location are so enticing that this might have been my first choice station were I a lightkeeper.

However, the fog signal seemed weak when we most needed it aboard *Steer Clear*—probably a trick of local "bounce." More than once when we were fogbound in Perry's Creek, the weather seemed to clear and we headed out. Down the Thorofare, visibility was good; but just as soon as we got near Browns Head and the Sugar Loaves, it turned to thick, impenetrable soup, and the horn on which I was depending became hard to hear, even close-to, because of some trick of bounce or breeze. This is not the best place to wait for a scale-up. The North Haven ferry to and from Rockland comes clipping through in all weather. And the big sardine carriers slow for no boat and no weather, and pay small heed to other craft as they make fast time to their cannery with their perishable cargo. At times I spotted as many as eight other cruising boats circling, waiting out here for the fog to lift a bit. They seldom saw each other in the fog, close as they were. When all eight, fearful of collision, blew their foghorns at about the same time, I made a slow run back to the peaceful safety of Perry's Creek.

Browns Head Light was automated in 1987—one of the last lighthouses in Maine to be unmanned. The Coast Guard destroyed the bell tower, but the bell is displayed by the Vinalhaven Historical Society.

Under the Maine Lights Program, the lighthouse buildings were transferred to the town of Vinalhaven in 1998, and while the Coast Guard maintains the light, it has become the office of the Vinalhaven town manager.

Goose Rocks Light, at the easterly end of the Thorofare, is the complete opposite of the comfortable station at Browns Head. Goose Rocks stands up in midstream—a caisson light, with no ground at all around it. It was a bachelor station, with no families allowed on it, except sometimes a wife would sneak in by rowboat, coming out from her home on nearby North Haven for a marital visit. But the keeper on Goose Rocks was isolated in his tower. When he arrived, his dory would be hauled up out of the water. Once inside the cylinder, the only sot for the keeper to get fresh air or exercise was the little walkway outside the lantern. He would have to walk eighty-eight times around it to get a mile of walking.

This caisson light was built in 1890 and keepers worked, lived, walked, and slept inside it for seventy-three years, until it was unmanned and automated in 1963. Yet Goose Rocks is a most handsome light and a splendid mark in the Fox Islands Thorofare.

Why is this passage called Fox Islands Thorofare? The reason dates back to 1603, years before the Pilgrims from the *Mayflower* set their feet on American soil. That year Martin Pring from Bristol, England, anchored in this passage in his 50-ton ship, the *Speedwell*, with a crew of thirty men and boys, accompanied by his smaller vessel, 26-ton

Built in 1890 at the eastern end of Fox Island Thorofare, Goose Rocks Light was automated in 1963 and remains an active aid to navigation. Courtesy of Philip Ziegler.

Discoverer, with thirteen men and boys aboard. In his log, he wrote of the catch of fine fish made here and of the fine wooded shores. Most of all he admired the pelts of the gray foxes that he saw loping in great numbers along both shores—so Pring named these islands the Fox Islands.

Today, the passage remains the Fox Islands Thorofare, although the names of the islands were changed. A Boston lobbyist by the name of John Vinal lobbied the Massachusetts Legislature in June 1789 to incorporate the two islands as townships, and in his honor, they were named Vinal Haven (now spelled as one word) and North Haven. John Vinal was also paid thirty-six pounds by the islanders for his lobbying work. The new town of Vinal Haven grew rapidly. By 1790, the population was 855; by 1880, when granite quarrying was at its peak, there were 3,380 people living on Vinalhaven. Today, population is around twelve hundred, which swells to six thousand during the summer months.

Running between Browns Head Light and Goose Rocks Light, through the Fox Islands Thorofare, big money surrounds you. Huge summer homes stand out on the shores of both islands. Here is the happy summer playground of the Cabots, Lamonts, Rhinelanders, Saltonstalls, the Watsons from IBM, and the Jennings from Standard Oil. However, here there is none of the lacquered gloss of citified society with which the summer colonies have overlaid Bar Harbor and Newport. They have not really marred nor marked these two Maine islands.

Even though the summer people now own most of the land and pay most of the taxes, they are migratory fowl who land here in July and August. Summer people own 75 percent of North Haven Island and 97 percent of its shorefront. The ferries arrive from Rockland packed with visitors. But it is the year-round natives who run the islands their way, to suit themselves, and run them well.

On Vinalhaven, Carvers Harbor is still a robust and vigorous fishing port. One of the finest medical clinics along the coast serves the people of Vinalhaven well. The great granite quarries are quiet almost all the year now. But granite from this island built scores of the greatest churches, hotels, post offices, skyscrapers, and federal buildings in the East.

——Saddleback Ledge and Isle au Haut Lights——

The good memories and the bad memories collide, but they do not intermingle.

In the margins of old charts on *Steer Clear*, staccato sentences summarize memorable legs of cruises past, and that day is raised from the dead file. On one chart, where the course is plotted from Matinicus into the Isle au Haut Thorofare, there is the notation "Gorgeous—all the way!"

On another, which summarizes the trip from Heron Neck Light (off the southern tip of Vinalhaven) to Saddleback Ledge and thence to Isle au Haut, is the note, "Tense and terrible: thick fog, bad seas all the way." The date is underneath each notation and that clues me into my log. I look up that date and read what I wrote that night, at anchor, and the details of that trip come to vivid life, raised from the dead file.

So it must be with every skipper who keeps a log not only about course and weather, but of feelings of fear and joy, too.

First the bad trip. Joy crowned even that and it came when we finally glimpsed the gleam of the Isle au Haut Light. Not even the relief that comes after an aching tooth is pulled, or after a throbbing boil is lanced, can match the glorious relief of coming safely onto your mark after tense passage. And tense passage it had been.

Almost as soon as we cleared Heron Neck, the fog came down like a blindfold. We were on compass course, and made our first mark, the N4 buoy; then altered course to sneak between Sheep Island and Sheep Island Ledge, heading for Robinson Point on Isle au Haut, about seven miles across the bay. We hoped in vain to catch sight or sound from the signal on Saddleback Ledge, off to starboard. All we heard were foghorns from other boats, but never a sight of them.

We crept across at low speed, taking almost two hours for the passage, more than twice the time of an open-weather run. When finally we reached what we hoped was Isle au Haut Light, and then saw its glimmer flashing in the opaque fog, we felt total relief. Part of the job at the helm is to pretend total confidence that you know exactly where you are, exactly where you are headed, and that the weather is not intimidating you and your seamanship. Underneath, it does. Doubt gnaws at the gut, despite the reliability of your instruments. You never realize how tense you are, until the tenseness drains out when you reach the safety zone and sense the comfort of security again.

The log for the run on a gorgeous, clear, calm day from Matinicus was a nicer story. North of Matinicus Rock, we passed barren Wooden Ball Island. The depth finder told us when we were over the ledge with that strange name of Shippershan, and we could see Saddleback Ledge directly ahead. Even Saddleback looks almost inviting on a calm and sunny day. But this was a brutal light station for the keepers who manned Saddleback Ledge Light for more than a hundred years, from 1839 to 1954.

Saddleback is little more than a small, barren ledge rising high from the sea. Just getting ashore must have been a terrible job when the seas were running, after a long, tiring row from Vinalhaven. Eventually, in 1885—after forty-five years of scrambling ashore on the right wave—a landing derrick or "boom" was installed, along with a Fresnel lens for the light. After this, a keeper on the ledge could send out the boom to pick up another keeper and haul him and his boat ashore in comparative safety. But one stormy, bitterly cold day in Jaunary 1925, when the boom was not yet working, Keeper W.W. Wells was capsized. Weighted down by hip boots, oilskins, three shirts, and a heavy sweater, Wells was drowning when a thirty-foot lobsterboat came alongside to rescue him. The rescuing lobsterman was also named Wells, George Wells.

As we cruised by Saddleback on one beautiful day, I recalled the story of a storm here, told by Keeper Wells to Robert T. Sterling, another keeper:

> The storm struck in the dead of night, the wind blew a sixty mile-an-hour gale. With it, came the seas ... One tremendous sea that boarded us shook us like a tablecloth. I thought it was going to clear away the works ... When daylight came, we ventured out to look things over. Things were certainly a mess. Over 128 feet of our boat slip was torn up and the cement breakwater built to protect the light was broken through in several places ... The storm threw a 140-gallon oil tank among the boats and jammed the winch ... Take it altogether, it was a hummer and did a lot of damage.

Keeper Wells told Sterling about his weirdest experience during his years as keeper on Saddleback Ledge—the night he was bombarded by ducks in a February storm of 1927.

> We keepers were setting in the kitchen talking about the World War when bang, bang, bang, something came against the windowpanes. We thought another war had started ... All at once I heard glass smash in the

lantern ... The bombardment started about supper time and lasted until midnight ... Crash! And a bird came sailing through a windowpane and landed at my feet. He began fluttering around on the floor, with one wing broken, and his bill telescoped almost through his head. Just when I thought the cannonading had stopped, one big sea drake struck the plate glass in the lantern tower, and came through without asking for a transfer. When he struck, he broke the works, put out the light, and broke the prisms out of the lens. The bird weighed over ten pounds ... Saddleback in darkness! What would people think on land and sea? The keepers got right to work to get the light going ... It was not long before old Saddleback was throwing her beams again as if nothing had happened ... In the morning, I picked up 124 birds around the tower, some dead, others just alive ...

The old keeper's house was blown up with explosives in a demolition exercise by the Special Forces of the U.S. Army. Its destruction was approved as the best way to reduce maintenance costs.

On that gorgeous day, we steered from Saddleback Ledge straight across to Western Ear at the southwest tip of Isle au Haut, so we could run down the island's spectacular and lovely western shore. Below the cliffs at Western Ear, seas surge mightily even on a calm day. We turned to make outside the Washers and then The Brandies rocks, and then poked briefly into a favorite haunt and anchorage at Duck Harbor.

Inside Duck Harbor there is just room enough for two, perhaps three, boats to swing on anchor. Open wide to the sea at its mouth, this harbor narrows to a bottle neck at its head, and there the land rises sharply up to the storm-beaten magnificence of Western Head. One day, on another cruise, I climbed that Head, beating my way through underbrush, because I had gotten badly off the trodden path. At the summit, I saw a lady, enjoying the splendor. She looked up as I came close and said: "This is where I go to church. This is the spot where I am awed by the majesty of Creation."

The harbor is called Duck because Indians drove sea ducks by the thousands into the funnel-shaped harbor, then snared them in nets stretched across the narrow head, smoked them on the spot that night, and took them inland to eat during the lean winter months.

We came out from Duck Harbor and cruised along to Moore Harbor, where fish weirs have been stretched to snare herring by the tens of thousands. Out again, we passed the impressive Bald Mountain and then we made the run toward Robinson Point, the Thorofare, and caught our first glimpse of Isle au Haut Light, gleaming and lovely in the sunshine.

This is one of the youngest and prettiest lights along the coast. It was not built until 1907, the only 20th-century light in Maine. A white bridge links the lighthouse to the shore and the handsome keeper's house. In 1934, to the disappointment of many who loved this station, the light was unmanned and the keeper's house offered for sale. It was lucky that an Isle au Haut man named Charles F. Robinson bought it, for it stands on Robinson Point. In summer, hundreds of cruising boats go to Isle au Haut or sail through the lovely Thorofare, with its views of the little town and churches, Kimball Island, and the Point Look-Out Club. So, if the light is not a major sea light, it is an indispensable beacon to many local fishing boats and thousands of cruising people every year.

The original fifth-order lens is on display at the Shore Village Museum in Rockland.

Isle au Haut is historic ground, where the discoverers of North America first made landfall. Giovanni da Verrazano in the 1520s first saw Isle au Haut, Mount Desert, and Monhegan. Italians have always had an eye for beauty and a tongue for the happy phrase. So Verrazano, politician as well as explorer, named these three islands "the Princesses of Navarre," after the three beautiful teenage daughters of his patron, King Henry of Navarre.

French explorer Samuel de Champlain, in 1604, mapped and named Isle au Haut. In the book about his voyages, Champlain wrote, "... nearly in the middle of the sea there is another island which is so high and striking that I named it Isle Haute."

The first white settler here was the unfortunate Seth Webb, who came in 1772. He hunted often with the Indian chief Orono. On a hunting trip in 1785, Webb was killed by his own musket, which accidentally fired when he was stepping out of his skiff.

By 1792, a man with the wondrous name of Peletiah Barter arrived from Boothbay, with his brothers William and Henry. Peletiah fathered ten children here before he died in 1832.

Isle au Haut was prospering. By 1820, Calvin Tuner had started his salt works, and his son Asa grazed four hundred sheep. Two dozen men were listed as shipmasters. Some caught the gold-rush fever of the 1840s. They built their own schooner here in the Thorofare and sailed her around the Horn to San Francisco, to take their chances among the frantic forty-niners.

More mundane enterprises flourished. A lobster cannery was started here in 1860 by a Boston firm, which shipped the cans to Crosse & Blackwell in London. Isle au Haut fishermen took freshly caught lobsters to New York City, making a round trip weekly, carrying 1,500 lobsters in their wet-smacks. By 1880, population year-round was up to 274. And then the summer folk started coming and formed the Point Look-Out Club. It was begun by Ernest Bowditch, grandson of the famous Bowditch who wrote the navigator's bible.

Miss Lizzie Rich was for years one of the great Isle au Haut fixtures, when she ruled as postmaster from the post office in the front room of her home. She was born on Isle au Haut in 1893, delivered by a midwife who charged $3. She began work in the post office in 1909, as a sixteen-year-old, and became postmaster in 1927. Miss Lizzie held the job until she was seventy, when federal government rules said she had to retire as postmaster. She did, and hired on right away as supervising clerk.

Just after dark in March of 1971, when she was seventy-eight, her hips gave way. "They just plumb cracked," Miss Lizzie told me.

> I fell to the floor. Inch by inch, I crawled and pulled myself across the room till I could reach my walkie-talkie. I called Stanley Dodge and he and some helpers came right over. They sat me up in my rocker, then lifted me in the rocker into the back of Stanley's truck and drove me to the town landing, where a boat was waiting. They carried me in the rocker onto the boat and strapped me and the rocker down tight in the cockpit. Off we went over six miles of open water to Stonington. I'd busted my hips at 5 p.m. By 8 p.m. I was all fixed up in my bed at the hospital ... Now that's some service.

Before long, Miss Lizzie was back at her post office, managing fine on walkers. Each day she made trips to her well out back, lugging in a pail of water. Each Sunday, using her walkers, she made it up the hill to the church she had been attending for more than seventy-five years.

"I take fifteen minutes now instead of two to get there. But I get there," she said.

Isle au Haut has been dwindling in year-round population, and is down to around forty or fifty today. One resident showed me a prayer tacked on her kitchen wall:

> Lord, we thank thee that thy Grace
> Has brought us to this pleasant place
> And most earnestly we pray
> That other folks will stay away.

Isle au Haut Light was built in 1907 and automated in 1934. It is still a working lightstation, but the old keeper's house has been restored as a bed-and-breakfast. Gannett file photo.

Eagle Island Light

Most summers for close to twenty years, *Steer Clear* made her passage up East Penobscot Bay. We would come from the east out of Stonington, on Deer Isle, or from the west out of North Haven and the Fox Islands Thorofare. And the light at Eagle Island was a joyous, handsome mark, standing out a bold 106 feet above the sea.

Thereabouts are favorite island beaches where we our swam and had picnics. Often our visits stretched to several days and nights of just poking around in the splendor of lovely islands and good anchorages. We have lain overnight in Lighthouse Cove on Eagle Island, more often in the sheltered coves on the eastern shore of Butter Island; and when a blow was coming, found good shelter among the little Barred Islands, between Butter and Great Spruce Head Island.

There is a lazy sailor's happy cruising ground, equal in many ways to the lovely multitude of idyllic islands between Stonington and Isle au Haut.

Butter Island, belonging to the Cabot family of Boston, is virtually uninhabited now. But it is visited by as many as a dozen boats a day in summer and sometimes it's an overnight stop for the crews of the Outward Bound boats. There was once a summer hotel, the Dirigo, a post office, and farms on Butter Island. Now there are only cellar holes and traces of old sheep pastures. There is a rough path to the highest point and, from there, 120 feet above the sea, you can get heart-pounding, magnificent views of all the islands in this part of the bay.

On the way up, in July, you can feast on hundreds of the lushest, juiciest raspberries ever to ripen anywhere in the world. One summer, while walking just inshore from a sweeping sandy beach, we came upon what seemed to be a Druid's altar: a rock with a jelly jar on it, filled with wilting wildflowers, and close by two low benches made from driftwood. It looked like someone's gentle paean of praise to this quiet and beautiful island. Later I was told that while on a school picnic, one youngster had drowned. Friends built this little altar as a memorial; probably it lasted only a brief time, but its simple eloquence was a song of love and beauty.

Some of the loveliest paintings and photographs of East Penobscot Bay were made by Eliot Porter and his brother. The Porter family lives on Great Spruce Head Island. Nearby on Bear Island lived Buckminster Fuller, the scientist-idealist who designed so many new forms of architecture and philosophy. In his last years, Bucky Fuller would sail his sailboat among these islands, with both of his hearing aids tuned to full power so he could hear the bell buoys.

There is a part of Eagle Island today on Great Spruce Head, though they are separated by a couple of islands and a couple of miles of water. It is the huge 1,200-pound brass fog bell, which stood near the light.

In 1964, when the Coast Guard was demolishing the keeper's house after the light had been automated, they made a bad mistake as they tried to dismantle the great fog bell (which was to be replaced by Eagle Gong Buoy). It got away from them and went bouncing down an eighty-foot cliff to the ocean below. That disposed of the giant bell, easily and quickly, and meant that the crew would not have to wrestle it from the top of the hill down to the wharf and then aboard the cutter.

Soon afterwards, a lobsterman named Walter Shepard, who was also caretaker at the Great Spruce Head, caught sight of the top of the giant bell as he passed close at very low tide. He told his employer, John F. Porter, about what he had seen. They decided to try to salvage the bell and erect it on Great Spruce Head.

Shepard got a chain around the bell and very slowly began towing it with his boat. It was a tricky operation, pulling a 1,200-pound bell behind a lobsterboat, but he got it to Great Spruce Head. A crew and tractor hauled it to the gallows frame he had made for it. There it is at this writing, ringing to summon Porters—out painting, photographing, sailing—home for mealtimes. Other authorities say that this bell is now in a church in St. George, Maine.

We know more detail about daily life and living on Eagle Island than almost any other light-station island along the Maine coast. This is due to the collaboration of John C. Enk and Captain Erland L. Quinn and their resultant book, *A Family Island in Penobscot Bay: The Story of Eagle Island*. The Quinn family lived on Eagle Island for generations and Enk was a historian who retired from teaching in New Jersey to live on the Maine coast, where he sailed and summered for thirty years.

Eagle Island Light was commissioned in 1839, when Martin Van Buren was president of the United States. Maine had been doing very well in the matter of getting lighthouses. In the fifteen years between 1824 and 1839, seventeen lighthouses were built in Maine—testimony not only to need but also to the political clout of Maine's delegation in

Congress, for Maine was then a very junior state, having just won statehood in 1820.

During these years, the new Maine lights were Monhegan (1824); Owls Head (1826); Pemaquid and Moose Peak (1827); Dice Head, Cape Elizabeth's Two Lights, and Hendricks Head (1829); Mount Desert Rock (1830); Browns Head, Marshall Point, and Curtis Island (1836); Nash Island (1838); and Eagle Island, Bear Island, and Saddleback Ledge (1839).

The enormous amount of shipping in and out of Bangor made a light at Eagle Island necessary. Eagle Island Light points the way from the ocean over Hardhead Shoals, on toward Dice Head Light, to Fort Point Light into the Penobscot River, and thence up to Bangor. Bangor was on its way to becoming the biggest lumber port in the world. In the span of fifty-six years, from 1832 to 1888, more than 8.7 billion feet of lumber were shipped out of Bangor. The records of the harbormaster in 1860 showed 3,376 ships arriving and 3,376 ships departing Bangor. The river was closed because of ice during several months in winter, so those arrivals and departures made for heavy, concentrated traffic that needed such aids to navigation as Eagle Light.

Originally, Eagle shone a fixed white light. Each night a lamp was carried up to the tower, while three spares were stored below in the service room. In the long nights of winter, the light was changed before bedtime, so there would be enough oil to burn through the night. The oils in the early period were fish oil, whale oil, lard, or colza, made from a mustard family plant. By 1877, all lamps were converted to kerosene, which was cheaper and gave a brighter light. After Eagle Light was automated, it used electricity provided from batteries and diesel generators.

There was a handsome four-bedroom house by the light for the keepers and families. Keepers lived in it for 120 years, until the Coast Guard demolished the house in 1963 for economic reasons.

Not until Senator Margaret Chase Smith of Maine took action was there a well for water (1947) or any toilet other than an outdoor privy (1949). During the years the light burned oil, keepers had the devil's own time lugging oil drums up the steep, rough path from the shore, especially in the snows of winter. Even after automation in 1959, Coast Guardsmen complained about the job of lugging the twenty-seven batteries needed from their cutter to the light, high on a hill.

The first keepers on Eagle Island had to supply their own boat. (Not until 1919 did the keeper get a government dory, and not until 1936 did the keeper get a fourteen-foot skiff; even then Uncle Sam did not supply the outboard to go with it.) They had to buy their own uniforms and they had to supply their own food. Making ends meet for a family man on the job was not easy, because pay began at a hundred dollars a month.

Yet some keepers stayed, father and son, for many years. Captain John Ball and then his son, Captain Howard T. Ball, kept the light between them from 1883 until 1913; and then the widow, Lucy Ball, kept the light briefly after her husband Howard died as the result of pneumonia, caught while guiding a fishing boat to safety in a sleet storm. Captain Charles W. Allen kept the light from 1919 till 1931. Another with a long span was his successor, the well-known Captain Frank E. Bracey, who was keeper from 1931 to 1945, when Coast Guardsmen replaced the civilians who had been keeping Eagle Light for more than 106 years.

In the Eagle Island Cemetery there are gravestones for twenty-two Quinns. Out of forty-five headstones, the next greatest number are marked "Unknown"—there are seven of these. Next come Howards, with five. And then there are the saddest ones of all, headstones of island babies who died in their infancy.

Erland L. Quinn lived on Eagle Island for forty years and later helped historian John Enk with much of the material for their book, *A Family Island in Penobscot Bay: The Story of Eagle Island.*

In 1844, Samuel Quinn bought all of Eagle Island, "except the Lighthouse Lot," for $1,500, including all the sheep on it, plus half of close-by Fling Island. Quinns lived on the island for more than the next hundred years. During the last of the 19th century, almost until World War II, there were two hotels and boarding houses for summer "regulars" on the island.

There are eight Eagle Islands along the Maine coast. The best known is the one in Casco Bay, home of Admiral Robert E. Peary, discoverer of the North Pole. It is now a state park, and the house is a fascinating museum.

Birds and animals crop up regularly in the names of Maine islands. There are twenty-one Ram Islands, thirteen Crow and thirteen Sheep Islands, eleven Hog Islands, eight Eagle Islands, seven Hen Islands, six Calf and six Cow Islands, four Bear and four Mouse Islands, and three Flea Islands.

Then there are the islands with wondrous strange names: The Ark, Ministerial, Grog, Burial, Pound of Tea, Smuttynose, Threads of Life, Boon, Seguin, The Cuckolds.

This Eagle Island is about $1^1/4$ miles long and half a mile wide, contains 263 acres, and the highest spot is 149 feet above the sea. There is no granite on this Eagle, but there are beautiful sandy beaches: Lighthouse Cove has a 350-foot beach, Wood Landing a 250-foot beach, and there are other large beaches at the West Cove and the old Quinn Wharf. Wild strawberries, raspberries, gooseberries, and cranberries grow profusely, but there are few wild animals. There are three freshwater springs on the island and one freshwater pond, though it's so close to the shore that salt spray blows into it during storms.

The last person to live year-round on the island was a woman named Miss Marian "Aunt Elva" Howard, relative of the Quinns. She was still living there alone when close to eighty years old. She had been born on Eagle Island, and graduated from the island school in 1912. Two years later, she was working on the nearby island of North Haven, where she was a telephone operator for fifteen years, and later went to the mainland to work in Camden as a taxi dispatcher. In 1953, Marian went back to her Eagle Island for a vacation—and never left for the next twenty or so years.

Winters were seldom as severe as the bitter "Arctic winter" of 1917–18, when the temperature dropped to 18° below. Erland Quinn, who was in his teens then, told historian John C. Enk what that winter was like: "The Bay and the Penobscot River were frozen over from Eagle Island to Bangor. Mainland traffic from Deer Isle crossed the Eggemoggin Reach by horsesled."

Similar crossings were made from Belfast to Castine and Islesboro. Deer and foxes also made the crossing. Quinn told of those winters on Eagle Island:

> Getting in and setting down the winter's food supply was serious business. Cod, haddock and hake, which had been sun-dried, were hung in a cold shed, or sometimes buried in the haymow. Tinker mackerel were put up in jars with vinegar and spices. Most families had a pig or two, as well as chickens and perhaps a cow. After cold weather set in, the men did the butchering, thus making it safer and easier to preserve the meat. Sides of beef were hung from beams in the cold wood shed. Some beef was "rolled up" and put in a pork barrel for corned beef. Pork was often put down in brine, in a stone crock or a pork barrel made of ash. Salt water and some pickle was added to the three pounds of pork in each barrel. It was salty enough when an egg would float on the brine.

The nearest doctor was a long journey away by boat. Islanders developed their own medicines and home remedies. Among them were onion and flaxseed poultices for lung congestion, niter to reduce fever, creosote or molasses and vinegar for coughs, salt-pork poultices to draw out infections, sulphur for the croup, clam boil as a laxative, and cobwebs from the barn to stop bleeding.

Islanders got little from and gave little to state and federal govern-ments. They ran their own government, not bothering with elections or taxes. Only when the nation was at war did the islanders feel the breath of the federal government. When the Civil War broke out, Maine fur-nished more soldiers and suffered more casualties than any comparable state: 73,000 Maine men went to fight in the Civil War; 9,000 never re-turned.

Two island men, subject to draft, simply left—disappeared to the "wild and wooly west." When the government sent two Army inspectors to the island to check on the draft dodgers, they were met by two island women. One, the wife of one of the missing men, had a tree limb in her arms and banged the inspectors so hard with it that they fled. Over at Loud's Island in Muscongus Bay, a major from the U.S. Army was bom-barded by hot roasted potatoes thrown by wives of the men he had come to draft into the army.

In 1972, the General Services Administration declared five of the six lighthouse acres on Eagle Island were no longer needed, after automa-tion, and would be given to a state or local government agency or put up for sale to private bidders.

Some lightkeepers' houses, such as the ones at Pumpkin Island in Eggemoggin Reach, Indian Island at the entrance of Rockport Harbor, Southern Island in Tenants Harbor (now the home of Andrew and Betsy Wyeth), had been sold privately.

Dice Head at Castine and Grindel Point Light at Islesboro had been turned into skeleton towers.

By the 1970s, Pemaquid Light, Two Bush Island Light, Saddleback Ledge Light, Rockland Breakwater Light, West Quoddy Head Light, Petit Manan Island Light, Moose Peak Light on Mistake Island (off Jones-port), and Curtis Island Light at the entrance to Camden Harbor, had all been automated. When lights are automated, the personnel are with-drawn, and the lightkeeper's home, the oil and fog signal buildings and so forth, are no longer needed. To reduce costs, the Coast Guard is com-pelled to be rid of them.

The Town of Camden took the house and land at Curtis Island and made it into a park and picnic area for local residents. Islesboro and Pe-maquid turned their lightkeepers' houses into local museums. The Samoset Hotel took the Rockland Breakwater Light from 1973 until 1989; in 1998, the City of Rockland applied for the property. The Friends of Rockland Breakwater Lighthouse are raising funds to create a living history museum for all to enjoy. Work began in 1999, when the exterior of the lighthouse was refurbished with the help of volunteers.

But the lighthouse-keeper's home and outbuildings on Eagle Island were not bought by individuals nor taken by local government. So the Coast Guard had to set them all to the torch. It broke the hearts of the islanders who saw the destruction. Coast Guardsman Ralph K. Banks, who had kept the light from 1949 till 1952—and who had also served on Seguin, Two Bush, Libby Island, and Little River Lights—wrote about how he felt:

> On Eagle Island, for the first time in my life, I found real friends and neighbors. There are no words to express how I enjoyed my relations with the people of Eagle Island.
>
> I can only express my feelings toward this island as the best place I have ever lived in my life. My wife and children agree with me on that. My wife and I went back to Eagle Island in 1971 to visit the light where we had lived and were dismayed at what we saw.
>
> The house we had loved so well had been torn down, all of the outbuildings were gone. Nothing was left but the light tower. The floor of the bell tower was rotted through. It didn't seem possible that this was the same bell tower where I had spent many a night operating it by hand when the fog signal mechanism had failed. Or that this was the same light station that I had received a letter of commendation for as the best-looking lighthouse from Maine to Texas.
>
> It was a heartbreaking sight.

Mark Island Light, Deer Island Thorofare

The western approach to Deer Island Thorofare is marked by the handsome light station on Mark Island. The light was built almost 150 years ago, and went into service in 1857 as a family station.

Fishermen and deepwater seamen from Deer Isle had been pressuring for a light to guide them into the Deer Island Thorofare as they navigated through the dozens of islands in East Penobscot Bay.

One vital fact to remember about the buoy system here is that coming to the Deer Island Thorofare from the west—from the Fox Islands Thorofare—you are going out to sea and not returning to harbor. This, of course, means that you leave the red buoys on your left and the black ones on your right. Making for the light on Mark Island, remember this because you must leave the red buoy at West Mark Island Ledge on your left and steer between it and the Mark Island Light. The same "red on the left, black on the right" applies to all buoys through the Deer Island Thorofare, heading to the east.

This light on Mark Island shines brightly in the cruising memories of *Steer Clear*. Most of them are happy. Every summer we loved our days spent among the anchorages around the Fox Islands: Perry's Creek, Long Cove, and others; then we left with the foretaste of the beauties of the islands in Merchants Row just ahead to make our leaving tolerable. On many lovely summer days, the short haul to Mark Island has spelled ideal cruising.

But I also remember vividly the reverse side of that coin.

We had been fogbound for three days and nights in Crockett Cove on the western side of Deer Isle, in a pea-souper so thick we could not see the shore—a hundred feet away—for forty-eight hours. On the third day, we eased slowly out into the murk, decided against it after a spell, pulled inshore, and tucked *Steer Clear* behind Moose Island to wait for the wind to blow and the fog to lift.

When the wind picked up, it came in strong from the southwest. The fog did not lift, but our anchorage became so rough and rolly, facing into the blow, that we decided to make a run for it. We started out on a course that would take us to the light on Mark Island, from where we would lay a new course for the buoy and monument marker at Channel Rock, outside the entrance to the Fox Islands Thorofare.

It turned out to be a bad trip. We would have been happier staying on our bouncing anchorage.

By the time we came near to Mark Island, the fog was thick, the seas were rough, and the wind was howling. *Steer Clear* was shipping green water over the bow, and sometimes over the cabin top. She was rolling so badly that all drawers flew open, all closet doors flew wide. Foodstuffs, glasses, books crashed to the decks from their safe stowage places. Holding a compass course was next to impossible, because the rough seas were running wild and mixed, and I had to keep swinging the helm to point the bow into the highest of the seas that were battering us. As we came by Mark Island Light, I wavered, wondering whether to backtrack or to keep going for North Haven. We plunged on slowly, banging and bouncing every yard of the trip.

From time to time, I'd glance back longingly toward Mark Island, trying to spot its light and to keep it astern in the right place. Bruised, wet, and tired, we made it into the shelter between North Haven and Vinalhaven. Within the next hour, the weather turned amiable. The seas smoothed, the wind dropped, the fog cleared, and, by evening, the sun came out to say goodbye to that beastly day. As so often in Maine waters, the swift change from awful to wonderful was incredible. We looked out at the calm and peaceful stretch toward Mark Island and could scarcely believe the hell it had been getting across it only a few hours earlier.

Here are, I believe, the finest, most beautiful cruising waters in the world. Circumnavigating Deer Isle itself, with its dozen snug harbors, its handsome watery corridor, the Eggemoggin Reach, its multitude of outcropping islands, is a joy to the eye. It is also a reminder of man's muscle and man's mind—the sea knowledge of Billings Diesel and Marine boatyard; the big, successful Fisherman's Co-op; the granite quarry at Webb Cove, now silent; the big pond of water lilies, coral pink and ivory white in a beautiful blanket of a thousand intertwining patterns; the bold granite ledges; the art at Haystack School; the plain, unpolished, haphazard beauty of Stonington; and the hundreds of years of pioneering and seagoing that mark the founding families of Deer Isle, whose descendants have never left this special spot.

Burnt Coat Harbor Light

Cruising east from Stonington, *Steer Clear* left astern jaunty Grog Island, comes between Saddleback and Shingle Islands, and from the bell buoy there set course across the splendidly named Jericho and Toothacher Bays for Burnt Harbor Light on Hockamock Head on Swans Island.

Burnt Coat is, many say, a corruption of the French name Brule Cote, a name given this spot in the 17th century because the land had been burned over by a wildfire.

Steer Clear had a hard time making this harbor on our first trip here. We had been running slowly in fog from the bell of Halibut Rocks, four miles away, on a well-held compass course to the bell by Harbor Island, near the entrance to Burnt Coat.

We didn't hear that bell when we thought we should and so made a very easy slow turn from where we thought the bell should be and put our bow toward the light and fog horn on Hockamock Head, hoping to spot the light glimmering through the fog or hear the horn. Neither. Nothing.

We cut the engines to watch and listen hard, and lay wallowing in the slow swell, with the wind on our stern. Then I heard the clang of the bell buoy behind us. With relief, I slipped into forward gear and eased slowly ahead, ears pricked for the fog signal, eyes peeled for a glimmer of the light. Suddenly, an enormous blast of the fog horn made me jump almost out of the cockpit. The noise seemed right upon us. Indeed, we were close abreast of the fog signal. The wind had been carrying its sound inland, over the island; but on the seaward side we heard nothing. Later, local fishermen told me they had the same trouble. They had complained for years to the Coast Guard, asking for a noise reflector to bounce the sound back seaward when wind was blowing it inland. They never got their noise reflector.

We never did see the light, fog enshrouded it so thickly. We crept slowly into the harbor and anchored. Late that night the wind picked up—but more of that nasty adventure in a moment.

Burnt Coat Light was built in 1872 under President Ulysses S. Grant. It had two towers, called range lights. In 1885, the captain of a ship that wrecked here complained to the Lighthouse Board that the two tower lights were confusing, and soon afterward one of the towers was torn down. Wrecks continued.

On November 13, 1887, a schooner bound for Portland was lost, but the four-man crew was rescued. A few weeks later, on January 27, 1888, a schooner out of Nova Scotia, with a crew of six, bound for Boston, was wrecked while trying to find shelter in Burnt Coat. The men were saved, but the cargo—a load of turnips—was ruined.

On January 4, 1900, an American schooner under a Captain Tuttle was driven ashore, trying to make Burnt Coat. On New Year's Day 1902, a British schooner tried to ride out a storm at anchor by Harbor Island at the entrance. At the height of the storm, her anchor hawser parted and she was blown onto Scrag Ledge at the opening into Burnt Coat.

The next victim was an American coal schooner, with a crew of five aboard, that hit on Johns Island Ledge while trying to take shelter in Burnt Coat. She was carrying coal to Bar Harbor and was laden deep and hit hard. She broke open on impact. The crew managed to get off in a boat before she foundered and went down. Bar Harbor homes may have gone cold and coal-less, but not so on Swans Island. That winter there was plenty of coal and all free for those who filled their boats.

The last in this log of international wrecks of vessels trying to make Burnt Coat Harbor was the Italian ship *Emiliard*, with eleven in crew. She had sailed from Scotland to pick up a cargo in Maine at Stockton, when she ran ashore here.

Steer Clear had a troubled time on that first trip into Burnt Coat, largely because of the tricks played by the wind on the fog signal. That night the wind picked up to fifty miles per hour, and we began to drag anchor in a strange harbor. So it was out of the bunk, into the oilskins, and onto the bouncing bow in the teeth of the wind. We upped anchor and used full power for a few moments to try another, better-holding ground. No sooner was the anchor down than the gale gusted even higher. That set our anchor in deep and we rested secure until morning came and the wind moderated; the sun came out, and the fog left.

We went ashore to find that Burnt Coat was the harbor where the first settler on Swans Island (then called Burnt Coat Island) dragged his boat ashore. He was Thomas Kench, a deserter and deranged soldier from the Revolutionary Army. He lived here as a hermit, alone on the six thousand acres. Kench arrived in 1776. Then in 1791, fabled "King

David" Smith arrived, fathered twenty-four children and more than fifty grandchildren, bossed the island, ruined Kench's solitude, and lived to reach eighty years.

Kench's old army commander, Colonel James Swan, then bought the island and twenty-four nearby islands. He paid two English pounds an acre for nine thousand acres in all. He planned to create a feudal kingdom here, with himself as king, and he named the place Swans Island.

Swan, a swashbuckling entrepreneur, left his native Scotland at age eleven and landed in Boston. By the time he was seventeen he had published a fiery tirade against the slave trade. As a young, hot-blooded member of the Sons of Liberty, Swan helped dump the 342 chests of English tea into Boston Harbor.

While still in his twenties, Swan became secretary of the Massachusetts Board of War, adjutant general of the Commonwealth, and a member of the Legislature. He parlayed his money into a new fortune, lived extravagantly, and drove the fanciest carriage in all of Boston. He entertained Washington, Rochambeau, and Lafayette at his grandiose house at the corner of West and Tremont Streets.

To establish his island empire, Swan brought in twenty families as new settlers, built a sawmill, established fisheries and a school, and built an enormous mansion for himself. Then his investments went sour and he was thrown into a Paris jail for twenty-two years, where he died in 1830.

Great Duck Island Light

Ducks gave Great Duck Island its name. When there was a pond in the middle of this 250-acre island just east of Mount Desert Rock Light, many thousands of ducks came here to lay eggs and raise their young on this pond.

Great Duck Island has long been a haven for birds. Now it will be forever preserved as such, because in 1984 the Maine Chapter of The Nature Conservancy bought the island from a psychiatrist who had used the isolated site as a counseling center. The Nature Conservancy estimates that this one island supports 20 percent of Maine's nesting seabirds. Most important, it is the nesting site for sixteen thousand pairs of Leach's Storm Petrels, which is 85 percent of that bird's total population in the United States. Petrels are secretive, nocturnal birds, that burrow into the soft forest soil to nest. They winter in South America and spend their lives at sea except during the summer nesting season.

Great Duck Island is also home to the largest colony of Black Guillemots in the East. More than four hundred pairs of guillemots nest in the deep crevices of the island's rocky shore.

In the 1930s, the Audubon Society leased part of the island as a gull preserve. The gulls would arrive in huge numbers in April—the mating season—and drive the keepers half crazy with their incessant mating cries. Then thousands of young gulls would be hatched. Gulls usually lay three eggs. If one egg is taken from the nest, the mother will return and lay another egg. If two eggs are taken, the nest is abandoned.

In August, the thousands of gulls would start leaving, their young flying away with them, and the keepers—who had been driven half crazy by the cries of mating gulls and then cries of young, hungry gulls—would miss their summer company.

Great Duck Island Light was built in 1890 during the presidency of Benjamin Harrison, and still stands much the same as when it was built. It was one of the last remaining lighthouses in Maine still manned by lightkeepers in the mid-1980s. It was automated in 1986.

The island light has seen its share of shipwrecks, survivors, and drowned sailors.

Long ago, a sailing ship was wrecked here, with all hands lost. Some time after the wreck, islanders found two of the crew dead and washed up, and held in the grip of a pair of rocks. The two men were frozen stiff, arms around each other. The islanders carried the iced bodies to a field, dug a shallow grave, and laid them to rest.

The families of the dead sailors, notified that they had been found, came to the island to take away their bodies. But they were so moved by the island grave, they gave them a more formal burial where they lay and fenced that burial ground with a white picket fence. For years, keepers of the light who had come to this station long after the tragedy placed flags and flowers on these graves each Memorial Day.

And there was the strange story, told by Robert Sterling in his book on Maine lighthouses, of the shipwrecked African-American who swam ashore close to death about a hundred years ago, before the light and the keepers were here. It was summertime and the sailor gathered berries to eat and salvaged washed-up boards from the shore to build a shelter. There he lived for several months. When found, he was thin as a skeleton and wild and wooly as a cannibal. In isolation, he had lost the ability to speak. After rescue by the sheriff of Hancock County, he was brought back to normal speech and normal weight, and sent off to his distant home.

In another shipwreck, the captain and crew abandoned ship and clambered into a long boat. The ship's dog tried to jump in with them, but a scared crewman swung at the dog with an oar and knocked the animal into the raging sea, where the dog presumably drowned.

But drown he did not. The dog made it ashore to Great Duck Island and came shivering and scratching at the door of the keeper's house. The wound from the blow of the oar still bled from his head. For two years, the keeper's young daughter fed and fondled the dog, and named him Seaboy. Then one day the captain of a fishing vessel came ashore, saw the dog, and called out to him. The dog came running, wagging his tail at the sight of his old master.

For the next two days, the dog and his old master enjoyed a happy reunion, and when it was time for the captain to leave, the dog ran down to the beach with him. The keeper's daughter wept to think Seaboy was lost to her. She cried out as the dog jumped into the dory. The dog heard her, leaped out, and ran to jump into the arms of the girl who had nursed him back to life.

Great Duck Island held the record for the greatest number of children in a keeper's family—sixteen. These sixteen youngsters belonged to Keeper Nathan Adam Reed and his wife, Emma, who began keeping the light in 1902. He was transferred in 1912 to Nash Island, where he died a few months later. But Keeper Reed got a school started on the island for his children, the children of two other keepers, and the children in the big family of a lobsterman who lived on Great Duck. Finally, one of the Reed daughters, Rena, went to the mainland and graduated as a qualified teacher from Castine Normal School. She returned to teach her brothers and sisters and the other pupils.

Libby Island Light

Keepers at Libby Island Light have endured peril just trying to get on and off their light, the most eastern primary light in U.S. waters at the entrance to Machias Bay.

Early on the morning of June 18, 1918, Samuel Holbrook and Julian Foss, the assistant keeper, were fishing just off Libby Island. A big incoming breaker capsized their skiff and both men were thrown into the sea. Foss clung to the boat. Holbrook, who could not swim, was drowned.

Young Naval reservists, stationed on Libby Island during World War I, saw what had happened, and swam out to help. They rescued Foss, still holding on to the capsized craft. But they found no sign of Holbrook.

The Coast Guard sent out a tender and tried dragging to recover the body. When that failed to find any corpse, they threw dynamite sticks into the ocean, but this also failed to raise the body. Two months later, Holbrook's body was found, washed ashore many miles to the west at the island of Isle au Haut.

Six years later, in the cold of December 1924, the keeper and his assistant took a small boat to row the five miles to shore to get supplies and mail at Starboard Village. They finished their chores and headed back to the light. They had gone about one mile back when a sudden wave capsized the skiff they were towing. They ran for shelter into the lee of Stones Island.

By now the wind was blowing hard, so the two men decided to row the mile back to the mainland rather than risk a four-mile passage out to the light. The December day was so cold that the spray and waves kicked up by the high wind turned to ice as it hit their boats. As the ice encased them with more and more weight, they sank lower and lower in the water until they were almost without freeboard and risked sinking with every wave. They made it back safely into Starboard Cove, and sheltered there for two days until the storm and cold moderated. Meanwhile, the third keeper, alone on Libby Island, kept the light and fog signal working.

Earlier, on the icy morning of December 9, 1910, Keeper Henry

Cuskley—who had been keeper since 1903—had a narrow escape. When he was pulling out from the slip in his power boat, the long tie-up line fell overboard and wrapped around his propeller. It snarled in tightly and he was dead in the water with no power. The waves drove him hard onto the ledges, with such force that he was thrown overboard.

Luckily, others in the light-station crew had seen his difficulty, ran to the rescue, and pulled him safely and quickly from the icy waters. They winched the powerless boat back to the slip, but it was a total loss.

Accidents like these were always happening at one station or another. Keepers who had to use small boats in bad weather were always at risk.

Libby Island Light was built early, in 1822, under President James Monroe. It must have been one of the best-built lights, for it stood for more than 150 years just as it had been originally built, a granite, conical tower, ninety-one feet above the sea.

Thick weather and bad storms and icy winters played havoc with the fishing boats and coastal schooners plying these down east waters in the last century. Old journals from the Libby Island Light report thirty-eight major wrecks between 1856 and 1906. Thanks to the bravery of lightkeepers, only nineteen lives were lost in these thirty-eight wrecks.

Keeper Cuskley, mentioned above, gave this staccato account of one:

> The three-masted schooner *Ella G. Ells*, bound light from N.Y. to St. John, N.B., ran ashore during a heavy fog on July 4, 1906, on the outside of the larger Libby Islands and all hands but the captain were lost. The captain floated ashore on the roof of the ship's cabin.

There are actually two Libby Islands, joined at low tide by a sandbar. But at high water, it appears that there is a seaway between the two, and ships have gone aground trying to sail through this deceptive passage at high tide.

One of the worst wrecks was the schooner *Caledonia* in the early morning of December 3, 1878. Under Captain Davidson, *Caledonia* left Yarmouth, Nova Scotia, in the morning of December 2, and was making good time when late that night a storm broke from the southeast. Captain Davidson decided to seek shelter in Machias Bay. But the storm increased and the small craft was getting badly battered. Davidson had an impossible job trying to hold course.

As he was rounding the end of Big Libby Island, a huge sea almost swamped *Caledonia*; but as she shook it off and righted herself, she crashed hard onto the deadly ledges. Two passengers, sheltering inside the after cabin, escaped the fate of the captain and his crew, who were working on deck. The giant breaker that had carried the ship onto the ledges swept the captain and his crew overboard and drowned them.

By morning, the sun was out and the seas were calm again. There on the sands of Big Libby were the bodies of the captain, the steward, and the deckhand. The vessel was hard aground. The two scared passengers were clinging to the rigging high in the mainmast. A boatload of volunteers from Starboard, five miles away, came out and rescued the passengers.

That deceptively inviting water, which at high tide totally covers the sandbars joining Big and Little Libby, was where the ship *Princeport* sailed to her death.

It happened during one bad September night in 1892, when hurricane winds and raging rain drove a careful captain to seek shelter. Captain John Brown, bound from Port George to Boston, ran for the shelter of Machias Bay. He spotted Libby Island Light and ran toward it. But he mistook the water between the two Libby Islands for the safe Eastern Passage and hit the bar, and stuck, with the storm beating him harder and harder aground and battering his ship to pieces.

At daybreak, Keeper Daniel French spotted the wreck. Little was left of the ship after the long night. The crew was huddled on the only part left, a bit of the bow and fore hatch. The keepers reached the stranded men and got them ashore. Had they been fifteen minutes later, men and bow would have been swallowed by the sea.

Another heroic rescue was performed by Keeper W.A. Aerman Wood and his assistants, when they rescued twelve from a crew of fifteen aboard the bark *Fame*. Keeper Wood was watching *Fame* through his glass, bucking a heavy gale, trying to head into the calmer water of Machias Bay. He saw her being blown toward the island, then saw her try to change course to set farther off the ledges. But the bark was driven ashore.

The keepers waded hip-deep into the surf, threw lines to the crew, and rigged a hawser from ship to shore. Then they rigged a bo'sun's chair and hauled twelve men safely to shore. But two other crewmen and Captain McDonald were lost.

The beautiful three-masted schooner *F.C. Lockhart*, bound for Nova Scotia with a load of fertilizer, drove hard onto the ledges on May 26, 1923. She hit at such high speed there was no way to winch her off. There she stayed, helpless, until she broke up in the spring storms.

In March of 1925, the barkentine *John H. Myers*, with a deckload of pulpwood, went aground here. The Coast Guard at Cross Island rescued all the crew. The only casualty was a broken leg suffered by the second mate. The *Myers*, like many before and since, had mistaken the water between the two Libby Islands for the Eastern Passage.

A big square-rigger—the *Africa*, 679 tons, owned and captained by T. E. Masters of Huntsport, Nova Scotia—met death the same way. This disaster happened at 2:30 in the morning of October 19, 1902. Captain and crew abandoned ship and got into their yawl boat. They were pulling hard through high seas, trying to get ashore on Big Libby. The side of their yawl boat was stove in as they were being hurled by breakers through the outcrop of rocks.

Before leaving his ship aground on the bar, the captain had thrown two anchors out to hold *Africa*. Each weighed five thousand pounds, but they didn't help at all. Soon *Africa*, only ten years old, was pounded into flotsam and jetsam. But the two anchors are still there and can be seen in a finely preserved state.

Petit Manan Light

Petit Manan is shortened in speech to "Titmanan," and sometimes Anglo-Saxonized and abbreviated further to "Titman." Petit Manan Light is beautiful and graceful, and the tallest lighthouse in Maine after Boon Island. From high-water mark to the top of the lantern is 123 feet. (Boon Island Light is 137 feet high.)

The light, authorized by President James Monroe, was first built in 1817. There is little available information about the light and its keepers in its earliest years; but by the time it was fourteen, it was in real trouble.

The auditor of the Treasury in charge of lighthouses was Stephen Pleasonton, and in 1831 he wrote an upbraiding letter to John Chandler, superintendent of lights for Maine:

> Petit Manan ... is stated to be in "Very Bad Condition" indeed—built of worse materials than Desert Light—the lantern is in good working order, but otherwise the place is positively dirty; dwelling house much out of repair and leaking badly; the keeper has gone off, being tired of his state of independence and left his wife in charge of the whole concern ...You will cause the necessary repairs to be made: and if the keeper has actually left the establishment to his wife, another appointment will be recommended."

The keeper's name was Leighton and he had indeed left his wife to run the lighthouse. He was fired, took ill, and died a year later. His wife did apply for his job, saying that she had been doing it for years and therefore knew the work well. But she was refused, and the job was given to Patrick Campbell.

Inspectors came again to Petit Manan in 1851, during the time when all lighthouses were inspected because of a scandal in the Lighthouse Department of Treasury. The 1851 inspectors reported that the light, of the lowest or fourth order of lights, was too weak and that its beam could not be seen more than eight miles away. They ordered a fog bell installed, because the island waters suffered from even more fog than the rest of Maine, and recommended that the tower be rebuilt and the light upgraded to a second-order light.

These improvements were carried out four years later. But the new tower was too weak. In a storm of 1856, a year after reconstruction, the high tower swayed and was loose in its upper part. Each huge storm that swept the island weakened it more.

By 1869, the keeper had this weird and frightening experience: The huge weights from the clockworks in the top of the tower came crashing down and fell to the lower floors of the light with such tremendous force that they snapped away eighteen steps of the cast-iron circular staircase. Luckily, no one was climbing on them at that moment.

In the same year of 1869, a steam fog signal was installed. But this, too, had problems. The water supply for making steam was drawn from a swamp, and was so filled with rotting vegetable matter that it was useless. So rain-catchers were put on the roof of the keeper's house, and rainwater was collected in barrels in the cellar. Pipes carried the water to the fog signal, where it was heated into steam to sound the horn.

Petit Manan in those days was a scary station. The tower swayed badly in gale winds. Keepers up in the tower working on the lantern felt as though whole top sections were going to be blown off, taking them to their deaths.

In the summer of 1887, radical repairs were made. The watch room and the lantern room above it were better secured to the rest of the tower by six iron tie rods driven through the granite walls to a huge bolt thirty feet below. Just as well, too, because in December of that year, the coast was battered by a series of severe gales that would likely have sent the tower crashing had the repairs not been completed.

The view from atop Petit Manan is spectacular, commanding all of Frenchman Bay and the inlets of Gouldsboro, Dyer's, Pigeon Hill, Narragaugus, and Pleasant bays, and the towns of Milbridge, Steuben, and Prospect Harbor. From the watch room, keepers kept a weather eye on the lobsterboats fishing out from nearby Corea and other fishing harbors.

Sometimes all the keepers could do in winter was just keep an eye on the boats. They could not go to their rescue because the waves breaking over Petit Manan froze the launching ramp for the rescue lifeboat, and it could not be launched.

One such instance happened in the winter of 1934, with Keeper Edward A. Pettigrew in charge. Pettigrew had barely survived the gale storms of January 28, 1928, when he was keeping the light at nearby Avery's Rock. In that storm, Captain Pettigrew said, his bell tower was smashed, his boardwalks ripped away, and his dwelling left knee-deep in water. While Pettigrew struggled to keep the light working, he worried about his wife and mother in the dwelling house. Seas had put out the furnace, and temperatures were below zero. The women fought uselessly against the seas pouring into their house, smashing windows and doors. Their clothes and their beds were drenched. They survived for days, hanging on till the weather eased enough for the buoytender *Hibiscus* to get them off Avery's Rock.

Now in 1934, Pettigrew was keeping Petit Manan, living through yet another gale and ice storm. The telephone in the watch room rang. A call from Corea reported one of the lobstermen was long overdue, and asked that Pettigrew keep a sharp lookout. It was 10 p.m. when the keeper saw a distress signal—a flaming torch far in the distance. Pettigrew, knowing his ice-bound lifeboat could not be launched, phoned the Coast Guard stations at Cranberry and Great Wass Island, giving them the position of the distress signal.

Fishermen from Corea and the Coast Guard tried, but could not locate the lobsterman in distress. And then a blinding snowstorm shut down all visibility, stopping all rescue efforts. When the snow stopped thirty-six hours later, the keepers saw a sail on the horizon and phoned again to the lobsterman's family in Corea. A rescue party set out, despite 60-mph. winds. The keepers saw the rescue boat come alongside the lobsterman, and take him off onto their boat. Somehow the fisherman had survived; his legs and arms were frozen, but he survived and by summer was fishing again.

The Petit Manan Light, built in 1817, was unmanned in 1972. Its second-order Fresnel lens is on display at the Shore Village Museum, Rockland. The beautiful lens stands almost ten feet tall and was manufactured in Paris, France, and installed at Petit Manan in 1855. The old fog bell from Petit Manan has found a home, too. It is mounted at the elementary school in Milbridge, Maine.

Nash Island and Moose Peak Lights

Nash Island Light, on the smaller of two Nash Islands, marks the entrance to Pleasant Bay, leaving Cape Split to starboard. This has long been prime lobstering ground for fishermen from Jonesport, and lobster buoys can be thicker than flies. First built in 1838 under President Martin Van Buren, it was rebuilt and greatly improved in 1873 under President Ulysses S. Grant.

When Captain John F. Purrington was keeper, he had so many children there, five miles out from Jonesport, that he had a schoolroom built and a teacher hired for them. After they had finished grammar school on the island, they were sent to board on the mainland during term, so they could attend high school in Jonesport.

The light was unmanned and automated in 1958, 120 years after it had been first built.

Moose Peak Light, on the point of Mistake Island, was built in 1827, while John Quincy Adams was president.

Jonesport, five miles away, is the nearest town for mail and supplies. In summer, keepers could take the inside passage behind Head Harbor Island, past the Spectacle Islands, and into Moosabec Reach to do their chores ashore at Jonesport. But in winter, it was a hard run outside Head Harbor Island down to Mark Island, and thence along the Reach to town. Either required careful seamanship, for, during the sixteen years between 1919 to 1935, Moose Point Light endured more dense fog than any other spot along the Maine coast.

This light was unmanned in 1972, after being run by keepers since 1827—a total of 145 years. The light stands seventy-two feet above the sea and has a beam of 1.1-million candle-power, compared to Libby Island Light, nine miles away, which stands ninety-one feet and has a 25,000-candlepower light.

West Quoddy Head Light

West Quoddy Head Light, despite its name, is built on the easternmost tip of the United States. The water border with Canada runs through the middle of Quoddy Narrows, which the light overlooks. Across the Narrows lies the island of Campobello, most recently made famous because President Franklin D. Roosevelt summered there in the Eleanor Roosevelt family cottage. It was here he first showed signs of the polio that was to cripple but not handicap him. There is a state park now on West Quoddy Head, where Arctic tundra grows, set off by several species of arctic wildflowers and plants. The views from these cliffs are spectacular, including the panorama of Grand Manan, the huge Canadian island to the south.

The light is one of the six oldest lights in Maine, an indication of the heavy shipping traffic into Passamaquoddy Bay two hundred years ago. This was the earliest light built in far Down East Maine. It was first lit in 1808, nine years before Petit Manan and fourteen years before Libby Island Light. The station was built first by order of President Thomas Jefferson, and rebuilt fifty years later, in 1858, under President James Buchanan. The first keeper here, appointed by Jefferson, was Thomas Dexter.

The job was not much of a political plum financially. Dexter collected only $250 a year and complained that this was not enough for a family man to support his wife and children. His gripe was that the soil near the light, where the tundra grows today, was so poor that he could not raise a garden; in addition, he had to travel to Lubec, five miles of hard pulling or sailing away, to get supplies. So in 1810, Dexter's pay was raised to $300.

West Quoddy also got one of the first fog signals. This was installed in 1820. Since God seems to make fog mostly in the nearby Bay of Fundy, the fog signal here was in almost constant use. The keeper, in blunt words, told his superiors just how much extra work he had to put in with ringing the fog bell. Seven years after its installation, the keeper was paid an extra seventy dollars a year for constantly ringing the bell to warn ships off from the dangers of Sail Rocks, as they made their turn into Lubec Channel. But ship captains had trouble hearing the bell and wrote lots of complaints from the start. So the bell was continually changed; four different kinds of bells were tried in seventeen years.

The first bell in 1820 was a 500-pound affair, and was replaced by a 241-pounder, supposed to send out a higher-pitched, more penetrating sound. It did not. So, in turn, it was replaced by a huge 1,565-pounder. This still didn't solve the problem. The authorities took a quite different tack: They installed a triangular steel bar that measured fourteen feet in overall length. In 1837, lighthouse inspector Captain Joseph Smith, aboard the revenue cutter *Morris*, surveyed the effectiveness of this cast steel bar and found it poor: "I believe that a sharp-toned bell of some 4,000 pounds weight, struck by machinery properly constructed and proportioned to the bell, would answer all the purposes," he wrote in his report. In 1858, the light and the fog signal were entirely rebuilt.

Now the light, standing eighty-five feet above the sea, flashes twice every fifteen seconds, sending out a beam visible eighteen miles away. The station is equipped with a radio beacon and the diaphone horn is as powerful as they make them. West Quoddy Head Light is one of the few candy-striped lights, painted in conspicuous red and white stripes. The lighthouse was automated in 1988, though unlike most of the Maine lighthouses, it has kept its original optic—a third-order Fresnel lens.

A photograph of West Quoddy Head when it was still manned by the U.S. Coast Guard. Built in 1808, it became automated in 1988. Gannett file photo.

Avery Rock Light

On the chart, Avery Rock Light sits at the south entrance to Machias Bay. Clearly it is little, but it doesn't look frightening. But frightening it was to Connie Small, who as a twenty-two-year-old bride came to live here in 1922 with her lightkeeper husband, Elson Small.

I met Connie Small when she was eighty-three, chipper, pretty, and looking sixty-three, in the living room of her garden apartment in Kittery. From the day she married at age twenty, Connie Small lived and raised her family on lighthouse stations. Yet details of life on Avery Rock sprung vividly to her mind even sixty years after she moved there. "Avery Rock," she said, "is one of the roughest light stations in the nation, though on the chart it may not look it."

The light stands on a quarter-acre of barren rock, battered by some of the worst seas and gales in the North Atlantic. Because the ledge called Avery Rock is so small, the light and the lightkeeper's house were both under the same roof. The light tower simply jutted up out of the roof of the keeper's house like a big finger pointed to heaven.

The light was built in 1875, by order of President Ulysses S. Grant. For fifty-nine years, until it was unmanned in 1934, many keepers and their families came close to being swept away, house and all, by seas that raged across the quarter-acre ledge.

"To keep our house from being swamped by stormy seas," Connie Small told me, "we had shutters four inches thick on all windows and the doors were like watertight barriers."

The weather was so bad for so long one year in the 1920s that young Connie and her family were marooned on Avery Rock for seven months. All fall and winter, the sea stayed too rough to launch or land any boat.

In another terrible storm, a gale topping seventy miles an hour blew without letup for three days and nights, with seas of more than forty feet. "The Coast Guard did not think we would live through that one," recalled Mrs. Small, whose husband died in 1962, eleven years after his retirement.

The Smalls made it through that storm, though the house was awash. Six months later, after the Smalls had been transferred to Seguin

Light, the next keeper and his family were not so lucky. Captain Edward Pettigrew and his wife and mother almost lost their lives on Avery Rock in a gale that demolished the light and the house. Since then, Avery Rock Light no longer exists. It has been replaced by an automated big flashing buoy, not far from where this light shone for fifty-nine years.

St. Croix Light

Go off this tiny, lovely island called Dochet, at the entrance to the St. Croix River, and you are in Canadian waters. St. Croix is the first light in the First Lighthouse District of the United States. There is a marker set in the ledge on the highest place on the island that says, "International Boundary." Today, the true boundary between the United States and Canada runs through the river, just east of the island.

Another more stirring historical marker set in a boulder reads:

> 1604-1904. To commemorate the Discovery and Occupation of this Island by De Monts and Champlain, Who naming it L'Isle Sainte Croix, Founded here 26 June 1604, the French Colony of Acadia, then the only Settlement of Europeans north of Florida. This tablet is erected by residents of the St. Croix Valley in 1904.

French historian Marc Lescarbot, describing the first landing here, wrote that the island was "one half a league in circuit, ground most excellent and fruitful, strong of nature, easy of defense, but difficult to be found."

Lescarbot, writing about De Monts's and Champlain's voyage to North America, says:

> All New France was contained in two ships, when they left Port Du Mouton for the purpose of discovering new lands in the Western Continent. They followed the coast line until they came to a large river [the St. Croix] where they fortified themselves on a little island [Dochet] which Champlain had discovered and viewed.

Those French settlers endured for only one winter on this island. Thirty-five of the seventy-nine who landed here died from scurvy. The forty-four survivors sailed away the next summer to settle in Nova Scotia. But Champlain and De Monts left an enduring mark upon the United States.

Samuel de Champlain, navigator for Sieur De Monts, left the camp on Dochet Island two months after they had set up headquarters there. Champlain took a seventeen-ton ketch, twelve sailors, and two Indian guides and went exploring.

One September day in 1604, he discovered Mount Desert. "This island," he wrote, "is very high and cleft into seven or eight mountains all in a line. The summits are bare and deserted. Nothing but rock. I named it Isle des Monts-deserts." Champlain called the region La Cadie, which later became L'Acadie, which became today's Acadia National Park.

Champlain, with his dozen sailors and two guides, sailed on to explore and map much more of the Maine coast, including the Cranberry Isles and Isle au Haut. Later, he left Maine to become the founding father of Quebec.

The St. Croix Light was built in 1857, when James Buchanan was president. It was rebuilt and modernized in 1901 during the presidency of Theodore Roosevelt. The light was unmanned in 1957, one hundred years after it was built.

To generations of lightkeepers, many of whom had seen rough and dangerous duty on remote stations, keeping the St. Croix Light seemed like paradise. The island is lovely, with good soil for a garden, plenty of spruce trees and birches, and spectacular scenery. The keeper's house was large, airy, and comfortable. When the light was automated, the keeper's house was left empty, without even a caretaker on this historic ground. Since Dochet Island is very close to the mainland and easy to reach by rowboat, it became a hangout.

One night in 1976, some youngsters, getting away from the arm of the law for some minor infringement, made an escape to Dochet Island. They took shelter from the night inside the old keeper's house. To keep warm, they started a fire. Due to a high wind blowing, their fire got out of control. The house and all other wooden buildings on this historic island were burned to ashes.

Mount Desert Rock Light

"Why here? What mad misanthrope chose to build a lighthouse on this hostile, forsaken rock, twenty-six miles offshore in perilous ocean?"

Mount Desert Rock is exposed to some of the most savage seas and gales of any light on the Atlantic Coast. Yet someone picked this place to erect a light to help mariners find the way to Mount Desert Island and Frenchman and Blue Hill bays on either side of it. And he ordered that the light be built upon a rock barely out of the ocean. The rock is a mere chunk of volcanic outcrop, a speck in the wild Atlantic. The nearest harbor is twenty-six miles away on the mainland.

On a calm day, you can walk every yard of this world in a few minutes; it is six hundred yards long and two hundred yards wide. On a calm day you might even feel safe and enjoy the ocean, twenty feet below the highest point on the rock at low tide.

In a storm, however, run fast for cover—the fury of the sea submerges every inch of the rock on which the light stands. The force of those seas is incredible. In a storm of 1842, say federal records, a mammoth rock eighteen feet long, fourteen feet wide, and six feet thick, weighing fifty-seven tons, was hurled by the wild ocean as though it were a toy! In another storm, a boulder weighing seventy-five tons was rolled like a hoop sixty feet by gigantic waves.

Sail by Mount Desert Rock Light today and you are glad it is there, but you wonder about the kind of men and women who have been its keepers and how they endured life on this rock for more than 170 years.

The first keeper sailed out, came ashore, and lit the first beacon here in 1830; from then on, men and women tended the light for nearly one and a half centuries. Just in time for Christmas 1977, a helicopter landed on the wave-swept rock and took off the last two men to man this forsaken rock. They were two young Coast Guardsmen, Robin Runnels, twenty-two, from Hyannis, Massachusetts, and Douglas Nute, twenty, from St. Louis, Missouri. The light and horn were then fully automated.

How did a twenty-year-old stand life on the Rock?

Nute said he was ready to scream after he had spent a week out here as a relief fireman. He said the constant noise of the 24-hour fog horn,

Twenty-six miles out to sea, Mount Desert Rock Light was built in 1830. Keepers and their families lived on the Rock for 147 years before it became automated in 1977. Gannet file photo.

plus the Rock's constricted size, got him down. Nute had previously spent eighteen months at Great Duck Island Light, about halfway between Mount Desert Rock and the mainland, so he knew life on remote island lights. "At least on Great Duck," he said, "you had a mile and a half circumference you could walk, and trees, and grass, and birds and people over on the other side you could talk to. But on this Rock, there was nothing but the noise of the fog horn day and night."

The usual tour of duty on the Rock for four Coast Guardsmen is one year. Nute had been there one week. Runnels had been there six months.

To make life more endurable for these young men, the Coast Guard equipped the Rock with electronic video games, a pool table, books, radios, and lots and lots of cards, plus television sets. Even with these diversions, the men were on the Rock usually for only twenty-two days and nights at a stretch, and then went ashore for eight days' leave.

On a winter night in February 1956, the four men on duty thought their world had come to an end. The building was rocked by a huge explosion. All the windows were blown out. Plaster ceilings and walls fell in. The night sky, far out in the ocean, became an enormous flash of white.

The keepers were terrified, thinking an oil tank might have blown up. However, the cause of the violence was the explosion of a photo-flash bomb by a Strategic Air Command plane from Dow Air Force Base, near Bangor. A photo-flash bomb weighs about two hundred pounds, most of it magnesium. The intensity of the light when 150 pounds of magnesium is ignited is equal to about ten billion candlepower, and can be visible 150 miles away.

This time the Strategic Air Command forgot to notify the Coast Guard of the little surprise they had in store for the keepers of Mount Desert Rock.

The first lantern in 1830 was a simple affair, housed inside a second roof above the keeper's house. With the Rock twenty feet above sea level, and the keeper's house built atop that, and with the lantern room built atop the keeper's house, the light then had an elevation of fifty-six feet above sea level. But it was not enough for the traffic it served. A report to the Lighthouse Board in 1851 urged that the light be raised higher and that it be equipped with the most powerful lens money could buy.

The Lighthouse Board was then a new organization in its first year, and it took until 1855 before ten thousand dollars was authorized to be spent on improvements. By 1857, a new and higher tower was erected, a new lantern with a powerful Fresnel lens was installed, and a fog bell was added.

These were the only improvements for twenty years. By 1876, the keeper's house was leaking and falling apart. The place was so wet and cold that repairs had to be made if keepers and their families were to live there. So money was allocated in 1880 to build a new one-and-a-half-story frame house for the keepers. But the fog bell was of little help to ships. A bigger 1,000-pound bell had been brought to the Rock in 1877, and placed in a special new tower forty-five feet above the ground. But no matter how hard keepers or far-fetched mechanisms struck the 1,000-pound bell, the noise was not loud enough to be heard above the roar of waves and gales. So in 1893, a noisier fog horn was installed, given a blast for three seconds' duration, followed by twelve seconds of silence.

By 1893, a new light tower of cut granite, conical in shape, had been raised an extra twenty feet. This was a far cry from the original wooden lantern room on top of the keeper's house. The new granite tower had a very broad base and very thick walls, built to withstand tremendous seas. Inside the tower were four stories of rooms, and a watch room with the lantern on the top, shining from a height of seventy-five feet above the water. In 1898, the fixed white light was changed to flashing white, a two-second flash of 24,000-candlepower every fifteen seconds, supposedly visible for fourteen miles.

Wrecks and rescues mark the logs of lightkeepers of the Rock. Here are three such stories. First is the miracle of "the oilskin baby," who survived the wreck of the schooner *Helen and Mary* in the 1880s. The schooner, with a cargo of granite blocks in her hold and a cargo of lumber lashed to her decks, set sail from Halifax with owner Captain Jared Parker, his wife and baby aboard, plus First Mate Nelson White—who was brother to Mrs. Parker—and a crew.

Near Mount Desert Rock, a storm caught the schooner and swept away her deck cargo, and she began to founder from the dead weight of the granite in her holds. All hands were ordered into the lifeboats. The captain's wife and baby went into the first boat with some of the crew; and Captain Parker, First Mate White, and the remaining crew crowded into the second boat.

Just as they launched, the schooner went under, and the suction carried down the second boat. Mate White surfaced, saw nobody. Ahead, he saw the first boat floating bottom-up, capsized. Again, there was nobody near it.

White was alone in the stormy sea. He grabbed at some floating wreckage, a plank or spar, and climbed on it. Then he spotted a bundle of yellow oilskin and grabbed it. Inside was the infant baby of the captain's wife, White's sister. He held the infant—his niece—wrapped in oilskins; for more safety, he strapped the package tight to his chest, so he could use both hands to cling to the floating wreckage. White and the infant survived that day and night. The gale carried the spar to which he was clinging toward shore, to within ten miles of the coast. At noon the next day they were spotted and rescued by the lighthouse tender *Iris*. According to Mary Crowninshield, authority for the story, White and his infant niece were put ashore at Prospect Harbor and both recovered entirely from their ordeal. Nothing was ever heard or found of the ship *Helen and Mary*, or the rest of her crew, who were listed as drowned at sea.

One day before the turn of the 20th century, the keeper observed a Maine fisherman hauling his trawls off the Rock. The next day the keeper looked out, amazed to see the trawl still in the same spot on the ocean as it had been the day before. Fearing something was wrong, the keeper rowed out to the vessel and found nobody aboard, only a line over the side. The keeper hauled up the line and made the ghastly catch of the fisherman's body. The poor man had caught his hand in one of the trawling hooks as it went overboard and had been pulled over. But how? The keeper pulled in more of the trawl line and hauled in a huge halibut, weighing over a hundred pounds. Presumably the halibut had hit the trawl, the fisherman's hand had caught on a hook, and the fish pulled the fisherman overboard to his death.

The third story among the many from Mount Desert Rock began at 5 a.m. on December 9, 1902, when the ocean tug *Astral*—with a crew of eighteen aboard and a barge in tow—crashed against the northeast ledge of the Rock. An assistant keeper heard a whistle blowing seven frantic blasts—the distress signal—and rushed to waken the head keeper. The head keeper later told the tale of the night and day that followed to Robert Thayer Sterling, keeper of the Portland Head Light. Sterling set down the story in 1935 in his book on lighthouses. I will quote part of this account of the events of December 9, 1902, as told by the keeper of Mount Desert Rock:

> The vapor was flying so densely one could hardly see ten feet ahead. It was inky dark and blowing one of the worst gales I have ever seen. The thermometer had never dropped so low during the 13 years I had been on the Rock ... It was high tide and we could make out some kind of a steamer ashore on the northeast point; but the big seas were running so mountain-high it would have meant suicide for us to try to get out to her ... Not being able to see or hear anything or get any answer to our shouts, we stayed until we nearly froze to death ... We were chilled to the bone and could barely speak when we went back to the station to thaw.
>
> As soon as our fingers worked again, we got down ropes and life pre-servers as near the wreck as we could, but were compelled to wait until the tide went down and we could cross the point and get a line to the craft. We succeeded in rescuing seventeen men. There were eighteen in the crew, but one was frozen to death. They were all more or less frozen. The second engineer had to be carried to the station, his limbs being use-less ... He finally had to be put in a hospital where he stayed a year ... After we got them to the station, we treated their frostbites and dosed them with quinine pills and hot lemonade for fear pneumonia might set in.
>
> My wife got the government medicine chest down but through the excitement did not consult the doctor's book. We treated them for burns and later found we had handled the case just right ... These men re-mained with us six days and nights.

The wrecked tug *Astral* had a barge in tow when she hit. And what happened to the barge is another amazing story.

After the *Astral* hit, four hundred fathoms of towline kept paying out from her stern, letting the barge float off in the southerly gale. The ice on that freezing night was more than a foot thick over the windows of the pilothouse on the barge, so the crewmen aboard could not see out. They thought that the *Astral*, which had them in tow, had dropped anchor. With a foot of ice on the windows and vapor outside so thick that visibility was less than ten feet, the crew saw neither sight nor sound of the *Astral*.

> For ten hours or more at a stretch, each one of the crew took his watch at the wheel, keeping the barge headed into the wind. This was on Tuesday and the barge stayed there, on a 400-fathom line, lying in the lee until Thursday. Then the crew raised sail and set out for Rockland.
>
> The captain of the barge went ashore and called up the Standard Oil Company office in New York and told them what had happened. The company dispatched a wrecking crew from Boston to come to the Rock and get the tug's crew. The day they arrived was fine and the sea was never smoother. But the captain and crew of the wrecker were greatly afraid of being capsized as they tried to row ashore from their big boat, off at anchor. Seeing the big rollers shoot over the ledges terrified him, and he would row back out as if a bear were chasing him. I finally got him to row in as I directed and he landed without mishap ... Well, they got the crew aboard and left for Massachusetts.
>
> You should have seen the write-ups in the papers there. The captain had told how he and his crew had braved the seas ... a certain humane society fell for the story and rewarded the crew with $5 gold pieces.

From 1830 until 1977, keepers and their wives lived here, with no phones and no electricity, but they kept the light burning. It was so desolate a place that nothing grew there. Fishing-boat skippers, who were grateful for the light, would bring out a few baskets of dirt and hand the dirt to the keepers, who would row out in the dory to get it. The keeper and his wife would scatter the precious dirt into protected crevices and plant a few flowers or vegetables and raise a summer crop.

Come the first storm, the precious dirt would be torn away and the flowers and vegetables would be eaten by the ocean. But for a brief summer, flowers comforted the lonely men and women keeping the light at Mount Desert Rock.

No men, no wives, no children are on the Rock today—nothing but automated machines, though in summer, whale-watchers associated with the College of the Atlantic on Mount Desert Island often live out here for brief periods.

Little River Light

Little River Light marks the entrance to Cutler Harbor and is built on a small island, only a short row from the mainland in fair weather, but difficult to access in a blow. It was first lit in 1847 by order of President James K. Polk, and improved thirty years later because of the ever-increasing amount of coastal shipping and the mounting number of fishing boats working out of Cutler.

Cutler is the site of a key installation in American defense. The radio transmitting station that links the Navy Department to its underwater submarines has been located at Cutler. This very low frequency group of transmitters kept contact, for example, with the submarine *Thresher* when it was disabled and all aboard were killed in a freak and spectacular disaster at sea. The towers dominate the Cutler sky.

Keeping the light here had been a family tradition among the Corbetts. Captain W. Corbett kept the light for more than twelve years. His wife was the daughter of the former keeper, and had been raised as a girl at this light. After she married Corbett and returned to this light, she and her husband raised eight children of their own here.

One night when Corbett was ashore on errands, Mrs. Corbett heard a knocking at the door. A weak voice asked to be let in from the storm. He was a pilot who had been guiding a vessel from St. John, Nova Scotia, to the entrance of Cutler Harbor. There he had left the vessel to go on its way, while he took a dory to row ashore into Cutler. On the way, the wind shifted to the north and began to blow hard, so he could make very little progress against it. Spray soaked him and his boat. He began to freeze before he made it ashore to the island where the light shone. He said that when he clambered ashore, his hands were practically frozen to the oars. Mrs. Corbett took him in, put the pilot to bed, and nursed him back to strength.

There are two unmarked graves on the island, presumably sailors who perished and whose bodies were washed ashore and given burial there. There are no records of who they were, whence they came, or when they died.

The light was unmanned in 1975 and the old fog bell is on display in nearby Cutler, Maine. In 1980, the Fresnel lens was removed and the light was replaced by one mounted on a skeleton tower. Neglected, the property deteriorated, although some concerned residents of the area did occasional painting and repairs. In 1998, a nonprofit group called Maine Preservation added Little River Light to its list as one of the most endangered historic properties in Maine. In 2000, the property was leased by the American Lighthouse Foundation, which hopes to eventually restore all the buildings. That summer, the wooden walkway from the boathouse to the lighthouse was completely rebuilt by the Coast Guard, with financial help from the Foundation. And in October 2001, the lighthouse was officially relit after being dark for twenty-six years.

Lesser Lights Down East

Baker Island Light

Baker Island Light marks the entrance to Frenchman Bay. This is a light with handsome views to the skyline of Acadia National Park and the coast, and is a popular picnic spot in summer.

The light stands atop a stone tower, 105 feet above high water. It was built by order of President John Quincy Adams in 1828, one year after Matinicus Rock and one year before the light at Cape Elizabeth. To the sailor, its prime purpose is a warning of the many shoals and the sandbar that runs between Baker Island and Little Cranberry Island. Because there were so many wrecks hereabouts, the Coast Guard established a lifesaving station on Cranberry Island.

This light was manned for 138 years, from 1828 until 1966, when it was automated. The lens from the old light is on display at the Fisherman's Museum at Pemaquid Light.

Built in 1828, Baker Island Light rises 105 feet. With Mount Desert in the background, the light marks the western approach to Frenchman Bay. Gannett file photo.

Bear Island Light

Bear Island is joined to the mainland by a mudflat and there is too little water in that passage for good-size boats. The light marks the entrance into Northeast Harbor. It was a family light, built in 1839 under President Martin Van Buren, the same year as Eagle Island and Saddleback Ledge Lights, and was rebuilt in 1889 under President Benjamin Harrison.

A coaling station and a buoy repair and repainting depot were established here. So it became a busy place, manned by several men to re-coal the tenders working this region and to maintain the buoys brought in for repair and painting.

The light was automated in 1981. It is an important mark for the hundreds of pleasure craft coming in and out of Northeast Harbor every summer.

Built in 1839, Bear Island Light, off Northeast Harbor, was a favorite family station until automated in 1981. Gannett file photo.

Egg Rock Light

This light is built on a mass of ledges to the eastward of Mt. Desert Island, which is still a good fishing ground for vacationers. Steer a course northwest-by-north from the light and it'll take you into Bar Harbor.

This is an odd-looking light, with the tower built upon the roof of the old keeper's house. It was built in 1875 under President Ulysses S. Grant, and was unmanned and automated in 1966. Today a boathouse, oil house, and generator house still stand along with the lighthouse. Closed to the public, Egg Rock Light is passed by many tour boats and whale watches leaving Bar Harbor. The light remains an active aid to navigation and is managed by the Petit Manan National Wildlife Refuge.

Winter Harbor Light ————————————————

Built in 1856 under President Franklin Pierce, Winter Harbor Light was built to mark the entrance into a once-favorite, almost-landlocked harbor. When eastern Maine was a very busy place for coasting vessels, this harbor was filled to overcrowding on stormy nights.

In an economic move during the Great Depression, the lights at Winter Harbor and at Pumpkin Island in Eggemoggin Reach were sold at auction by the government to the highest bidder. Mr. George Harmon of Bar Harbor bought both of them. This has not been a functioning light for more than fifty years. Now privately owned, the station is not open to the public and is best seen from a boat.

Winter Harbor Light on Mark Island, near Bar Harbor, was built in 1856 and deactivated in 1933. Today, it is privately owned and not open to the public. Gannett file photo.

Prospect Harbor Point Light ——————————————

This light was built in 1850, rebuilt in the 1890s, unmanned in the 1930s, and automated in 1951. Prospect Harbor has been a busy fishing harbor since the mid-nineteenth century and was much used by coasting schooners. The light on a white tower stands on the eastern side of the inner harbor.

Today the light is on the property of the U.S. Navy, though it remains an active aid to navigation. The keeper's house is used as a recreational facility for Navy personnel and sometimes is used for overnight stays by active and retired military families. In recent years however, there has been ghostly activity in the building. A statue of a sea captain seems to change positions by itself, and some guests claim to have seen or heard a ghost at night.

Emms Rock Light

This is a twenty-eight-foot stone light at the east end of Moosabec Reach, between Beals Island and Jonesport. Emms Rock is an active aid to navigation and is solar-powered.

Dog Island Light

Dog Island Light has two minor claims to fame, even though it is only a skeleton tower thirty-two feet high on the riverbank on the eastern side of Eastport. It is one of the most northern lights in the United States, and is located at the site of Old Sow, considered by the Coast Guard to be the second-largest whirlpool in the world. The light was built in 1919 and rebuilt in 1977.

Lubec Channel Light

Lubec was for many years a town that lived by sardines. Canneries stood shoulder to shoulder along its waterfront. The town echoed with the sound of factory sirens summoning extra workers to cut and fillet the newly arrived catch, and pack the little fishes into millions of tin cans, headed for lunch buckets around the world.

Consequently, the traffic east and west through Lubec Narrows was heavy and constant. Those ships always faced near-disaster from the shallows that reached far out, close to the shipping channel.

Responding to demand, the Lighthouse Board, in 1889, under President Benjamin Harrison, built a kind of caisson light at the harbor's western entrance. It is a white conical tower shaped like a cylinder, standing fifty-three feet high out of a rock foundation. The bottom part is iron, sunk on rock, and the top part is made from brick, painted white. This was a stag station, with no room for a family, for it is a mere tower. It was kept by part-time bachelors for forty-nine years.

After an oil fire broke out in 1939, asphyxiating the keeper on duty, the light was automated; and in 1968, the old Fresnel lens was replaced by a modern optic.

A $700,000 renovation in 1992 restored Lubec Channel Light to its best condition in decades. Over time, the lighthouse had begun to tilt slightly, so part of the renovation was stabilizing the foundation. New plates were installed on the caisson and 200 cubic yards of concrete was pumped in. Twelve piles were then driven through the caisson into the bedrock. One of the piles was driven 149 feet. The lighthouse still tilts six degrees, but is considered stable.

Keeper Elson Small was at Lubec Channel Light in the 1920s, and his wife Connie Small's book *The Lighthouse Keeper's Wife* includes memories of the station. So, when the U.S. Coast Guard repainted the lighthouse in 2001, they honored Small by painting "Connie Small was here" on the tower.

Whitlock's Mill Light

At its beginning in 1892, the light on the southern or American side of the Calais River was nothing more than a lantern hung from a tree. It served the needs of its time. But as more shipping went farther upriver, there were complaints about the light. In 1910, a more permanent structure was built to house the light. It is the northernmost light in the United States and is one of Maine's youngest lighthouses.

The new lighthouse was named for Mr. Whitlock, who owned a nearby mill and had tended the original lantern. It had a fourth-order Fresnel lens and flashed a green light. The interior of the 32-foot lighthouse is lined with white ceramic tile—among New England's lighthouses, Rockland Breakwater Light was the only other to be lined with tiles.

Whitlock's Mill Light was automated in 1969 and the Fresnel lens was removed. Though it remains an active navigational aid, the light is not open to the public. The property is owned and maintained by the St. Croix Historical Society.

First Cousins to Lighthouses

Portland Lightships
Buoys
Fog Signals
Keepers of the Lights
Chronological Listing of Lights

Portland Lightships

Once there were 122 lightships in the United States. Today there are none. The era of stalwart lightships is gone forever. Yet the memory, the nostalgia, and the love of lightships live on.

Lightships live in the long memories of old immigrants heading from Europe to a new life in the New World. The first foretaste of their new world was the lightship that signaled they were at long last coming to their American harbor. Lightships live in the memories of mariners, to whom these special marks signaled the safe end of a long voyage. And lightships live in the memories—not always fond ones—of the men who served aboard these bouncing tethered sentinels of our coast.

Portland had a series of four lightships for seventy-two years, from 1903 until 1975, when the last *Portland* lightship was replaced by an automated, crewless, large navigational buoy.

Portland's first lightship came on station March 7, 1903, anchored in seabed selected by divers six miles east-southeast of Cape Elizabeth. This lightship, Number 74 in the annals of the Lighthouse Service, was three years late in reporting for duty. This delay was due, first, to delays in the shipyard that built her, the Parkersburg Iron Works in Virginia, and second, because no sooner had she been launched than she went hard aground in the James River.

The shipyard, however, was proud of the vessel it had built. Her keel was made from seasoned white oak, her planking was of seasoned, five-inch yellow pine, and her two masts were made of steel. She came on station under the command of Captain John E. Ladd. The mate was Thomas Ingersoll, a native of Portland. Captain Ladd commanded the vessel for twelve long years, until 1915. He reported that the small, round-bottomed ship was a devil for rolling as she lay anchored in 150 feet of water on the approach to Casco Bay. It was an isolated job for Ladd and his crew. Even though they were only six miles from Portland, there was no communication by radio or telephone. They might see Portland, but they never knew what was happening there or elsewhere in the world unless a lobsterboat came alongside and hurled aboard some out-of-date copies of the Portland newspapers. When that happened, the rush for the papers was something like a stampede, and more than once the papers got kicked overboard.

The staunch wooden vessel did her duty ably for twenty-eight years. Seven years after she had come on station, her name was changed from the original *Cape Elizabeth* to *Portland*, which since 1910 had been emblazoned in huge white letters on the red hulls of every lightship stationed there.

Portland's first lightship saw her full share of storms, fog, foul and fair weather, plus the occasional excitement of fire and rescue at sea, and the comings and goings of merchantmen, troop carriers, and U.S. Navy warships to Casco Bay during World War I.

In 1918, the schooner *James Young*, bound for Boothbay Harbor from New Jersey with a cargo of coal, was dismasted ten miles southeast of the lightship in a terrible storm. The seas that tore out her masts also dislodged her galley stove and set the ship afire. The four men aboard managed to get off in the lifeboat and, through the raging seas, make the trip to the lightship, which hauled them aboard and resuscitated them. When the storm had passed, a sub-chaser operating off Portland Head took them to the city.

Edwin L. Eaton knew the *Portland* lightship, old No. 74, too well. He served aboard as chief engineer for more than fifteen years. Long after his retirement, his memories of the *Portland* were still fresh. He gave the following interview to Robert Sterling, assistant keeper of Portland Head Light. Sterling used a lengthier version in his excellent book, *Lighthouses of the Coast of Maine and the Men Who Kept Them.*

> She broke away from her moorings twice while I was on the lightship. It stormed on the morning of February 12, 1912, and kept blowing hard until the night of the 15th. Boy, wasn't it a corker! Those big combers would come at you like a ton of bricks. One sea swept over the vessel from stem to stern and took everything with it.
>
> We steamed ahead all the time so as to take what pressure we could off the chain and anchors. But she was dancing around so, and surging back and forth, that in some way the anchor chain shackle unshipped. So we raised sail and worked her into Portland. I tell you they were some surprised to see us in the harbor with no orders ... We got a new anchor and chain and were soon back on our station.

Eaton remembered another time the *Portland* lost her mooring anchor:

> That was during a mull fog. The old twelve-inch fog whistle aboard had been hammering away for twenty-four hours. How long we had been adrift I could not say, but when the fog lifted, there were scores of fishing vessels around us. We dropped a spare anchor near Cashes Ledge.

Well, to see a lightship anchored off Cashes Ledge with the name *Portland* on her sides had the old skippers guessing! One old feller in a Gloucester vessel stood down to us and shouted, "Where the hell am I?" The old lightship had got them all guessing and I would bet there was a fleet of 25 fishing boats, standing back and forth, terrible confused. I saw one of the crew on a fishing boat run into the after-cabin and come back up the companionway with a chart in his hand. He laid it on top of the cabin and would look at the chart, and then at the lightship, and then back to the chart, seeing where the Portland Lightship was supposed to be anchored.

Eaton spoke about the life aboard:

I had an idea it must be terrible lonesome aboard one of them critters, but I had to go and find out and I did ... There is plenty to do to take up your mind, working on the upkeep of the ship ... As far as machinery goes, I had plenty to do keeping that in good running order.

Of course, you take them young fellows that never went to sea and don't know what it is to look death in the face, it comes pretty hard for them. I have seen boys or young men come on there and after a few days when the newness had worn off they would be thinking of home and mother. I would find them pacing the deck and looking inshore ... I used to try and console them. Sometimes I could and a great many times I couldn't. I have seen many of them go ashore for their first leave after a month, and never come back, like the old maid's tomcat ... When the tenders would come out to water us up or to coal the ship, they would bring our mail, and then those boys—Barnum never put on a better circus.

Eaton remembered the wartime days before he retired in 1918:

The most heartaching scene I ever witnessed was in those war days. Everybody was looking for a German submarine to blow us up most any time. These young Naval Reserve boys who came out to the vessel as wireless operators needed the sympathy of everybody. Some of them had never been at sea and when it came on an easterly, and a storm would make up, many a boy never left his bunk, he was so seasick and so scared ... I know I am safer on the old ship than trying to get across Congress Street in Portland on a Saturday afternoon. If there was any dodging to be done, we at least had plenty of searoom to do it in, and no traffic cop's whistle to get me excited.

But that old lightship was a terrible roller. During a storm of great intensity she would shiver and shake when the big seas struck, but she would always come out of those loon dives and again sit just as pretty on the water as a swan.

After twenty-eight years of buffeting by the North Atlantic, Number 74 was honorably retired to easier duty in 1931. Old 74 was a "coal-eater."

Steam-powered, her two boilers carried a hundred pounds per square inch, feeding a compound reciprocal engine with cylinder diameters of fifteen and thirty inches with a common stroke of twenty-two inches. She had to keep her boilers hot at all times for what used to be known as "open roadstead steam." This meant she burned a lot of coal—about seventy-five tons every two months. Resupplying her meant using either a large coal tender or taking the lightship off station and back into harbor for coaling. The wooden vessel was replaced by one with an iron hull, Number 90, 130 feet long.

She came with a big-port, big-city record. Number 90 had been the *Ambrose* lightship, operating for many years off New York Harbor, and before that at Cape May, New Jersey. Yet Number 90 was not a stranger to Maine. She had been here as a replacement for old Number 74 back in 1926, when the *Portland* vessel went in for biennial overhaul.

So Number 90 was by no means a new vessel. When she came to become the *Portland*, she was already twenty-three years old. She had been launched in 1908 as a coal burner and was converted to oil-steam in 1936, five years after becoming the *Portland*.

This was the year in which Number 90 had a close call with collision. On January 24, 1936, the four-masted lumber schooner *Alvena*, running light out of Portland on a return trip to Florida, was passing close by the lightship. Just then a strong gust of wind out of the northwest blew down upon her and swung her stern crashing into the lightship, hitting it near the port bow. The jolt broke loose the heavy spare anchor of the lightship, which went crashing down onto the *Alvena*'s quarterdeck, splintering her rails and breaking some of her planking. The damaged *Alvena* hove to off Halfway Rock for inspection, and then headed back into Portland Harbor for repairs.

After Pearl Harbor was bombed and the United States entered World War II, most navigation aids along the coast were extinguished. The *Portland* lightship was ordered to Key West, Florida, to join the Atlantic Coastal Defense Squadron. There she saw duty for more than three years.

In the summer of 1945, the *Portland* lightship came home under the command of Captain Asbury Hanna, a native Mainer from Round Pond. En route back home, Number 90 was assigned temporary duty as relief lightship at Chelsea, Massachusetts.

While Number 90 had been away from Portland, her replacement in Casco Bay was Number 112, the largest lightship in the world.

Portland during World War II was a major jumping-off place for some of the biggest convoys crossing the North Atlantic. Thanks to the huge natural harbor, more than eighty vessels and their escort warships were frequently in Portland Harbor. The job of Lightship 112 during those years was to act as a harbor control and examination ship, and she was generally stationed just outside the submarine net that stretched across the entrance to Portland Harbor to prevent enemy submarines from sneaking inside. After the war, Number 112 returned to her regular lightship duties as the Nantucket Shoals lightship.

Two years after the *Portland*—Number 90—was back on her home station, she was nearly finished in the terrible storm of March 4, 1947, the storm that shipwrecked the collier *Oakley L. Alexander* off Two Lights at Cape Elizabeth. The 80-mile-per-hour gale winds and 25-foot seas finally snapped her six hundred feet of anchor chains after hours of bucking.

When the crew tried to get the engines started, the crankshaft bent and left the vessel helpless and without power in the mountainous waves. The spare anchor was thrown over and together with the broken anchor chain, weighing tons, they served as a brake, or sea anchor, against the storm. Even so, the lightship was blown four miles off station and almost came to her death on Old Anthony Rock. Near those ledges she was rescued by the Coast Guard tender *Cowslip*, as the lightship was being blown fast toward the rocks and lighthouse at Cape Elizabeth.

The wild storm kept blowing with such strength that it was three days before the lightship could be safely towed into South Portland Coast Guard Station for repairs. Captain Hanna said this was the worst storm he had seen in forty years at sea, twenty-one of them on the *Portland* lightship. Hanna was on the bridge, without sleep, for seventy-two hours. Half of his fourteen-man crew was too seasick to work; the other seven worked three days and nights. A relief lightship from Boston took over the station while Number 90 was undergoing repairs.

Perhaps the worst fright in her life came to Number 90 just a year later, when she was rammed by the 487-foot Canadian tanker *Rincon Hills*, inbound with 116,000 barrels of Venezuelan crude for the Portland Pipeline. At 2 a.m. Friday, March 12, 1948, the big tanker hove to off the lightship, waiting for daylight. For some reason, her engines failed and could not hold her when a heavy wind and sea began to blow the tanker down upon the lightship in the darkness.

God was with the lightship that night. The tanker, almost four times the length and many times the weight of the lightship, struck only a glancing blow. It ripped a gash in the starboard bow eight inches deep and six feet long, mostly above the waterline. Almost no damage was suffered by the tanker, which unloaded its 116,000 barrels of crude oil at the Portland Pipeline later the same Friday, and then sailed at noon Saturday for Aruba and a new cargo of oil.

Eight months later, the *Portland* lightship was hit again, but this time it was not Number 90. She was in port for maintenance and had been relieved on station by relief Lightship 106. The weird accident occurred in daylight, with calm seas and clear visibility, on a peaceful Sunday afternoon. It was due entirely to gross human error by a helmsman who lost his head.

The Navy patrol boat PCE 851, attached to Portland Navy Reserve Training Center, was returning from Boston. The patrol boat passed 440 yards east of the lightship, then turned left to enter the shipping channel—but swung much too far to the left. The officer on the bridge, Lieutenant William P. Cline, USN, called for immediate correction, ordering hard right rudder and hard right turn.

The helmsman lost his head and performed the reverse—swinging the vessel yet more to the left, heading straight for the lightship. A petty officer jumped to the helm, threw off the befuddled helmsman, and frantically turned the wheel. But it was too late, even though the Navy ship now had both engines in full reverse. The patrol vessel crashed into the lightship at twelve knots.

The lightship, under the temporary command of BMC Malcolm Wood, had a crew of twelve aboard. The patrol boat had 851 aboard, plus twenty in regular Navy crew.

The prow of the Navy ship cut a long vertical gash in the lightship's port quarter. Luckily, the blow came at a rib where two steel plates overlapped and were further strengthened by rivets. "If the blow had come one foot away, on one side or the other, the ship's hull would have been cut through as if by a can opener," said crewman Harry Hawes, who had just left his bunk in the spot where the blow fell.

Lightship Number 89 came from Boston to act as relief, while the lightship already on temporary duty was sent to drydock.

A great storm on January 17, 1950, with winds clocked at more than eighty-three miles per hour, blew the *Portland* lightship three hundred yards off station (the ship number was 90 again), and thirty-foot waves swept her decks. That night, Number 90 extinguished her lights in accordance with Coast Guard regulations that any lightship off station shall not show her lights. But old Number 90 was back on station and secure by 8 a.m. January 19, and her lights were once again shining.

By 1952, Number 90 was forty-four years old. She had had a hard life. The time for her decommissioning had arrived. As Number 90 left her Portland station after twenty-two years of duty here, her replacement was a Maine-built ship, Lightship Number 111 (or WAL 533 under the new Coast Guard numbering system, which started when the Coast Guard took over lightships, lighthouses, and buoys from the old Lighthouse Service).

The new lightship in Portland had been built by Bath Iron Works. It, too, had seen big-city service earlier, having served as the *Ambrose* lightship outside New York Harbor. She was 132 feet long, 30 feet in beam, powered by 450 horsepower, 780-ton displacement, and made 8 knots. According to the well-laid plans of the Coast Guard, this was supposed to be the last lightship in Portland. All lightships, except for two, had already been replaced by automated buoys. But like so many well-laid plans, this, too, was not to work out.

This Bath-built lightship did duty in Portland from 1952 until 1969. In those seventeen years, she and her crew weathered their share of bad storms, thick fogs, and near misses. They lived through weeks of uneventful boredom, with little to do more exciting than fighting rust and corrosion, painting decks and topsides, polishing brass, and oiling machinery. Probably a million cups of coffee were consumed aboard during those years, and crewmen tried every bait known to mankind to catch the fish of Casco Bay. From time to time, the lightship left station for repairs and overhaul, turning over her duties to a replacement from Boston.

A severe gale in November 1955 broke her primary anchor chain and sent her ashore for a new chain and a new anchor. The cost of her new 7,000-pound mushroom anchor and 15 tons of new chain exceeded $10,000 in 1955. Divers searched in vain to recover the lost anchor and chain, though they knew they had been lost in a small, well-defined area of sea bottom. They did, however, find six hundred feet of old chain lost in a storm twenty years earlier. The commander of the Coast Guard station, Harry Stimpson, speculated the gear might have been lost in a deep hole, where there is 243 feet of water.

Her replacement faced a long journey from San Francisco. The new *Portland* lightship, a chipper twenty-one-year-old, had been built in Curtis Bay, Maryland, in 1950. She was 128 feet long, with a 30-foot beam and a draft of 11 feet, with a displacement of 600 tons. Her diesel engine could make no more than 11 knots, so the trip from San Francisco was a lengthy one. However, with fuel storage for 94,500 gallons, she could travel the distance without refueling.

After duty as the *San Francisco* lightship, she was being replaced there with a massive, million-dollar unmanned sea buoy.

Her trip, which began on June 26, 1971, had its bad moments. One day out from San Francisco, there was a burial at sea—not for a casualty of this trip, but for her former captain, Lieutenant Commander William A. Little, who had died ashore but had requested a ceremonial burial at sea by the Coast Guard in which he had served.

By July 4, the vessel was in the resort of Acapulco, Mexico, and

After 72 years, the *Portland* lightship era ended in 1975. Its duties are now performed by an automated navigational buoy. Gannett file photo.

celebrated Independence Day there. But on July 7, she lost a vital nut from her single-screw propeller, and that left her drifting helpless in high winds and big seas along the Mexican coast. A Mexican minesweeper came to her rescue and towed the lightship into the port of Salinas Cruz, on the Mexico-Guatemala border. There she stayed for three weeks, until a U.S. Navy ship towed her to Panama for repairs.

One incident on the voyage troubled superstitious members of the crew. They sighted an albatross, symbol to mariners of bad luck. But this huge oceanic bird, which seldom comes close to land, was hitchhiking aboard the back of a giant sea turtle.

The new *Portland* lightship served until February 1975, when she was replaced with a huge automated buoy.

Built by Bath Iron Works at a cost of more than half a million dollars, the LNB (large navigational buoy) does the job that lightships did for seventy-two years, and does it at a fraction of the cost. No longer must a fourteen-man crew be fed, housed, given shore leave, rotated, and relieved. No longer must a lightship be chipped and painted constantly. Even the initial cost of an automated buoy is millions less than the cost of a new lightship.

The new automated buoy weighed 104 tons, its deck was 40 feet in diameter, and its tower stood more than 40 feet above the water, capped by a 7,500-candlepower light, fog signal, and radio beacon. Beneath the deck are eighteen compartments entered through a hatch on deck. One major compartment houses the generator, the only mechanical sound in the sterile, unheated interior of this buoy. A second major compartment houses a standby generator. Each is air-cooled and runs on 3.5 kilowatts. The third and largest compartment, about seven by fifteen feet, contains sophisticated electronic equipment. In a box that looks like a medicine cabinet is the heart of the buoy—the link equipment that checks and measures every function performed by the other equipment on board.

Every five minutes, automatically, the shore station asks this monitor in the buoy, "Is everything functioning properly?" The buoy monitor then answers back, "Everything performing OK." If any part is malfunctioning, the buoy monitor names the part and informs the shore station.

An important function is the buoy's work as a homing beacon for shipping. The system contains a six-minute radio beacon sequence for the coast of Maine. On the first minute, Mount Desert radio beacon transmits its signal; on the second minute, Matinicus Rock Station comes in; on the third, Manana Island at Monhegan; on the fourth

Portland's Large Navigational Buoy is towed out to its duty station. This hundred-ton marvel is the automated replacement of the well-loved lightships. Gannett file photo.

minute, Halfway Rock; the fifth minute is for Eastern Point Light Station near Cape Ann, Massachusetts; and the sixth and final minute is reserved for the Portland LNB.

Another gray box contains the power-distribution panel for everything aboard. Near it is the foghorn equipment, battery-operated. If the power fails, the battery will power the foghorn for eight days and nights so ships eight miles distant can hear it. LNB foghorns often last three years. The closed equipment boxes are filled with nitrogen, a gas that helps prevent corrosion. Each compartment also contains its own flood detection and warning system. Deeper under the deck are compartments for ballast and others for a two-year supply of diesel fuel for running the generators.

Last but far from least is the vital box in the main hatchway, at the base of a ten-foot ladder. This contains the gas detector. Every time a man enters any of the compartments, he must first check the poisonous gas detector, which will give warning if there are any poisonous gases escaping from the generator, the batteries, the wiring, or any other equipment.

This complex, compact replacement for the manned lightship can do everything the lightship used to do. Though it cannot relay detailed weather reports to the National Weather Service, the space-age LNB records wind direction and velocity, as well as wave height and water temperature.

When the *Portland* lightship was replaced by the LNB, she had been one of only three remaining lightships in the nation. A month or so after the Portland lightship went off station for the final time, the Boston lightship was replaced by an LNB as well. That left only one lightship in the United States—the lightship at Nantucket. That is where the Portland lightship was sent for her final duty. On December 20, 1983, the lightship at Nantucket was replaced by an LNB, and the last stalwart lightship, which had seen duty as the *Ambrose*, the *Portland*, and the *Nantucket*, went off station. She was dispatched to drug-patrol duty in the Caribbean.

So ended the 154-year-long era of American lightships, which had begun in 1829 when the first American lightship—an old hulk, with lanterns hanging from her masts—had been anchored off Newport News in the Chesapeake Bay.

Buoys

Buoys are kissing cousins to lighthouses. But they are far smaller and there are many times more of them. In this First Coast Guard District, between Boston and the Canadian border, there are nearly three thousand buoys. Some are lighted, some have gongs, some are black, some are red, some have horizontal stripes, some have vertical stripes, some are pointed at the top, some are flat-headed, most are numbered, but some are numberless.

Buoys are road signs for boats, just as traffic lights, curve signs, danger ahead signs, and speed limit signs are for cars. All coastal shipping, from the smallest boat to the largest vessel, relies on buoys. So they must stay on station, doing their duty day and night, year-round, despite all the torments that natural forces of waves and wind heap upon them.

Buoys speak a language to boatmen far more detailed and more informative than landlubbers might guess. By their information, a foreign ship, with no knowledge of the local water, can be guided safely into harbor.

Buoys began when the nation began. President George Washington approved $264 to build a buoy for the Delaware. An act of 1797 provided for sixteen buoys in Boston Harbor. In 1843, all buoys on the Maine and Massachusetts coasts were spar buoys, painted black, white, and red, but without any system. They spoke no true language, and provided little information.

But in 1850, Congress passed a law requiring that buoys be colored and numbered. Since then, any vessel will invariably find red buoys with even numbers on the starboard or right side when entering a harbor. (Seamen have an alliterative phrase: "Red Right Returning.") Black buoys with odd numbers are always on the port or left side. The safe channel is to pass between, leaving red to right, black to left on entering, and the opposite on departing harbor.

But there are buoys without numbers, too. What do they mean? What do they warn against? Buoys without numbers but with horizontal stripes indicate rocks underneath—they may be passed on either side. Other numberless buoys are painted with black and white vertical stripes. These are mid-channel markers and again may be passed on either side, close-to.

Still other buoys are fitted with perches, cages, even signposts, and these mark abrupt turns in the channel or other obstructions.

Buoys are of different shapes, and this helps mariners even when the numbers on the buoy cannot be read. There are nun buoys and can buoys. The nun buoys are conical in shape and the can buoys have flat tops.

A vessel coming in from the sea leaves the nun buoys with pointed tops (and usually painted red) on the right-hand side and black, flat-topped buoys on the left-hand side. To give warning in fog and at night, many buoys are fitted with lights, bells, and whistles, so they can be heard if not seen. Bell buoys started about 1855; whistling buoys were invented in 1876 by J.M. Courtenay. Gas-lighted buoys came first to New York Bay in 1882. By 1910, lighted buoys, operated by compressed acetylene gas, came into many major harbors.

The action of waves triggers the bells on bell buoys. Their sound can be helpful, but often in fog there are no waves, so no sound is made.

Whistling buoys also get their power through wave action. When a wave lifts the buoy, it sucks in air, and then expels it with a whistle as the buoy drops down in the trough. Lighted buoys are triggered by the rising and the setting of the sun.

Buoys are far bigger than the part you can see. The biggest are more than sixty feet long and weigh over seventeen tons. Most of the regular buoys weigh between four and eight thousand pounds. Coast Guard tenders equipped with strong derricks and winches lift these buoys out once a year, take them ashore for overhaul, and replace them immediately with freshly painted, recently overhauled buoys. With about ten thousand buoys in the United States, this keeps the Coast Guard busy. No other nation has as many buoys as the United States.

A cannonball is attached under the exposed part of the buoy so it floats more or less upright. Without this weight, the buoys might topple over, and lie flat and invisible in seas or winds. Huge chains and vast anchors are used to hold buoys in place and on station. Often storms move them hundreds of feet off station, to the bewilderment—and sometimes the danger—of ships.

Gales and high seas have swept buoys away completely. Some from New England have been found weeks later on the coast of Ireland.

Fog Signals

New England leads the nation in the amount of fog, so New England led the nation with the first fog signal. Fittingly, the first fog signal was mounted by the first lighthouse, which was Boston Light. The fog signal was a gun, mounted there in 1719. The light was first lit in 1716 and the fog cannon came three years afterward, when the third lightkeeper was in charge (the first two having drowned). His name was John Hayes, and in June 1719 he asked the Boston merchants that "a great gun may be placed on the island to answer Ships in a Fogg."

The cannon was probably taken from defenses on Long Island and moved to Little Brewster Island. The cannon has long since been removed and now serves silently as a monument at the Coast Guard Academy in New London, Connecticut. The date engraved on its barrel is 1700.

I am oddly moved by the simple words of Captain John Hayes asking the Boston merchants "for a great gun to answer Ships in a Fogg." Hayes had long been a mariner himself in the days before there was a light—let alone a fog signal—at Boston Harbor. I feel a kinship with Hayes, who must have often lost his way in dense fog. It is not easy to convey to a landsman the eerie feeling of a mariner totally lost and disoriented in fog. It is not easy for boatmen today, with radar and loran or even more simple radio direction finders, to understand the total sense of disorientation that comes from being lost in thick fog.

It has happened too often to me in a small boat, and it is always frightening. Dense fog blots out all sight to the point where you cannot see the water under your boat, nor the bow of your boat, nor the stern of your boat. The sensation must be close to sudden blindness. This loss of being able to see anything leads to other losses. Your ears strain to hear something as they never strain when your eyes can see something. Most ears are unused to such intensive detective work.

Mine tense up and respond badly. I hear sounds from somewhere out in that fog and they are sounds I cannot categorize, sounds I cannot locate with certainty—for the sounds move and change and vanish. I know where I was on the chart when the fog came down; I know where

I am heading, thanks to my compass. But the lack of vision, the tricks played by my ears now induce tricks upon my brain.

My brain begins to feel a tiny doubt about my compass, to wonder if it is correct. It induces a stain of fear that the tide or wind may be setting my boat off from its compass course and that I may be heading toward a ledge just to the right (or left) of my plotted course. I have learned to acknowledge that fog distorts my brain, so I have installed two compasses close to each other, to offset the crazy thought that my compass is not telling me the truth. When two compasses tell me the same story, I am inclined to believe them rather than the idiotic whisperings in my ear.

These confessions make me sound like a blathering idiot in thick fog. That, I think, is an exaggeration, because to date we have never hit anything nor been hit by anyone. We have eventually gotten to our destination every time. But fog does take a heavy toll on mariners, at least on this one. After I have done a few hours at the helm running a fog course, and get to my destination, I feel exhausted in eyes, ears, brain, and legs. I admit these failings, because they are what gives me that feeling of kinship with John Hayes, mariner-keeper of the Boston Light, when more than 280 years ago he asked for a gun to signal ships in the fog.

In thick fog, a million-watt light won't help direct your boat any more than a tallow candle. You can't see either one. That is why Hayes wanted his gun, so that a fog-blinded ship could find its way to safety by following sound instead of light.

But it turns out that sound can be totally misleading.

Lots of people blame this on fog. They say that fog distorts sound; that fog kills sound, or deadens it; that fog can distort the direction of sound, because fog is so thick it can echo or deflect sound. Maybe there is a grain of truth in such allegations. But the basic fact seems to be that sound is not a reliable guide, even on a clear day or night.

Begin with a few commonplace events on dry land. You come home from work and shout, "Hi! Anybody home?" You get an answer back from your wife or child. Then the next question you shout is, "Where are you?" You need to know whether they are upstairs, downstairs, and in which room—because simply by hearing their voice once, you cannot tell their location.

Try this experiment with your dog. When the dog is sleeping, call its name. The wakening dog will recognize your voice. But the dog cannot tell where you are. The dog may jump up, but may run in different directions for a moment or two, until sight or scent plus ears point the dog so it comes bounding to you.

Take another situation: You are out walking or hunting in the woods with a friend, and you separate. You do not go far from each other. But as it grows dark, you want to meet, join up, and walk out of the woods together. So you shout back and forth to each other. You move in the general direction of each other's sounds. But each of you must keep repeating your shout back and forth, so each of you can keep correcting your course until you finally come together.

It is not only human ears that are imprecise. Startle a deer, or even a squirrel, as you walk through the woods. Up goes the head at the noise of your approach. But then the head turns in different directions, picking up smell or sight or more noise, before the deer or squirrel is certain about the precise spot where you are.

So ears are not very reliable guides to direction under the best of circumstances. In fog on the water, straining to hear a fog signal, they can be worse.

Like most seamen, I have been steering correctly toward a fog signal and hearing it clearly, seeming to hear it sound louder and louder as I steered closer and closer. Then suddenly I could not hear it at all anymore. The easy conclusion is to blame myself. I must have lost direction, because the fog signal is not moving and the fog signal has not stopped blowing. So the fault must lie in me.

This is not the case at all. Fog signals act as crazily as sailors. Time and again it has been scientifically documented that a fog signal that can be clearly heard from ten miles may not be heard at all from five miles away on the same compass course, in the same weather, on the same day. Then at three miles it might be loud and clear and at a half-mile distant, the sound may be so faint as to be inaudible. Take comfort. It is not you who is crazy, but the fog signal.

Look at the trouble the experts had with the fog signal at Whitehead Light. Whitehead, you will recall, is the light outside Tenants Harbor, Maine, at the westerly entrance to the Muscle Ridge Channel. It is venerable, ordered built by Thomas Jefferson. In 1852, it was ordered rebuilt and modernized by Millard Fillmore, thirteenth president. And soon thereafter it was a busy place, with all the granite quarrying operations going on at Dix and High islands as well as farther east on Vinalhaven.

But the fog signal was causing problems, and in 1870 the Lighthouse Board directed General Duane of the U.S. Army Corps. of Engineers to study the steam fog signals along the coast of Maine. In his report, General Duane wrote:

There are six steam fog-whistles on the coast of Maine: these have frequently been heard at a distance of twenty miles, and as frequently cannot be heard at a distance of two miles, and this with no perceptible difference in the state of the atmosphere. The signal is often heard at a great distance in one direction, while in another it will be scarcely audible at a distance of a mile. This is not the effect of wind, as the signal is frequently heard much farther against the wind than with it; for example, the whistle on Cape Elizabeth can always be heard distinctly in Portland, a distance of nine miles, during a heavy northeast snowstorm, the wind blowing a gale directly from Portland toward the whistle.

The most perplexing difficulty, however, arises from the fact that the signal often appears to be surrounded by a belt, varying in radius from one to one and a half miles, from which the sound appears to be entirely absent. Thus, in moving directly from a station, the sound is audible for the distance of a mile, then is lost for about the same distance, after which it is distinctly heard for a long time. This action is common to all ear-signals, and has been observed at times at all stations, at one of which the signal is situated on a bare rock, twenty miles from the mainland, with no surrounding objects to affect the sound.

That was part of an Army engineer's report. But the civilian scientific advisor to the Lighthouse Board made his own experiments at other fog stations and found the same kind of phenomenon.

British scientists were equally puzzled when they surveyed Whitehead fog signal, with Professor Tyndall of the British Lighthouse Board, writing:

The most conflicting results were at first obtained. On the 19th of May, 1873, the sound range was 3.5 miles; on the 20th it was 5.5 miles; on the 2nd of June, 6 miles; on the 3rd, more than 9 miles; on the 10th, 9 miles; on the 25th, 6 miles; on the 26th, 9.2 miles; on the first of July, 12.7 miles; on the 2nd, 4 miles; while on the 3rd, with clear, calm atmosphere and smooth sea, it was less than 3 miles.

Delving into these reports, which fascinated me because these experts reported bafflement just like the bafflement this seaman sometimes suffers, I came upon these comments by the assistant inspector of the Third Lighthouse District, Lt. Commander F.E. Chadwick, USN, written in the 1880s:

Fog, in my experience, is not a factor of any consequence whatever in the question of sound. Signals may be heard at great distances through the densest fogs, which may be totally inaudible in the same directions and at the same distances in the clearest atmosphere.

That fog has not great effect can be easily understood when it is known (as it certainly is known by observers) that even snow does not deaden sound. There being no condition of the atmosphere so favorable for the far reaching of sound signals as is that of a heavy northeast snowstorm, due supposedly to the homogeneity produced by the falling snow.

It seems to be well established by numerous observations that on our own northern Atlantic coasts the best possible circumstances for hearing a fog signal are in a northeast snow-storm ... The worst conditions for hearing sound seem to be found in the atmosphere of a clear, frosty morning on which a warm sun has risen and been shining two or three hours.

Here are examples of more quirky behavior by the fog signal at Whitehead.

On a night of thick fog in 1872, the steamer *City of Rockland* heard the Whitehead signal, a ten-inch steam whistle, from six miles away and continued to hear it with increasing intensity until the steamer was three miles away, when the sound suddenly ceased and was not heard again until the steamer was 440 yards from the station. It is known that the signal was operating all the time. And during the whole time, the fog-signal keeper was able to hear the sound of the steamer's six-inch whistle even when the steamer could not hear his ten-inch whistle. After getting lots of complaints of this sort, the Inspector of the First District, Commander H.F. Pickering, USN, decided to come to Maine and take a firsthand look.

He approached Whitehead from the southeast during a thick fog in July 1877, and reported that he heard the whistle from six to four miles away, then lost it completely and could hear nothing until he was within 400 yards, when the blast of the whistle hit him so hard he almost went overboard. The wind was then against the sound.

Later in September of the same year, Professor Henry, secretary of the Smithsonian Institution and the chairman of the Lighthouse Board, made a further investigation at Whitehead. They conducted their experiment in clear weather with a southwest wind of 12 mph, temperature of 67 degrees, and the barometer at 28.9. As they steamed windward away from the fog signal and as soon as they were a quarter to a half-mile distant, they lost the sound completely until they were a mile away, when it came in faintly and then continued to grow louder until they were four miles away, when they heard it with great clarity. They then reversed course and observed the same phenomenon in reverse order. For three successive days they repeated similar experiments and got similar results.

Inventors have tried hard over the years to devise a sound signal for sailors in a fog. They tried cannon, guns, sirens, trumpets, steam-whistles, bell-boats, bell-buoys, bells struck by weird Rube Goldberg machinery, rockets, and gongs.

Professor Henry tells of a huge 24-pound cannon used at San Francisco Bay in 1856–'57, that helped guide ships into harbor, day and night, in fog. The gun was fired every half-hour day and night in thick weather, except when there was not enough powder. It was an expensive business. During the second year, there were 1,582 discharges. A gun was also tried at West Quoddy Head, Maine, far down east. It was a cannonade, five feet long, with a $5^1/2$-inch bore and charged with four pounds of powder.

The gun was fired on foggy days when the Boston steamer was approaching from St. John, and the man at the gun was able to hear the steamer's fog whistle. He usually heard the ship's whistle when she was six miles away, and he began loading and firing as fast as he could manage. "But the signal was abandoned," wrote Professor Henry, "because of the danger attending its use and the brief duration of its sound, which renders it difficult to determine its direction with accuracy."

The United States tried bells instead of guns, and by 1890 there were 125 bell signals along the coast, some weighing three thousand pounds. But General Duane, the Army engineer, said they were of little use because half the time they could not be heard a mile away, even in good weather; and in rough weather, the sound of surf and waves and wind drowned out the sound of the bell entirely.

The international code of shipping then required all ships to ring bells in foggy weather. The only exception made was for Turkish ships. They were allowed to ring a gong instead, because the ringing of bells is forbidden on religious grounds to the followers of Mohammed.

A Mr. J.M. Courtney of New York made a nice pile of money from his invention of the whistling bell, an iron, pear-shaped bulb, twelve feet across at its widest part and floating twelve feet out of the water. He installed more than sixty-five of these at a price of $1,075 each during the 1880s. They helped sailors, but were a bane to anyone on shore living within earshot. Courtney's whistling buoys let out an inexpressibly mournful wail that could scare children and keep parents awake all night for miles around. General Duane, a Maine man who had a home in Portland, said he could hear the ten-inch steam whistle at Cape Elizabeth, nine miles away.

Next came the trumpet, invented by C.L. Daboll of Connecticut. It was a mammoth and weird contraption. The biggest ones had a trumpet seventeen feet long with a flaring mouth more than three feet across. Air is driven through the trumpet by hot air or machinery at a pressure of fifteen to twenty pounds, and the trumpet is capable of emitting a shriek that can be heard at a great distance for a number of seconds each minute.

After the trumpet left the scene, an ear-splitting siren took center stage after being unveiled at the Paris Exhibition in 1867. Those spectators who rallied around to see the invention never forgot its diabolical noise. After Professor Frederick Holmes of Great Britain had demonstrated his siren blast just once, the Paris authorities forbade a second performance. Yet in clear weather, the Holmes siren could carry twenty miles to sea.

By 1890, the United States had about a hundred fog signals of various types giving out shrieks along our coast. It had cost more than $600,000 to install them and more than $100,000 a year to operate them.

Maine had some of the first. The bell originally installed at West Quoddy Head in 1808 was replaced four times with different types of bells in the next thirty years. None worked very well, nor did the experimental cannon. This is an indication of the amount of materials, labor, time, and money spent to build fog-signal stations. There are more than a thousand of them along the coasts of the United States. Fog may be the worst menace to navigation in Maine—and Maine has plenty of it.

For example, one year the fog signal at Seguin blew 2,734 hours. Pity the poor keepers—that averages out to the fog signal blowing one out of every three hours for the entire year. Seguin is the second foggiest place along the coast of Maine. On average, it has fog 1,829 hours a year. The record is held by Whitehead, which takes the prize with an average of 1,920 hours of fog each year. Matinicus Rock runs in third place, averaging 1,718 hours of fog a year.

Considering the fact that between May and October, Maine offers the finest small-boat cruising in the world, these seem discouraging figures. Yet, take courage! For the entire coast of Maine, the average amount of fog is 874 hours a year, with more than half of that during the months that nobody is pleasure-cruising. Even so, that works out to thirty-six days and nights of fog in a year, with an average of fifteen of them in the summer. That is one reason why books take up more room than clothes aboard my boat, the *Steer Clear*.

There is a masochistic fascination with these fog figures. So here are a few more: The average number of fog days, taken over many years, is fifty-nine days at Eastport; forty-two at Portland; eleven at Boston; eighteen at Nantucket. Based upon figures taken at twenty-one fog stations, fog signals were in operation at the Maine stations for 1,145 hours a year; in New Hampshire, for 688 hours (a very small coastline); and in Massachusetts, 776 hours a year. Fog in Maine is a frequent companion, if seldom a friend.

Yet, as I have been writing this, I am appalled at how little I know about fog signals, even in my own back yard. After cruising the Maine coast for twenty years, I should know the distinguishing sounds of a dozen fog signals. But here I sit, wracking my memory, and I cannot with certainty sound out the signal of any fog horns—often as I have listened to them. Every time I am steering a fog course, I must refer to the chart and look up the signals, even for the most familiar horns I hope to hear.

I can tell you the bends in the road, the turns, the hills and landmarks to watch for as you drive to my house. Certainly I should be able to call off the fog signals from Manana, Pemaquid, Seguin, and so on. I cannot. Can you call off the signals in your home waters?

Of course, we have radar, radio direction finders, loran, and GPS these days to make fog less of a menace to life and ships. Yet even fifty years ago, some ships never slowed down for fog. The *Queen Mary* once reported dense fog all the way from England to New York, day and night. The captain hardly slept since leaving Cherbourg. But he docked his liner in New York only four hours late. These days a ship that is two hundred miles off our coast can get radio bearings. But only since 1931 has there been a radio beacon on *Ambrose*, in New York Harbor. Now these beacons are all along the coast. Together they have added almost two million more square miles to the area served by U.S. aids to navigation.

But after the mention of these modern aids, I will end with a story of the oldest aid, and one of the strangest, used in Camden Harbor. We have talked about the use of eyes and ears. Now it is the nose. Some sailors can use their nose and smell their way in the fog. Phil Rynes of Camden, a local lobsterman, smelled his way for years. "Phil uses his nose to navigate Penobscot Bay in thick fog," said the local legend. A few good sniffs and Rynes knew which shore of which island he was coming on.

Among old-time Maine coasters there was a saying: "The right crew for every coaster is a man, a boy, and a dog." The job of the dog in dense weather was to go forward on the bow and bark. If the boat was heading toward a cliff or high ground, the bark would bounce back as an echo, and the skipper altered course. If the boat was heading toward a flat beach, however, the skipper would get a different clue. Near a beach, there are usually houses. Where there are houses, there are dogs. And if the dogs on the beach heard another dog barking out there in the fog, they would bark right back. So when a skipper heard barking dogs, he knew he was heading too close to shore and altered course.

Keepers of the Lights

"The Keepers of the Lights"—there is a ringing majesty to that title. It tempts us to invest keepers of the lights with an aura of superhuman dedication to duty; with a special resilience to storms and loneliness and hardship; to imagine them as a breed apart, a special strain of monk, mariner, saint, and hero.

Yet of course, they were humans—men and women with clay feet, head colds, bad tempers, arthritis, with some weakness for candy, spirits, dried codfish, tobacco, or gossip. They raised children who got sick, disobeyed, and lit up their lives. They had chickens that would not lay eggs, seed that would not grow, money that ran out, and oarlocks that got lost.

The little army of men, women, and children who have been the keepers of the lights for two hundred years were commonplace people. Herein lies the fascination.

Ordinary men and women have been changed into legendary heroes and heroines, not once or twice, but hundreds of times. And this miracle has happened year after year for two centuries along our coast. Do so many ordinary human beings have this stuff of greatness born in them? Or is it the lightkeeper's job that develops these potentials? Certainly lightkeepers were not carefully selected for their sterling qualities of character. Yet the crises of their jobs transformed them at moments into human beings of unforgettable courage, who laid their lives on the line—and sometimes lost them—to save sailors and ships they never knew.

At the start, the job of lighthouse keeper was a political appointment. It was part of the spoils system, and had little to do with merit, knowledge, or training. The surprise is that anyone wanted those early jobs, and that our greatest presidents—including Washington and Jefferson—personally wrote the letters appointing the lightkeepers.

George Washington himself chose Joseph Greenleaf to be the first keeper of the Portland Head Light on January 7, 1791. It was more honor than cash for Greenleaf. The poor chap could not collect his pay for two years, a paltry $160 a year. Even then, he did not live to enjoy it long; two years later, he died on the job of a heart attack while rowing his skiff.

There is a letter in Jefferson's handwriting: "The appointment of William Holms to be the keeper of the Lighthouse at Sands Point is approved. Salary $250."

And another signed J.Q. Adams, that says: "Let John Whalton be appointed keeper of the floating lights on Carysfort Reef with a salary of $700 a year." Andrew Jackson fired lightkeepers for purely political reasons, so he could install men who would vote for him and and his party.

Abraham Lincoln abused the lightkeepers for his party's political spoils. Between 1859 and 1863, Lincoln kicked out three-quarters of all keepers so their jobs could go to men who had a political lever into the Lincoln White House. This was not the fault of Honest Abe. He was a victim of the spoils system and freely admitted it. He is reported to have said early in his term:

> I wish I could get time to attend to the Southern question ... but the office seekers demand all my time. I seem like a man so busy letting rooms in one end of his house that he has no time left to put out the fire that is burning and destroying the other end. Sitting here where all the avenues to public patronage seem to come together in a knot, it does appear to me that our people are fast approaching the point where it can be said that seven-eighths of them are trying to find out how to live at the expense of the other eighth.

The job of lighthouse keeper was certainly part of the spoils system—yet the jobs could not have been political plums because the pay was only $350 to $400 a year in Lincoln's time.

After President Garfield was assassinated by a disgruntled office-seeker, the nation tried to rid itself of the political spoils system, and in 1883, President Arthur signed the Civil Service Act. It took another thirteen years before lightkeepers were covered by these Civil Service regulations. Their jobs were removed from the spoils system and put under Civil Service, thanks to some artful backstage work by President Grover Cleveland in 1896. This got rid of the dreaded "Extinguished Service Check." This was a printed form about the size of a check. All too often it had carried, over the signature of the regional collector of revenue, this bad news:

> You are superseded as keeper of_____Light Station on (month, day, year) by_____, the bearer of this notice.

That was the brutal way lighthouse families were fired and hired too often, up until the twentieth century. In walked a new political appointee, with the Extinguished Service Check in his hand, and the old keeper, wife, and family were booted out of light and home, bag and baggage.

Most lightkeeping jobs in the year 1897 paid about a $1,000 a year, and carried no retirement or survivors' benefits. Those didn't come until 1919, won for the keepers after a hard fight by George Putnam, the Commissioner of Lighthouses. Despite low pay and few benefits, and the vicissitudes of political jobs, most keepers performed their jobs loyally.

Women became keepers after their husbands died on the job. That happened often, because the men usually had an earlier career as a mariner or fisherman. They were middle-aged or older when they became keepers. But keeping the light burning was often a husband-and-wife job; and the wife or daughter or son usually became a well-trained assistant keeper. So when the keeper died, his widow was often named to his post.

By 1830, there were women keepers in New England. By 1851, when the Lighthouse Board took over from the Treasury, the roster showed thirty widows working as lighthouse keepers. When the Civil War started, the number was down to fifteen. Thereafter, as heavy lenses, machinery for steam-driven fog horns, coal-fired boilers, internal combustion engines, and other heavy mechanical equipment came on station, the number of women keepers dropped.

The last woman keeper was Mrs. Harry Salter of Maryland, appointed by President Calvin Coolidge in 1925, to succeed her husband. She stayed on as keeper of the tiny Turkey Point Light in the Upper Chesapeake until she retired in 1948 because she found the job "too hard on the feet." Two southern women ran up records for length of time lightkeeping. One was Mrs. Maggie R. Norwell, who retired in 1932 after forty years as keeper of lights in Louisiana. Another was Mrs. Younghans who cared for the light at Biloxi, Mississippi, for fifty-one years and was succeeded by her daughter.

Lighthouses have always enjoyed the reputation of being kept "neat as a pin." This is probably due to the influence of the women who shared duties with their husbands. A district superintendent in the 1930s said:

> I know of no other branch of government service in which the wife plays such an important part. Every keeper gets a rating in part on his skill, in part on his faithfulness to duty, and in part on the cleanliness and spotlessness of his lighthouse.
>
> When I'm on an inspection trip, I can see a kitchen shining and a stove so brightly polished you'd think it was never used. But I can see a tower that needs a bit more paint, or a light that needs more polishing.

In other words, the woman is neat and the man is a bit sloppy. So I take the woman aside and compliment her on her spotless house and then say to her, "I had to speak to your husband about the way the tower looks—I know you'll jack him up." She does. And the next time I go back, everything is fine. But, if it's the other way around, I'm in a real scrape. If the man is neat and the woman is sloppy, I know the woman is boss and her husband won't dare tell her to spruce up. If I ask him to, it only gets him in bad. If I speak to her, well, that's dangerous too. In most cases, however, the man who has courage to be a lightkeeper has wit enough to pick a good housekeeper.

George R. Putnam was a high-ranking executive on the administrative side of the lighthouse fraternity. Part of his splendid service to the keepers were the books he wrote about them and their lights. His book *Lighthouses and Lightships of the United States*, published in 1917 by Houghton Mifflin, includes many stories of lightkeepers. The experiences of keepers were alike, no matter where they worked, from Portland, Maine, to Portland, Oregon. One amazing fact about these keepers is their ripe age. In 1916, when Putnam was finishing his book, there were ninety-two people in the Lighthouse Service who were seventy years old or older, and twenty-four who had served for more than forty years.

Their pay was poor and their retirement pensions did not exist. Yet these men grew so accustomed to their life and their lights that they stayed on the job for a lifetime. As to pay, the average salary was fixed by law in 1867 to not exceed $600, and that was not changed until after the United States entered World War I. The top pay, sometimes reaching $1,000, went to the keepers of the remote offshore lights, while part-time keepers of post lights along inland rivers earned only $10 a month. When Putnam was writing in 1917, the nation's lightkeepers received no pension on account of age, long service, or disability resulting from their work.

A few keepers wrote to the secretary of the Treasury or to the head of the Lighthouse Service, asking for more money. One was a keeper of the Gay Head Light in Massachusetts, with the remarkable name of Ebenezer Skiff. He wrote to Albert Gallatin—a secretary of the Treasury who admired lightkeepers—and Skiff won a raise of fifty dollars more a year. President Jefferson himself approved increasing Skiff's annual salary to $250.

Ten years later, in 1810, Skiff wrote again to his boss, now the Commissioner of Revenue, and again asked for more money. Skiff wrote a colorful letter, reciting the plights of a keeper's life. Here are a few paragraphs from it:

Sir: Clay ochre and earth of various colors from which Gay Head derived its name ascend in a sheet of wind to catch on the glass of the lighthouse, which glass requires to be often cleaned from the outside: Tedious service in cold weather and not needed in any other of the New England States.

The spring water has become useless. I cart the water used by my family more than half a mile and it is necessary to keep a horse and cart for that purpose. Frequently have to travel on foot five miles over hilly common to find the horse.

My firewood is bought from the Mainland and is more expensive. It is eight miles to a grist mill, and creeks are not fordable at all seasons.

When I hire an Indian to work, I usually give him a dollar when the days are long and seventy-five cents when the days are short and give him three meals. Now supposing the meal's worth twenty-five cents, they amount to seventy-five cents a day, which is seven cents more than my service both day and night.

In duty bound, I humbly pray you take this Matter into your wise consideration and afford me relief by granting an increase to my Salary.

I am sir with all possible respect yours to command—Ebenezer Skiff, Gay Head, 2nd November 1815.

This time President James Madison approved a $50 increase, raising Skiff's salary to $300 a year.

One keeper of an island station on the coast of Maine had sixteen children, many born on the island. Another keeper raised twelve children at Isle Royal Lighthouse on a lonely rock on the north side of Lake Superior. This man had helped build the station and applied for the job, but he was a bachelor, and the inspector told him that he wanted a married man for the job. So he went to the mainland and got married.

The keeper of a minor light on the upper Hudson River died in World War I after keeping the light for fifty-two years. His son then became keeper, starting the job at age sixty-five.

At his light in South Carolina, a keeper heard a "terrific buzzing sound" as he climbed close to the beacon. He found a huge rattlesnake curled around the warm light box. He beat the snake off with an oar, forcing it into the water. The angered rattlesnake, instead of making off, swam back to the beacon and proceeded to climb up it, winding his body in and out between the steps. This time the keeper got a bigger oar and attacked savagely, beating the dying snake into the water where it floated away.

Women, as wives, daughters, or widows of keepers, have done well keeping lights. But in 1912, the inspector at Staten Island was surprised to get this letter:

I am writing to you for a position as keeper in a lighthouse anywhere from New York to Portland, Maine. I am the daughter of a barge captain and I also have a pal and we are both willing to do hard work and I know I would enjoy the lonesome life of keeping the light burning. I know how to row and run an engine and steer a boat ... I am afraid we will not get this position on account of being girls but we shall wear trousers instead of skirts ... I think that two strong girls like us could manage a lighthouse and keep a good log, and trusting Uncle Sam will only be kind to us.

A few keepers felt no one else could run their light. A keeper in Oregon took two days' leave in twenty-three years, and one of these was to get married.

The keeper of the Key West Light stayed at his post thirty-five years and refused to take a day off. He died at the light, past seventy years old.

Caspar Murphy grew up almost a hundred years ago, on island lighthouse stations in Maine. I was lucky to meet him and hear his stories. I met Caspar Murphy in a Waldoboro nursing home in April of 1984. I was delivering two hundred daffodils on Daffodil Day, the American Cancer Society's day of hope, when it distributes daffodils to all shut-ins, hospital patients, and those who are spending their last years in nursing homes.

Murphy was in a wheelchair, far into his eighties, his head bald, his skin stretched taut over high cheekbones, his striking blue eyes shrunk deep into his skull. It was hard to picture him as a six-year-old boy growing up on Mount Desert Rock Light—a station so remote and so exposed to raging seas and howling gales, twenty-six miles out in the Atlantic—that no keeper has lived there for many years. But that is where Caspar Murphy grew up as a boy. His memory of it is vivid:

I was six when I went to live there with my Aunt Lucy and Uncle William Dodge, who had been made second assistant keeper there in 1902.

We shared a two-family house with the keeper, Fred M. Robbins. The first assistant keeper and his family had a house of their own. I used to play with his boys, Arthur Newman, five, and Lawrence Newman, four. We played in the fog bell tower, played boats on Herring Puddle, walked on stilts, and tried to play croquet on the volcanic rock.

The littlest Newman boy, Charlie, was three years old. They kept him tethered to a spike beside the house for safekeeping. One day he had toddled too far out on a ledge and the sea knocked him down and nearly drowned him. Their big Newfoundland dog, called Prince, rescued him. Pulled the kid out of the sea and dragged him up on the ledge. Took a piece out of the boy's ear while he was dragging him.

Then Prince grabbed the boy's wet cap in his jaws and ran with it to the boy's father. And the father ran down and pumped the water out of the boy. After that, they kept him tethered.

The father went on to become keeper of Pumpkin Light on

Eggemoggin Reach. Arthur Newman grew up to be a mechanic and was elected selectman in Brooksville. Young Lawrence was going into the ministry, but dropped dead in his twenties, washing down a yacht.

I asked Caspar, as he sat in his pajamas on the side of his nursing-home bed, how they got fresh water and food out to the Rock, twenty-six miles in the Atlantic.

We got fresh water from a spring. But only one bucketful a day. We caught rainwater from run-offs on the roofs. But only when it was calm. In stormy weather, with the spray and wind blowing, the rain was briny with salt, and undrinkable. Even in calm weather, we had to let the rain first wash off the salt collected on the roofs for half an hour before we collected any water. Then we added half a cup of bleach whitening so the water wouldn't bite our lips.

In dry spells, lighthouse tenders would bring us fresh water in vinegar casks. Three times a year, the government boats brought food supplies—huge hams, slab sides of bacon, canned mutton, salt horse, salt pork, kegs of sour pickles, barrels of dried apples, and hardtack. We ate well.

When the sea was calm, fathers and sons caught lobsters. And we could keep the 'shorts,' because we were twenty-six miles out to sea. We caught pollock three feet long and lots of big codfish. We had to split and dry the fish on racks, out in the sun. On wet or foggy nights, we'd bring the drying fish inside.

The old, frail man, sitting in his nursing home, enjoyed talking about the sea lights. He recalled one of the many shipwrecks and rescues he saw as a boy:

This happened one December when the temperature was minus 20 and a hard gale blowing 70 miles an hour and seas to 50 feet high. We heard distress signals from a boat driven on the ledges. But the vapor was so thick we could not see her. Then we did make out her shape, but we couldn't get near her. The seas were like mountains, breaking over the tower, fifty feet up.

When the tide dropped, the keepers rigged a line and breeches buoy out to the ship and one by one hauled the crew to shore, all freezing they were. The mess boy froze to death on deck before they could get him ashore. My aunt and uncle and the other keepers' families nursed those seventeen men day and night for a week or more and saved the lives of all. Finally the ocean calmed enough to get a rescue boat close enough so we could rig a contraption so they could get the seventeen shipwrecked men off the Rock and back to the mainland.

Murphy was talking to me with the fluency of an educated man. But he said he only had six months of school in his life.

My Aunt Lucy MacMullen Dodge schooled me every day on the Rock for hours. Then at later stations too. She taught me reading, writing, grammar, and history. I learned a bit of mathematics and mechanics from working alongside the keepers on the engines and lights and fog signals. We had to be able to repair anything.

By the time Caspar was ten, his Uncle William was transferred to Seguin Light, and the boy and Aunt Lucy of course went along. The biggest difference between the Rock and Seguin was that on Seguin, they had trees and fields and room to walk around.

There was not one pound of dirt on all Mount Desert Rock. On the Rock we could grow nothing. But on Seguin we had a big vegetable and flower garden and fertilized it with rockweed and fishheads. And we were close enough to row to the mainland. And we were more part of the world. Every day we could see ships close-to, going east and west and going in and coming out of the Kennebec River and Bath.

Caspar still remembers the fog at Seguin, after seventy years:

Fog at Seguin rolled in and stayed thick for weeks on end. It was specially bad when they were burning cranberry bogs on Cape Cod and the wind blew the smoke our way. The big fog horn blew four times a minute, day and night, weeks at a time. My bed was only inches away from it.

Again, as at the Rock, Caspar had young people for company on Seguin. The head keeper had a son and three daughters:

Lighthouse girls grow up to marry lighthouse men. One daughter married Frederick Grant and they went to keep the light on Matinicus Rock. Another daughter married lightkeeper Merton Tolman, who later became a ship chandler in Portland.

Caspar Murphy's next move with his Uncle William and Aunt Lucy Dodge was to Egg Rock Light. It was built in 1875 by order of President Grant, and stood at the entrance to Frenchman Bay on a mass of barren ledges. The station was a nasty comedown after the space and trees and gardens on Seguin. Here was nothing but ledge and storms as savage as those on the Rock. After several years of duty here, with Caspar now eighteen, the next tour was a great improvement in living—Grindel Point Light on Islesboro Island.

That is the only time I ever remember a keeper deliberately putting out his light. My Uncle William did that the winter all Penobscot Bay froze over thick and solid. No shipping could move in the Bay. So my Uncle William extinguished his light, got a horse and sled and drove Aunt Lucy and me across the ice from Islesboro to Belfast and we went shopping and ate a meal at a restaurant.

Caspar Murphy was tiring and his voice was weakening. He stretched out on his nursing-home bed to rest. But he looked happy. "You can lose your health," he said. "You can lose your money. You can lose your home. But no one can take away your memories."

What is it like to be the wife of a Maine lightkeeper? When I spoke with her in the mid-1980s, Connie Small was a young-looking eighty-three-year-old widow living in Kittery. After twenty-nine years as a lightkeeper's wife, lighthouses are imprinted in her mind and blood. Although it had been thirty-six years since her last light station, she subconsciously thought of lighthouses even when sleeping. "When I wake up in the middle of a foggy night, and see it is thick of fog outside, my first thought still is, 'Get the fog bell going!' "

Lighthouses were all around her in her waking hours, too; in paintings on the walls, in models on the tables, in needlepoint on the cushions, in lamps shaped like lighthouses.

Constance Scovill married lightkeeper Elson Small in December 1920 in down east Lubec, when she was twenty years old. For the next twenty-nine years she lived on Maine light stations until her husband retired in 1949.

"For his last tour of duty, Elson was given a mainland light, the Fort Point Light in Portsmouth. We spent three years at Fort Point Light, from 1946 through 1949. There we had electricity and running water for the first time in more than a quarter-century of marriage. Elson went wild. The week we moved in, he bought an electric toaster, an electric refrigerator, an electric washing machine and dryer, and this electric coffee pot, which I'm still using today." Elson Small died in 1960, eleven years after his retirement.

Elson and Connie Small lived and worked together, manning the lights at Avery Rock in Machias Bay, at Seguin, at St. Croix Island, and finally at Portsmouth. Connie was not with Eldon on his first station, the stag light at Channel Rock, in the channel between Lubec and Campobello Island.

Connie Small talks mostly of her happiness as a lightkeeper's wife, "but it wasn't all sweetness and light," she says:

Cooped up together on a rock for months on end, seeing no one else, talking to no one else, we'd sometimes get mad at each other. Then Elson would stalk off to be by himself down in the engine house. Or I'd go stand alone on a ledge by the sea for a couple of hours. After a while, he'd cool off or I would and we'd come back into the house together. Then we'd talk out our differences, and the trouble blew over. Good communication, a good airing out of our differences, talking about the things that griped us, was our secret to being able to live together happily, alone on a rock for months on end.

When Connie became engaged to Elson, she looked forward to life as the wife of a sea captain, to running a sea-captain's handsome home, and to occupying her position in a coastal community as the wife of a man of prestige. These were her expectations because Elson Small was then an officer in the Merchant Marine, running regularly from New York to Rotterdam. But when World War I was over, the U.S. Merchant Marine fleet dwindled fast. Jobs at sea became scarce. Chances of Elson making captain vanished. He was laid off. So when Elson was offered a job in a secure, new career as a lightkeeper, he took it.

Connie Small told me, "I was really disappointed to see my dreams of life as the wife of a ship captain vanish. Then one day in Lubec, Elson took me down to the waterfront to look out to Channel Light. He turned to me and said, 'Connie, do you love me enough to be a lightkeeper's wife?' When he put it to me that way, I answered, 'Yes, I do.' "

Channel Light is a caisson light—nothing but an iron and brick cylinder sticking up out of the ocean, half a mile out from Lubec. It was a stag station, for bachelors only—no women were allowed to live there. Connie knew that. Her uncle was the keeper there, and Elson was to join him as assistant keeper.

The sea, wrecks, and shipwrecked sailors were in the blood of Constance Scovill long before she married Elson Small. Not only was her uncle the keeper of Channel Light, but her father, Ira Scovill, was one of the original crew who manned the Quoddy Head Lifesaving Station when it opened on June 5, 1887. Connie, at eighty-three, vividly remembered the day three-quarters of a century earlier, when her father was terribly injured during one lifesaving rescue:

There had been a wreck on nearby Sail Rock, the graveyard of so many sailing ships and just as far east as you can get and still be in United States waters. It was terribly cold, with the temperature at minus twenty-seven degrees. My father went out on the rescue lifeboat. His foot got badly frostbitten. I was only six years old at the time, but I can still feel the shock and amazement at seeing the skin of my father's foot and ankle peeling off, complete and intact in one piece, even including his toenails. The doctor came every day for months to treat and to save that foot. Finally Father got well enough so he could walk on it. He immediately went to rejoin the lifesaving crew. He wasn't allowed to go out on rescues anymore, so he worked as the cook at the Quoddy Head Lifesaving Station.

After Connie and Elson were married, Elson had to stay alone on the stag station at Lubec Channel. Connie would row out to visit on calm days. To get into the tower, keepers had to climb a vertical thirty-foot iron ladder, jumping from their dory to grab the bottom rungs.

"I refused to make that jump," says Connie. "So when I went out to visit, Elson would attach ropes around both ends of my dory and winch me and the dory together up out of the ocean up to the little iron walkway around the light tower."

After two years, Elson was sent as keeper to Avery Rock in 1922. On this barren, storm-beaten ledge at the entrance to Machias Bay, twenty-two-year-old Connie spent her next four years as a new wife, keeping a lightkeeper's house. It was a hard post, pounded by the worst of Atlantic gales and seas, which often swept through the house. One long winter, the weather stayed bad and violent for so long that Connie and Elson were marooned on Avery Rock from October 10 until April 30. Two people, man and wife, isolated in foul weather for seven long months, facing, seeing, hearing, eating, sleeping with the other for 210 days and nights: one wonders how much tolerance, how many inner resources, how special a love it took, to come through those seven months.

After four years, Elson and Connie (now twenty-six) were sent to Seguin Light, where they were stationed from 1926 to 1930.

"What relief! What wonderful change, just to be able to have dirt for a garden, to have trees, to have room to walk, to have different places to sit and watch from!" says Connie, as though these everyday things were a special blessing.

She remembers getting a real scare one Sunday afternoon, when Elson was away from the house:

> A big boat from Gloucester had anchored in the cove on Saturday and was still there on Sunday, when Elson left. I looked up from the kitchen and saw 25 men trooping across the fields toward me. They were from the Gloucester gillnetter. They came right on up into the house, a lot of them talking Italian or Portuguese. They came into the living room and sprawled over the floor, the chairs, the sofa.
>
> I couldn't believe it right away when they told me they had come to listen to the opera on my radio. They heard every aria. Gentle as big lambs. Next day they brought us a thank-you present: a 65-pound codfish.

On days when the fog rolls into Kittery, Connie sometimes seems to hear the fog signal blowing on far-off Seguin. "One year we were on Seguin, that fog whistle blew day and night without stopping for three weeks. It is a powerful one, loud enough to be heard by ships fifteen miles away. And our keeper's house was right beside the fog whistle."

A banker's wife may be married many years and know nothing about banking, but a keeper's wife knows her husband's light. Connie worked to keep the lenses and the brass, the endless brass, shining and spotless. "We won many awards for the best-kept light in New England," she says with pride. But Connie learned more than the housekeeping side of a lighthouse.

> Sometimes, over twenty-nine years, Elson would get sick; run a high fever, turn delirious. I'd nurse him of course; but then it was my duty to keep the light burning and the whistle blowing. When Elson's arm was caught in a winch while he was trying to repair the fog-whistle engine, he was out of commission. I could not fix the machinery. So rang the whistle by hand, pulling hard on the emergency ropes and clangers for hours, so my hands were bleeding from the work.

Lightkeepers, like ship captains and other men at sea, developed hobbies to pass the time in their isolated jobs. Some made toys for their children, some gardened, some did needlepoint, some made boats, some painted.

Augustus Wilson, assistant keeper of the Spring Point Light in Portland Harbor, whittled. "Gus whittled every spare moment," said Fred Anderson of South Portland, who had spent many hours with his friend Gus, as a boy. Some of Gus Wilson's whittlings have become expensive treasures in American folk art. One of his carvings of a seagull sold for $3,800 at an auction in 1970. When Wilson had carved that gull down at Spring Point Light, he sold it for a dollar, and was glad to get that much. Wilson carved duck decoys by the hundreds and sold them for seventy-five cents each to Walker and Evans, a hardware and sporting goods store in Portland.

Lynn Franklin, a reporter for the *Maine Sunday Telegram*, talked to Fred Anderson about keeper-carver Gus Wilson, and the long interview was published April 25, 1976. Thanks to that, we know quite a lot about Keeper Wilson and his carvings.

Gus Wilson came from Manset, down east on the Maine coast. He was born in 1864 and died in 1950, in Gray, Maine. His brother was keeper of the Spring Point Light when Gus was assistant keeper there. Anderson knew Gus Wilson for more than ten years, when Anderson was a schoolboy and Wilson lived next door.

> He carved constantly, not just for money—there was precious little of that—but because it was his art. Over the ten years I knew him, Gus carved six days a week. He wouldn't work on Sundays. He'd get all dressed up, though he didn't go to church. He'd put on his white shirt, a tie, a suit of clothes and sit in the living room and thumb through the Bible, this passage and that, and that's how he passed his Sundays."

At 3 p.m. every afternoon, Gus would walk to Fort Preble, from his home at Willard Beach in South Portland, and get into the skiff tied there and row out to relieve his brother at Spring Point Light.

To make his carvings, Gus preferred to use cedar wood, but he'd use any wood he could get. For example, Anderson's grandfather found an old spar buoy floating off by Peaks Island, the kind that used to mark a channel before can buoys were used. This spar was about sixty feet long and thirty inches in diameter, a tremendous spruce tree. He towed the spar over to South Portland and gave it to his grandson, Fred Anderson. Fred and Gus cut it up and it made tremendous decoy wood for Gus. Later, Gus even used old railroad ties.

> As for Gus's tools, they were nothing special either. He'd rough out with a hatchet and for general use he used a Boy Scout jackknife. He thought it was the greatest tool he'd ever seen. He'd buy four at a time because they didn't last long. Terrible steel. He was always delicate with the can opener, the prick punch corkscrew, the great wide blade. He had that Scout knife and a chisel and a little plane he used to smooth the wood— and yes, a brace and a bit. What made him the carver he was, was style and imagination.

Gus Wilson turned out thousands of duck decoys, gulls, snakes, birds, and tigers, using pictures for his models. But he knew nothing at all about paint. Schoolboy Anderson, whose father was a cabinetmaker, taught Gus about paints.

> Old Gus had no idea at all about paints. He'd just see a can of paint on the shelf and read the label—Brown, Green, Blue, Yellow—and he bought it. Whatever else was on the label meant nothing to him.
>
> Sometimes he'd put Automobile Duco on decoys, making them bright and metallic and we'd have to sand them down again to dull them. So I told him about the flat paint my father used on furniture. He was fascinated. I bought him some and he put it on some scooters. It dried right out, fine and flat. "Isn't that something" said Gus. "Where did you get that kind of paint?"
>
> So at 75, Gus learned how to paint. Before that he had one tube of color, Prussian Blue ... my father explained about umbers and siennas and we got Gus an assortment of tubes.

Gus Wilson could carve anything. In the early 1930s, he carved a tiger about five feet long. He invited a neighbor to see his tiger, who said, "That's the goddamndest thing I ever saw. It's too skinny. Tigers aren't like that." So Gus carved another, much fatter, eighty-two inches long. He tried to give it away, but nobody would take it. Today it is a museum piece, part of an exhibition entitled "Masterpieces of American Folk Art."

Gus Wilson died when Fred Anderson was in high school, back in the 1950s. In the 1970s, Anderson began going to auctions to find duck decoys for the collection he had started.

> I went to an auction down in Hyannis, and saw some of the decoys there fetching high prices, and they were listed as "Maker Unknown."
> "My God," I said, "this man is not unknown. He lived next door to me. He kept the Spring Point Light. Those duck decoys are Gus Wilson's."

That was the auction where the prices for Wilson's decoys ranked in the top ten.

Lightkeepers and their wives frequently became skilled hobbyists. To pass the long and lonely days and nights, and to give them something else to do other than tend the light and look at and talk to each other, they took up carving, or painting, or rug-working. Others played a musical instrument, sometimes a guitar or penny whistle or flute, which was often homemade. Some even wrote poetry. Others memorized long sections of Scripture.

Usually these hobbies were more a way of keeping their sanity than outbursts of artistic creativity. Hobbies were an important part of their lives. Yet it is not easy to find examples of their work today. Much of it was thrown away when keepers changed stations, retired, or died. Some remnants surely exist, buried in attics and cellars or basements of grandchildren and great-grandchildren.

When I see this handiwork, I see a fragment of Americana that is almost outside the comprehension of Americans today—the lonely, isolated, self-reliant lives of the men and women who kept our lighthouses.

——— Chronological Listing of Maine Lights ———

1.	Boston Light	1716		45.	Portland Breakwater	1855
2.	Portsmouth Harbor	1771		46.	Winter Harbor	1856
3.	Portland Head	1791		47.	Kennebunk Pier	1856
4.	Seguin Island	1795		48.	Blue Hill Bay	1857
5.	Whitehead Island	1804		49.	Tenants Harbor	1857
6.	Franklin Island	1806		50.	Deer Island Thorofare	1857
7.	Wood Island	1808		51.	St. Croix River	1857
8.	Passamaquoddy	1808		52.	Bass Harbor Head	1858
9.	Boon Island	1812		53.	Manana Island Fog Signal	1870
10.	Petit Manan	1817		54.	Halfway Rock	1871
11.	Isles of Shoals	1821		55.	Burnt Coat (Range I)	1872
12.	Pond Island	1821		56.	Burnt Coat (Range II)	1872
13.	Burnt Island	1821		57.	Avery Rock	1875
14.	Libby Island	1822		58.	Egg Rock	1875
15.	Monhegan Island	1824		59.	Little Diamond Island	1875
16.	Owls Head	1825		60.	Cape Neddick	1879
17.	Matinicus Rock (North)	1827		61.	Ram Island	1883
18.	Matinicus Rock (South)	1827		62.	Rockland Breakwater	1888
19.	Pemaquid	1827		63.	Crabtree Ledge	1890
20.	Moose Peak	1827		64.	Goose Rocks	1890
21.	Baker Island	1828		65.	Lubec Channel	1890
22.	Hendricks Head	1829		66.	Great Duck Island	1890
23.	Dice Head	1829		67.	Moosabec Reach	1891
24.	Cape Elizabeth (West)	1829		68.	Cuckolds Fog Signal	1892
25.	Cape Elizabeth (East)	1829		69.	Whitlock's Mill	1892
26.	Mount Desert Rock	1830		70.	Seavey's Island (Range I)	1893
27.	Whaleback Ledge	1831		71.	Seavey's Island (Range II)	1894
28.	Browns Head	1832		72.	Frost's Point	1896
29.	Marshall Point	1832		73.	Jerry's Point	1896
30.	Goat Island	1833		74.	Ames Ledge	1896
31.	Fort Point	1836		75.	Spring Point Ledge	1896
32.	Negro (Curtis Island)	1836		76.	Two Bush Island	1897
33.	Nash Island	1838		77.	Perkins Island	1898
34.	Bear Island	1839		78.	Squirrel Point	1898
35.	Eagle Island	1839		79.	Doubling Point	1898
36.	Saddleback Ledge	1839		80.	Doubling Point Range (I)	1898
37.	Minot's Ledge, Mass.	1847		81.	Doubling Point Range (II)	1898
38.	Little River	1847		82.	Fort Popham	1899
39.	Prospect Harbor	1848		83.	*Cape Elizabeth* lightship	1903
40.	Indian Island	1850		84.	Abbagadasset Range (I)	1903
41.	Grindel Point	1850		85.	Abbagadasset Range (II)	1903
42.	Narragaugus	1853		86.	Ram Island Ledge	1905
43.	Pumpkin Island	1854		87.	Robinson's Point,	
44.	Heron Neck	1854			Isle au Haut	1907

Index